1

BREAKING THE
SPANISH
BARRIER

LEVEL ONE
BEGINNER

John Conner

Student Edition

BREAKING THE BARRIER, INC.
THE LANGUAGE SERIES WITH ALL THE RULES YOU NEED TO KNOW
THE FASTEST PATH TO TRUE LANGUAGE FLUENCY

For Lisa, Jamie, Hannah, Alexandra and Sarah

ACKNOWLEDGMENTS

Thanks to Guillermo Barnetche for the artistic vision, Barbara Peterson, contributing editor, for her wonderful suggestions, and to Ann Talbot for her stylish layout. A special thanks to Miguel Romá for his brilliant editing.

AN INVITATION

*We invite you to join many of our readers who, over the years, have shared their suggestions for improvements as well as their personal knowledge of the Hispanic world. In doing so, they have become our partners. We are grateful for their invaluable contributions as the evolution of **Breaking the Barrier** belongs, in part, to them.*

BREAKING THE BARRIER, INC.
63 Shirley Road
Groton, MA 01450
Toll Free: 866-TO BREAK (866-862-7325)
Fax: 978-448-1237
E-mail: info@tobreak.com
www.tobreak.com

ISBN: 0-9712817-2-6

PREFACE

BREAKING THE **S**PANISH **B**ARRIER is a core text, workbook and handy reference all-in-one. It can stand alone, or complement the multitude of Spanish language resources currently available.

We believe the fastest path to fluency is built upon a rock-solid understanding of grammar. **BREAKING THE SPANISH BARRIER** provides the essential roadmap for this journey.

In the following twelve lessons, you will find country maps, vocabulary, a review of key grammatical concepts, explanations of new material, many practice exercises, an exciting dialogue series, as well as review tests. A companion audio CD set provides further opportunity to sharpen your Spanish skills — by hearing, modeling, and conversing with native speakers. Sentences throughout the book highlight current people, places and events from the Spanish-speaking world. You will find the tone of these pages informal and conversational — a one-on-one session between teacher and student.

WE LOOK FORWARD TO ACCOMPANYING YOU AS YOU
SET OUT TO **B**REAK THE **S**PANISH **B**ARRIER.

¡BUENA **S**UERTE!

JOHN **C**ONNER
Author and Series Editor

CINDY **B**EAMS
Publisher

TABLE OF CONTENTS

FIRST STEPS

*Long before you learned any grammar rules in your native language, you had learned to speak beautifully. As a child, you added vocabulary little by little, figured out how to put sentences together, and discovered how to imitate the sounds of the language. As you begin to **Break the Spanish Barrier**, you will learn — right from the start — some useful vocabulary, expressions, and tips about pronunciation . . . all before you learn any grammar rules. For a little bit, you will have to be willing to leave some of your questions unanswered. Never fear, however! By the end of this book, all of your questions will be answered. These first ten steps will get you speaking Spanish right away.*

STEP ONE — ¿CÓMO SE LLAMA USTED?

 When you want to learn someone's name, you can ask him or her:

¿Cómo se llama usted? (What is your name?)
> *Me llamo María.* (My name is Mary.)
> *Me llamo Juan.* (My name is John.)

You can also ask someone to tell you who another person is. Here are some possible questions you might ask:

¿Cómo se llama su profesora? (What's your teacher's name?)
> *Mi profesora se llama señora Sánchez.* (My teacher's name is Mrs. Sánchez.)

¿Cómo se llama su madre? (What's your mother's name?)
> *Mi madre se llama Ana.*

¿Cómo se llama su amigo? (What is your friend's name?)
> *Mi amigo se llama Andrés.*

¿Cómo se llama el presidente de México? (What is name of the president of Mexico?)
> *El presidente se llama Felipe Calderón.*

 This symbol lets you know where you can practice along using the Audio CD set.

Here are some common Spanish names:

Adela	*Elena*	*Lucía*	*Paco*
Ana	*Gabriel*	*Luis*	*Penélope*
Andrés	*Gisela*	*Lupe*	*Pilar*
Arturo	*Inés*	*Manolo*	*Ramón*
Carlota	*Isabel*	*Marcos*	*Raquel*
Carmen	*Javier*	*María*	*Ricardo*
Chita	*Jorge*	*Miguel*	*Rosaura*
Cristóbal	*Juan*	*Nicolás*	*Tomás*

 PRÁCTICA

Answer the following ten questions aloud or on paper.

1) **¿Cómo se llama usted?** Me llamo _____.

2) **¿Cómo se llama su profesor?** Mi profesor se llama _____.

3) **¿Cómo se llama su amiga?** Mi amiga se llama _____.

4) **¿Cómo se llama su dentista?** _____.

5) **¿Cómo se llama su papá?** _____.

6) **¿Cómo se llama su mamá?** _____.

7) **¿Cómo se llama usted?** _____.

8) **¿Cómo se llama su amigo?** _____.

9) **¿Cómo se llama el presidente?** El presidente se llama _____.

10) **¿Cómo se llama su profesor de matemáticas?** Mi profesor de

matemáticas _____.

PRÁCTICA DE PRONUNCIACIÓN

a, e, i, o, u

TRACK 3 DISC 1 The five vowels in Spanish are so important to learn! Fortunately, these sounds don't change from word to word. They are crisp, short sounds, unlike many English vowel sounds that seem to drag on. Oftentimes, English speakers think that Spanish speakers talk so fast. This observation is made, in part, because the sounds of the vowels are shorter.

In order to feel at ease with these new sounds, practice them frequently with the help of your teacher or the CD.

a – This letter sounds like the "a" when you sing the notes "la-la-la."

Repita (repeat!): *casa, bata, mamá, masa, papá, alma, mala, arte, taza, salsa, lata, Nacha*

e – This letter sounds like the "a" in the word "chaos."

bebé, leche, de, té, pele, bese, entender, teme, Enrique

i – This letter sounds like the "ee" in "tee."

sí, misa, pizza, linda, cinta, amiga, misa, chico, di

o – This letter sounds like "o" in the word "nose," but it is actually almost half the sound. You have to try to chop off the last part of the long English "o."

ola, olé, nota, mole, bota, bolo, Lola, onda, chocolate, solo, cola

u – This letter sounds like the "oo" in "soon." Once again, the sound is shorter and crisper.

uno, luna, mucho, cuna, buche, lunes, bambú, fumas, pluma

STEP TWO — ¿DE DÓNDE ES USTED?

When you want to find out where someone is from, you can ask him or her:

¿De dónde es usted? (Where are you from?)

    Soy de Chicago. (I'm from Chicago.)

    Soy de Santo Domingo. (I'm from Santo Domingo.)

You can also ask someone to tell you where someone else is from. Here are some possible questions you might ask:

¿De dónde es su padre? (Where is your father from?)

    Mi padre es de Nueva York. (My father is from New York.)

¿De dónde es su amiga? (Where is your friend from?)

    Mi amiga es de Los Ángeles.

¿De dónde son los mexicanos? (Where are Mexicans from?)

    Los mexicanos son de México.

¿De dónde son los colombianos? (Where are Colombians from?)

    Los colombianos son de Colombia.

Here are some well-known cities, countries, and geographical locations around the world with Spanish names. How many could you locate on a map?

Amarillo	*España*	*Panamá*
Argentina	*Fresno*	*Paraguay*
Barcelona	*Guatemala*	*Perú*
Bolivia	*Honduras*	*Puerto Rico*
Chile	*Los Andes*	*La República Dominicana*
Colombia	*Los Ángeles*	*Río Grande*
Costa Rica	*Madrid*	*San Francisco*
Cuba	*México*	*San Juan*
Ecuador	*Nevada*	*Uruguay*
El Salvador	*Nicaragua*	*Venezuela*

PRÁCTICA

Answer the following ten questions, aloud or on paper, in complete sentences.

1) **¿De dónde es usted?** Soy de _____.

2) **¿De dónde es su madre?** Mi madre es de _____.

3) **¿De dónde es su profesor de español?** _____

   _____.

4) **¿De dónde es su amigo favorito?** _____

   _____.

5) **¿De dónde es Ricky Martin?** _____

   _____.

6) **¿De dónde son los californianos?** _____

   _____.

7) **¿De dónde son los africanos?** _____.

8) **¿De dónde son los chilenos?** _____.

9) **¿De dónde es su padre?** _____.

10) **¿De dónde es usted?** _____.

PRÁCTICA DE PRONUNCIACIÓN

y, d

 In this section and the remaining ones of First Steps, we will look at Spanish consonants. A number of Spanish consonants are pronounced exactly as in English, while others are completely different. Using your teacher or the CDs as a model, practice and repeat the following:

y – This letter, in fact, has two different sounds — the first is vowel-like, and the other like a consonant. When the letter "y" stands by itself or when it comes at the very end of a word, it sounds just like the "ee" in "tee," except a bit shorter and crisper.

y, ley, buey, ay, hay, Uruguay, Paraguay, soy, muy, hoy

When the letter "y" is found in any other position, it is pronounced just like the "y" sound found in the English word "yes."

ya, yema, yo, cuyo, suya, hoyo, mayo

d – This consonant has different sounds, depending upon where it is placed in a word or sentence. At the beginning of a word or breath group, or following a consonant, it sounds pretty much like the "d" in the word "dentist."

Diego, diablo, dice, doctor, diente, de, dolor, donde, andar, dan, doce, Dalí

Surrounded by vowels, the "d" loses most of its "voiced" sound, and sounds more like the "th" in "lather."

código, lado, helado, comido, aliado, frustrado, modo, Estados Unidos

Finally, at the end of a word, the "d" still sounds like the "th" in "lather," but it is even weaker or "breathier."

comed, edad, ciudad, universidad, facilidad, facultad, id, capacidad

When you want to find out how someone is feeling today, you can ask him or her:

Buenos días. ¿Cómo está usted hoy? (Good morning. How are you today?)

    Estoy bien. (I'm well.)
    Estoy así-así. (I'm so-so/O.K.)
    Estoy mal. (I'm bad, i.e., not feeling well.)

    To add some extra emphasis to your answer, you can add the word *"muy"* meaning "very."
    *Estoy **muy** bien.* (I'm very well.)
    *Estoy **muy** mal.* (I'm very bad.)

You can also ask someone to tell you how another person is doing. Here are some possible questions you might ask:

Buenas tardes. ¿Cómo está su amiga hoy? (Good afternoon. How is your friend today?)

    Mi amiga está bien. (My friend is fine.)

¿Cómo está el profesor? (How is the teacher doing?)

    El profesor está mal. (The teacher isn't feeling well.)

Buenas noches. ¿Cómo están sus padres? (Good evening. How are your parents?)

    Mis padres están así-así. (My parents are so-so/O.K.)

¿Cómo están los animales? (How are the animals?)

    Los animales están muy bien. (The animals are very well.)

When you want to say "goodbye" to someone, you could say:

Adiós. Hasta luego. (Goodbye. See you later.)

Answer the following ten questions, aloud or on paper, in complete sentences. Use as many different responses as possible.

1) **Buenos días. ¿Cómo está usted?** Estoy _____.

2) **¿Cómo está su madre?** Mi madre está _____.

3) **¿Cómo está su padre?** _____.

4) **¿Cómo está su amigo favorito?** _____.

5) **¿Cómo está Shakira hoy?** _____

_____.

6) **¿Cómo está su profesora de historia hoy?** _____

_____.

7) **Buenas tardes. ¿Cómo están sus amigos hoy?** Mis amigos están _____

_____.

8) **¿Cómo están sus padres hoy?** _____

_____.

9) **¿Cómo está su tío** (uncle) **hoy?** Mi tío _____.

10) **¿Cómo está usted?** _____.

PRÁCTICA DE PRONUNCIACIÓN

h , q , s

 Here are some more consonants:

h – This letter is <u>completely</u> silent in Spanish. It requires your making no sound at all, no matter what position it is in! Ever!

hotel, historia, hilo, Alhambra, rehén, hielo, hombre, hospital, ahora, hijo

q – This letter is always followed in Spanish by the vowels "ui" or "ue." The "u" in these combinations is silent. The sound of "qu" is like the English "k" in the word "kind."

que, quien, quiero, Raquel, Quito, adquirir, queso, quepo, Querétaro, quiosco

s – This letter sounds like the "s" in the word "song."

sosa, sin, flores, casa, playas, chiste, masa, seta, seis, siete, San Salvador

 ## STEP FOUR — ¿ES USTED NORMAL?

 When you want to find out what someone is like, you could ask him or her:

¿Es usted normal? (Are you normal?)
> *Sí, soy normal.* (Yes, I'm normal.)
> *No, no soy normal.* (No, I'm not normal.)

¿Es usted popular? (Are you popular?)
> *Sí, soy popular.*
> *No, no soy popular.*

¿Es usted interesante? (Are you interesting?)
> *Sí, soy interesante.*
> *No, no soy interesante.*

You can also ask someone to tell you what someone else is like. Here are some possible questions you might ask:

¿Es generoso su amigo? (Is your friend generous?)

> *Sí, mi amigo es generoso.* (Yes, my friend is generous.)
> *No, mi amigo no es generoso.* (No, my friend is not generous.)

¿Es sincera su amiga? (Is your friend sincere?)

> *Sí, mi amiga es sincera.* (Yes, my friend is sincere.)
> *No, mi amiga no es sincera.* (No, my friend is not sincere.)

¿Cómo es su amiga? (What is your friend like?)

> *Mi amiga es generosa y popular.* (My friend is generous and popular.)
> *Mi amiga es fantástica.* (My friend is fantastic.)

Adjectives that end in "o" when describing a male change to "a" when describing a female.

¿Es muy diplomático su padre?

> *Sí, mi padre es muy diplomático.*
> *No, mi padre no es muy diplomático.*

¿Es muy diplomática su madre?

> *Sí, mi madre es muy diplomática.*
> *No, mi madre no es muy diplomática.*

The adjectives used so far in this section should sound quite familiar to an English speaker *(normal, popular, interesante, generoso, diplomático)*. It is because these words are <u>cognates</u> — they come from the same Latin roots — that they are easily recognizable. They look and sound quite similar to many English words you know. Here are some other Spanish adjectives whose meanings you could probably guess instantly:

ambicioso/a	*conservador*	*fantástico/a*	*posible*
artístico/a	*cordial*	*importante*	*práctico/a*
atlético/a	*elegante*	*imposible*	*religioso/a*
brillante	*estúpido/a*	*liberal*	*romántico/a*
cómico/a	*famoso/a*	*paciente*	*sincero/a*

Using the adjectives that you learned in this section, answer the following ten questions aloud or on paper. Try not to use the same adjective more than once.

1) **¿Es usted normal?** Sí, soy _____.

2) **¿Cómo es su amigo?** Mi amigo es _____.

3) **¿Es liberal su profesor?** _____.

4) **¿Es religiosa su madre?** _____.

5) **¿Es atlético Tiger Woods?** _____.

6) **¿Es atlética Lorena Ochoa?** _____.

7) **¿Cómo es su amiga?** _____.

8) **¿Es popular su profesor de español?** _____

   _____.

9) **¿Es romántico Enrique Iglesias?** _____.

10) **¿Cómo es usted?** _____.

m, n, ñ

 Here are three more consonants:

m – This letter is pronounced just as in English. The Spanish "m" sounds like the "m" in the word "mouse."

mapa, Madrid, Miami, malo, cama, imposible, masa, limpia, mitología, maestro

n – This letter is always pronounced just as in English. The Spanish "n" sounds like the "n" in the word "night."

hermano, piano, nata, Candela, Nicaragua, norte, chimenea, cementerio

ñ – This letter is not found in the English alphabet. However, the same sound exists in English. The "ñ" is just like the "ny" in "canyon" or the "ni" in "onion."

niño, año, caña, cumpleaños, reñir, teñir, viña, mañana, Nuñoz

STEP FIVE — ¿QUÉ ES ESTO?

 When you want to find out what something is, you could point at it and ask:

¿Qué es esto? (What's this?)
> *Es un libro.* (It's a book.)
> *Es una silla.* (It's a chair.)

The word *un*, meaning "a" or "an," is used before "masculine nouns" — ones that end in "o" and many others, while the word *una* (also meaning "a" and "an") is used before "feminine nouns" — ones that end in "a" and many others.

Here is some useful vocabulary that you can use in the **classroom** or at **home**.

LA CLASE y LA CASA					
(una) alcoba	→	bedroom	*(una) mesa*	→	table
(un) baño	→	bathroom	*(un) papel*	→	paper
(una) cama	→	bed	*(una) pluma*	→	pen
(una) casa	→	house	*(un) profesor*	→	teacher
(un) coche	→	car	*(una) profesora*	→	teacher
(una) cocina	→	kitchen	*(una) puerta*	→	door
(un) comedor	→	dining room	*(un) reloj*	→	watch/clock
(una) escuela	→	school	*(una) sala*	→	living room
(un) lápiz	→	pencil	*(una) silla*	→	chair
(un) libro	→	book	*(una) ventana*	→	window

 PRÁCTICA

I. *Study the words carefully that were presented in this section. Once you feel that you have them fairly well memorized, draw a little picture of the five words presented below. Try not to look back at the list as you do this exercise!*

1) **una ventana**

2) **un profesor**

3) **una casa**

4) **un lápiz**

5) **un papel**

II. Now answer each question, following the model presented.

Example: ¿Qué es esto? *Es una pluma.* _____

1) **¿Qué es esto?** _____

2) **¿Qué es esto?** _____

3) **¿Qué es esto?** _____

4) **¿Qué es esto?** _____

5) **¿Qué es esto?** _____

PRÁCTICA DE PRONUNCIACIÓN

c, ch, p

TRACK 11 DISC 1 Here are some more consonants:

c – This consonant has a number of different pronunciations. As in English, before an "a," "o," or "u," this letter sounds like the "c" in "cool."

casa, cama, coche, rica, Cuba, acumular, coco, costa, colina

Again, as in English, when "c" comes before "e" or "i," it is most often pronounced like the "s" in "song." In some parts of Spain, however, the "c" in this position would be pronounced like the "th" in "thin."

celos, cielo, reciente, producir, cinta, cenicero, sinceros, cine

ch – Until recently, this consonant has normally been considered a single letter in the Spanish alphabet, although it certainly looks like two! This "ch" sounds like the "ch" in the word "chocolate."

chica, coche, chiste, chicle, Conchita, Chiapas, rechoncho, relinche

p – This letter is basically like the "p" found in the English word "pizza." At times, the "p" in English "explodes" a little bit, with a fair amount of breath coming out of the speaker's mouth. The Spanish "p" is a little more restrained, but to most people not really distinguishable from the English "p." If you put a candle close to your lips when saying the name "Peter," you might blow out the candle. In Spanish, the flame would barely flicker when saying *"Pedro."*

pelo, postal, padre, reportero, ropero, pico, picante, suplicar, aplicado

 ## STEP SIX — MI FAMILIA

 If you want to learn about someone's family, you might ask him or her:

¿Tiene Ud. (usted) hermanos? (Do you have brothers and sisters?)
>*Sí, tengo un hermano.* (Yes, I have one brother.)
>*Sí, tengo una hermana.* (Yes, I have one sister.)
>*No, no tengo hermanos.* (No, I don't have brothers or sisters.)

¿Tiene Ud. (usted) abuelos? (Do you have grandparents?)
>*Sí, tengo un abuelo.* (Yes, I have one grandfather.)
>*Sí, tengo una abuela.* (Yes, I have one grandmother.)
>*No, no tengo abuelos.* (No, I don't have grandparents.)

You might want to ask someone about another person's family. If so, you could ask:

¿Tiene María hermanos? (Does Mary have brothers and sisters?)
>*Sí, María tiene un hermano.* (Yes, Mary has a brother.)
>*Sí, María tiene una hermana.* (Yes, Mary has a sister.)
>*No, María no tiene hermanos.* (No, Mary doesn't have brothers or sisters.)

¿Tiene su amigo muchos primos? (Does your friend have many cousins?)
>*Sí, mi amigo tiene muchos primos.* (Yes, my friend has many cousins.)
>*No, mi amigo no tiene muchos primos.* (No, my friend doesn't have many cousins.)

The following is a list of useful vocabulary related to the **family**:

LA FAMILIA

abuela	→	grandmother	*nieta*	→	granddaughter
abuelo	→	grandfather	*nieto*	→	grandson
cuñada	→	sister-in-law	*padre*	→	father
cuñado	→	brother-in-law	*prima*	→	cousin (female)
esposa	→	wife	*primo*	→	cousin (male)
esposo	→	husband	*sobrina*	→	niece
hermana	→	sister	*sobrino*	→	nephew
hermano	→	brother	*suegra*	→	mother-in-law
hija	→	daughter	*suegro*	→	father-in-law
hijo	→	son	*tía*	→	aunt
madre	→	mother	*tío*	→	uncle

PRÁCTICA

I. *After studying the list of vocabulary about the family, answer the following questions in complete sentences.*

Example: *¿Tiene Ud. primos?*   <u>*Sí, tengo primos / No, no tengo primos.*</u>

1) **¿Tiene Ud. (usted) muchos primos?** _____.

2) **¿Tiene Ud. una hermana?** _____.

3) **¿Tiene Ud. un hermano?** _____.

4) **¿Cómo se llama su abuelo?** Mi abuelo se llama _____.

5) **¿Cómo se llama su tía? Mi tía** _____.

6) **¿Cómo se llama su madre?** _____.

7) **¿Tiene Ud. un cuñado?** _____.

8) ¿Tiene muchos primos su amigo? _____

_____.

9) ¿Tiene esposo Penélope Cruz? _____

_____.

10) ¿Tiene Ud. muchos primos? _____.

II. Fill in the following spaces with appropriate vocabulary from this section. A few
of the sentences have more than one possible answer!

1) El padre de mi padre es mi _____.

2) La madre de mi madre es mi _____.

3) El hermano de mi padre es mi _____.

4) El hijo de mi hijo es mi _____.

5) La hija de mi tío es mi _____.

6) La hija de mi abuela es mi _____.

7) La esposa de mi padre es mi _____.

8) El hermano de mi esposa es mi _____.

9) El hermano de mi prima es mi _____.

10) La hermana de mi hijo es mi _____.

PRÁCTICA DE PRONUNCIACIÓN

z, l, ll

 Here are some more consonants:

z – In most of the Spanish-speaking world, this consonant sounds like the "s" in "sailor." In parts of Spain, it sounds like the "th" in "thin."

zapato, zona, lápiz, Zaragoza, azúcar, alzar, realizar, azul, azulejo

l – This consonant is pronounced just as in the English word "lost."

lindo, listo, luego, alto, leal, hotel, loco, lástima, Los Ángeles, líquido, limón

ll – This is another consonant that historically has been considered one letter in the alphabet. In most places in the Spanish speaking world, it is pronounced like the "y" in "yes." In parts of Spain, it resembles the "lli" in "billion," while in Argentina, it sounds like the "Zsa" in the name "Zsa-Zsa."

millón, relleno, callado, calle, valles

STEP SEVEN —
¿LE GUSTA EL ELEFANTE AZUL?
¿HAY TIGRES EN ÁFRICA?

 If you want to find out if someone likes something, you could ask him or her:

¿Le gusta el elefante azul? (Do you like the blue elephant?)
  Sí, me gusta el elefante azul. (Yes, I like the blue elephant.)
  No, no me gusta el elefante azul. (No, I don't like the blue elephant.)

¿Le gusta el cocodrilo verde? (Do you like the green crocodile?)
  Sí, me gusta el cocodrilo verde. (Yes, I like the green crocodile.)
  No, no me gusta el cocodrilo verde. (No, I don't like the green crocodile.)

If the thing you like is plural, the sentences will be a little different:

¿Le gustan los elefantes azules? (Do you like [the] blue elephants?)*

    Sí, me gustan los elefantes azules. (Yes, I like [the] blue elephants.)

    No, no me gustan los elefantes azules. (No, I don't like [the] blue elephants.)

*Note: If the speaker is talking about elephants in <u>general</u>, the English translation would not include the word "the".

¿Le gustan los cocodrilos verdes? (Do you like [the] green crocodiles?)

    Sí, me gustan los cocodrilos verdes. (Yes, I like [the] green crocodiles.)

    No, no me gustan los cocodrilos verdes. (No, I don't like [the] green crocodiles.)

If you want to find out if someone else likes something, you could ask:

¿Le gusta el elefante azul? (Does she/he like the blue elephant?)

    Sí, le gusta el elefante azul. (Yes, she/he likes the blue elephant.)

    No, no le gusta el elefante azul. (No, she/he doesn't like the blue elephant.)

¿Le gustan los cocodrilos verdes? (Does she/he like [the] green crocodiles?)

    Sí, le gustan los cocodrilos verdes. (Yes, she/he likes [the] green crocodiles.)

    No, no le gustan los cocodrilos verdes. (No, she/he doesn't like [the] green crocodiles.)

> **Helpful Tip:** Do you notice that these questions all start with the word *"le"*? *"¿Le gusta(n)?"* can mean either "Do you like?", "Does he like?" or "Does she like?"

Here is a list of names of **common animals** in Spanish. (The corresponding definite article — "the" — is written in parentheses before each word . . . *el* is used for masculine nouns and *la* is used for feminine ones.)

LOS ANIMALES			
(la) ballena	→ whale	*(el) pájaro*	→ bird
(el) caballo	→ horse	*(el) perro*	→ dog
(la) cebra	→ zebra	*(el) pez*	→ fish
(el) gato	→ cat	*(la) rana*	→ frog
(la) jirafa	→ giraffe	*(el) ratón*	→ mouse
(la) llama	→ llama	*(la) serpiente*	→ snake
(el) león	→ lion	*(el) tigre*	→ tiger
(el) oso	→ bear	*(la) vaca*	→ cow

> **Helpful Tip:** A handy word to learn now is *"hay."* It means "there is" and "there are." *¿Hay tigres en África? ¿Hay un perro en la casa? ¿Hay una llama en el parque?* (Are there tigers in Africa? Is there a dog in the house? Is there a llama in the park?)

This next list has the names of **common colors**. (You may have noticed that these adjectives are placed after the nouns that they modify . . . e.g., *elefante rosado, cocodrilo verde.*)

LOS COLORES				
amarillo/a	→ yellow	*morado/a*	→	purple
anaranjado/a	→ orange	*negro/a*	→	black
azul	→ blue	*rojo/a*	→	red
blanco/a	→ white	*rosado/a*	→	pink
gris	→ gray	*verde*	→	green
marrón (café)	→ brown			

 PRACTICA

I. Answer the following questions in complete sentences.

1) **¿Le gustan los gatos amarillos?** Sí, me gustan _____

_____.

2) **¿Le gustan los perros negros?** _____

_____.

3) **¿Le gusta su casa?** Sí, me gusta mi _____

4) **¿Le gusta su escuela?** _____.

5) **¿Le gustan las casas verdes?** _____

_____.

6) **¿Le gusta más (more) Nueva York o Chicago?** _____

_____.

7) ¿Le gustan más los perros o los gatos? _____

_____.

8) ¿Le gustan más los caballos grises o los caballos negros?

_____.

9) ¿Le gusta su casa? _____.

10) ¿Qué animal le gusta más? _____

_____.

11) ¿Hay una serpiente en la casa? _____

_____.

12) ¿Hay perros en la escuela? _____.

II. Fill in the following paragraph with names of colors and animals from this section.

En mi casa tengo un _____. El color de mi

_____ es _____. Mi amiga, Elena, tiene una

_____. No es blanca; es _____. Mi

_____ se llama Fido y su _____ se llama

Kermit. ¡Son animales fantásticos!

PRÁCTICA DE PRONUNCIACIÓN

$$\boxed{\textbf{b, v}}$$

 The consonants in this section — "b" and "v" — are pronounced exactly the same way!

b and v – At the beginning of a word or following another consonant, the "b" and "v" sound just like the "b" in "buffalo."

> *bello, bola, barco, barba, béisbol, Bogotá, bilingüe, bizcocho verde, vamos,*
> *vértigo, Venezuela, voz, votamos, invierno, valle*

If a "b" or "v" is found between vowels, however, the sound is different. You start to say the "b" sound as in "buffalo," but you don't close your lips all the way. You'll have to practice this one a bit. You can try placing a thin pencil lengthwise between your lips to prevent them from closing during the sound.

> *abuelo, cubo, sabemos, labio, nubes, caminaban, cabido nueve, ave, lívido,*
> *uvas, tuvimos, llave, caverna, Oviedo*

 ## STEP EIGHT — UNO, DOS, TRES . . .

 In this section, you will learn to count from one to thirty-one. Here is the vocabulary that you will need:

LOS NÚMEROS (1-20)			
uno	→ one	*once*	→ eleven
dos	→ two	*doce*	→ twelve
tres	→ three	*trece*	→ thirteen
cuatro	→ four	*catorce*	→ fourteen
cinco	→ five	*quince*	→ fifteen
seis	→ six	*dieciséis (diez y seis)*	→ sixteen
siete	→ seven	*diecisiete (diez y siete)*	→ seventeen
ocho	→ eight	*dieciocho (diez y ocho)*	→ eighteen
nueve	→ nine	*diecinueve (diez y nueve)*	→ nineteen
diez	→ ten	*veinte*	→ twenty

Note: Did you notice that the numbers 16–19 can be written either as one word or as three?

This list will take you through to thirty-one:

LOS NÚMEROS (21-31)		
veintiuno (veinte y uno)	→	twenty-one
veintidós (veinte y dos)	→	twenty-two
veintitrés (veinte y tres)	→	twenty-three
veinticuatro (veinte y cuatro)	→	twenty-four
veinticinco (veinte y cinco)	→	twenty-five
veintiséis (veinte y seis)	→	twenty-six
veintisiete (veinte y siete)	→	twenty-seven
veintiocho (veinte y ocho)	→	twenty-eight
veintinueve (veinte y nueve)	→	twenty-nine
treinta	→	thirty
treinta y uno	→	thirty-one

Note: The numbers 21–29 can be written in Spanish either as one word or as three. However, you must write thirty-one, thirty-two, etc., as three words.

 PRÁCTICA

I. After studying the numbers in this section, fill in the following spaces with the appropriate number to complete the sequence.

1) uno, dos, _____, cuatro, cinco

2) dos, cuatro, seis, _____

3) diez, once, doce, _____, catorce, quince

4) cinco, diez, quince, veinte, _____, treinta

5) nueve, ocho, _____, seis, cinco

6) _____, tres, cinco, siete, nueve, once

7) dos, cuatro, _____, ocho, diez, doce

8) uno, once, dos, doce, tres, _____, cuatro, catorce

9) veintiuno, veinticuatro, _____, treinta

10) veintinueve, _____, veintiuno, diecisiete

II. In the following exercise, first read the mathematical equations aloud, and then
write them out. Follow these models:

$$1 + 1 = 2 \quad \underline{uno\ y\ uno\ son\ dos}$$
$$5 - 2 = 3 \quad \underline{cinco\ menos\ dos\ son\ tres}$$
$$2 \times 5 = 10 \quad \underline{dos\ por\ cinco\ son\ diez}$$

1) $2 + 4 = 6$ _____

2) $9 - 3 = 6$ _____

3) $2 \times 2 = 4$ _____

4) $5 + 5 = 10$ _____

5) $14 + 4 = 18$ _____

6) $7 \times 4 = 28$ _____

7) $12 - 4 = 8$ _____

8) $1 + 1 = 2$ _____

III. Write the corresponding number next to the figures.

1) _____

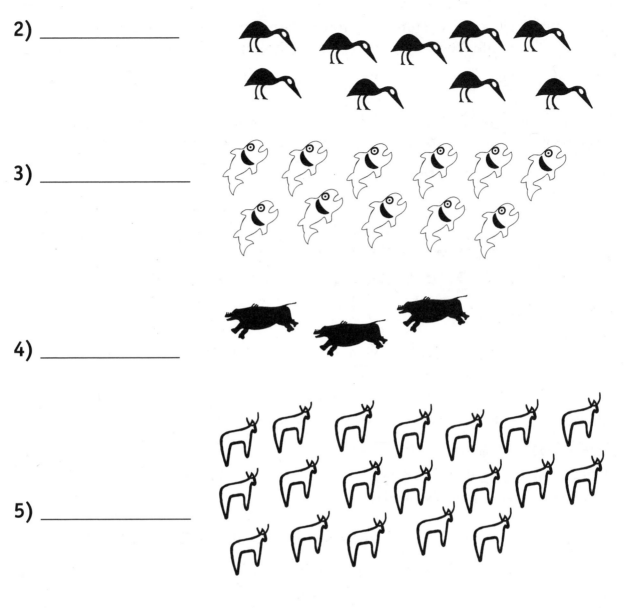

2) _____

3) _____

4) _____

5) _____

PRÁCTICA DE PRONUNCIACIÓN

r , rr

 TRACK 17 DISC 1 Here are two more consonants:

r – The Spanish "r" is different from the English "r." It is a "rolled" r . . . it sounds as though you were imitating the sound of a motor of an airplane. A number of years back, a famous advertisement for *"Ruffles"* potato chips presented this "r" sound with the line *"Ruffles* have ridges." Some have learned this sound by repeating the

word "butter" or "kitty" ten times in a row as fast as possible. The rolled "r" sound starts to come to life. You will have to practice this one with your teacher and CD.

caro, pero, hablar, comer, irse, arte, comercio, carta, puerta

rr – The "rr" is also considered a single consonant in Spanish. It is almost like the "r" sound, but it has even more force and roll.

perro, carro, barrera, carrera, correo, errar, errante, zorro

 # STEP NINE — ¿QUÉ DÍA ES HOY? . . . ¿QUÉ TIEMPO HACE HOY?

 In this section, you will first learn to find out what day, month and season it is. You will then learn how to talk about the weather.

When you want to find out what day it is, you can ask someone:

¿Qué día es hoy? (What day is it?)
> *Hoy es lunes.* (Today is Monday.)
> *Hoy es martes.* (Today is Tuesday.)

When you want to find out what day tomorrow is, you could ask:

¿Qué día es mañana? (What day is tomorrow?)
> *Mañana es jueves.* (Tomorrow is Thursday.)
> *Mañana es viernes.* (Tomorrow is Friday.)

Here is a list of the days of the week:

LOS DÍAS DE LA SEMANA			
lunes → Monday		*viernes* → Friday	
martes → Tuesday		*sábado* → Saturday	
miércoles → Wednesday		*domingo* → Sunday	
jueves → Thursday			

If you want to find out in what month someone's birthday falls, you could ask:

¿En qué mes es su cumpleaños? (In what month is your birthday?)

> *Mi cumpleaños es en agosto.* (My birthday is in August.)
> *Mi cumpleaños es en noviembre.* (My birthday is in November.)

Here is a list of the months of the year:

LOS MESES DEL AÑO					
enero	→	January	*julio*	→	July
febrero	→	February	*agosto*	→	August
marzo	→	March	*septiembre*	→	September
abril	→	April	*octubre*	→	October
mayo	→	May	*noviembre*	→	November
junio	→	June	*diciembre*	→	December

If you want to ask someone which season is his or her favorite, you could ask:

¿Qué estación le gusta más? (What season do you like best?)

> *Me gusta más la primavera.* (I like the spring best.)
> *Me gusta más el verano.* (I like the summer best.)
> *Me gusta más el otoño.* (I like the fall most.)
> *Me gusta más el invierno.* (I like the winter most.)

When you want to find out what the weather is like, you can ask someone:

¿Qué tiempo hace hoy? (How's the weather today?)

> *Hace frío.* (It's cold.)
> *Hace calor.* (It's hot.)

If it is particularly hot or cold, a person might respond:

> *Hace mucho frío.* (It's very cold.)
> *Hace mucho calor.* (It's very hot.)

Here are a few common expressions that describe the weather:

EL TIEMPO					
Hace calor.	→	It's hot.	*Hace viento.*	→	It's windy.
Hace frío.	→	It's cold.	*Llueve.*	→	It's raining.
Hace sol.	→	It's sunny.	*Nieva.*	→	It's snowing.

PRÁCTICA

I. Answer the following questions using vocabulary from this section.

1) ¿Qué tiempo hace hoy? _____.

2) ¿Qué día es hoy? _____.

3) ¿Qué tiempo hace en diciembre en Minnesota? _____.

4) ¿Hace mucho viento en Chicago? _____

_____.

5) ¿Qué estación le gusta más? _____.

6) ¿En qué mes es su cumpleaños? _____.

7) ¿Le gustan más los lunes o los sábados? _____

_____.

8) ¿Cuántos (How many) **meses hay en un año?** _____

_____.

9) ¿Cuántos días hay en una semana? _____

_____.

10) ¿Qué tiempo hace en San Juan, Puerto Rico? _____

_____.

II. Complete the following lists using vocabulary from this section.

1) **lunes, martes, miércoles, jueves, _____, sábado**

2) **enero, marzo, mayo, _____, septiembre**

3) **sí-no, día-noche, frío-_____**

4) **primavera, verano, otoño, _____**

5) **lunes, el veintidós de octubre, miércoles, el veinticuatro de octubre,**

_____

  ## PRÁCTICA DE PRONUNCIACIÓN

j, g

 Here are two more consonants:

j – The Spanish "j" has a rather harsh sound, kind of like an English "h" that got caught in the back of your throat. At times, it sounds as if one were clearing one's throat.

jota, jamón, rojo, reloj, jaca, lejos, junio, julio, jarabe, justos

g – The "g" is pronounced in two different ways. As in English, when a "g" comes before an "a," "o," or "u," it sounds just like the "g" in "goose."

gota, gozar, lago, Gutiérrez, gato, lúgubre, Galicia, gobierno

Note: The groupings "gui" and "gue" are pronounced in Spanish in a special way. The "u" sound in both of these groupings is completely silent. The purpose of the silent "u" is to make the "g" sound like the one in "goose."

guitarra, guerra, guisar, llegue, merengue, guisado, guiñar, sigue

When a "g" is before an "e" or an "i," however, it sounds just like the "j" described above.

gente, gitano, gesto, girar, ágil, generoso, general

STEP TEN — ¿QUÉ HORA ES?

 In this final "**STEP**" section, you will learn to tell time.

When you want to find out what time it is, you can ask someone:

¿Qué hora es?

>*Es la una.* (It's one o'clock.)
>*Son las dos.* (It's two o'clock.)
>*Son las tres.* (It's three o'clock.)

Here are some other useful constructions to use when talking about time:

>*Es la una y cuarto.* (It's quarter after one.)
>*Son las dos y cuarto.* (It's quarter after two.)

>*Es la una y media.* (It's one-thirty.)
>*Son las cinco y media.* (It's five-thirty.)

>*Es la una menos cuarto.* (It's quarter of one.)
>*Son las nueve menos cuarto.* (It's quarter of nine.)

>*Es la una en punto.* (It's one o'clock sharp.)
>*Son las once en punto.* (It's eleven o'clock sharp.)

>*Es la una y veinte.* (It's one-twenty.)
>*Son las nueve y veinte.* (It's nine-twenty.)

>*Es (el) mediodía.* (It's noon.)
>*Es (la) medianoche.* (It's midnight.)

Here are some possible questions you might ask when you want to find out when an event is taking place:

¿A qué hora es la clase de español? ([At] what time is the Spanish class?)

>*La clase de español es a las diez.* (The Spanish class is at ten.)

¿A qué hora es el partido de fútbol? ([At] what time is the soccer game?)

>*El partido de fútbol es a las tres.* (The soccer game is at three.)

¿A qué hora es la fiesta? ([At] what time is the party?)

>*La fiesta es a las ocho.* (The party is at eight.)

PRÁCTICA

I. Answer the following questions in complete sentences.

1) **¿Qué hora es?** _____ .

2) **¿A qué hora es su clase de español? Mi clase de español es a**

_____ .

3) **¿A qué hora es su clase de historia?**

_____ .

4) **¿A qué hora es su programa favorito* de televisión?**

_____ .

> Why does *"favorito"* end with "o" when *"programa"* ends with "a"? Good question! *"Programa"* is an exception — it's a "masculine" noun!

5) **¿A qué hora hace mucho sol?**

_____ .

6) **Son las cinco ahora. ¿Qué hora es en treinta minutos?**

_____ .

7) Son las cuatro menos cuarto. En veinte minutos, ¿qué hora es?

_____ .

8) Es la una y media ahora. En una hora, ¿qué hora es?

_____ .

II. Using the following clock faces, tell what time it is.

1)   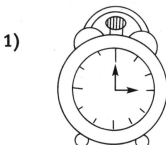   _____

2)      _____

3)      _____

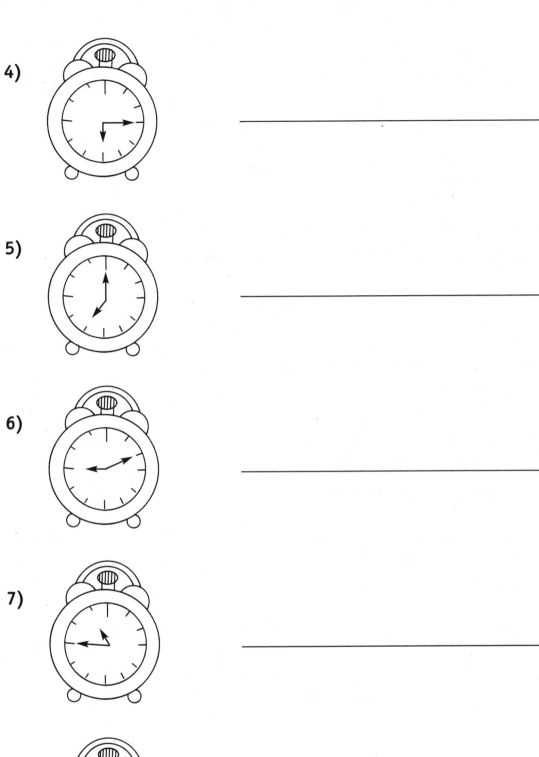

4) _____

5) _____

6) _____

7) _____

8) _____

PRÁCTICA DE PRONUNCIACIÓN

f, t, x

 Here are the last three consonants!

f – Here is an easy one. This consonant sounds like the "f" in "finger."

fe, fiel, café, filosofía, farol, alfabeto, Rafael, física, fideos

t – This consonant is similar to the English "t" in "toss," except that it has a bit softer sound. There is not the same explosion of breath, however, that follows the English "t." If you put a candle close to your lips when saying "Tom," you might blow out the candle. In Spanish, the flame will barely flicker when saying *"Tomás."*

taco, tentar, té, coyote, atleta, tío, temperatura, tostado, tela, timbre, Tomás

x – Depending on its position, the "x" has different sounds. Between vowels, it sounds like the "x" in the English word "exactly."

examen, exigir, éxito, exactamente, exacto

When the "x" comes before a consonant, however, it can sound like the "s" in "soap" (Spain), or like the "x" in "exactly" (Latin America).

extraño, extraordinario, experimental, extraterrestre, explicación

Note: The words *"Texas"* and *"México"* are pronounced "Tejas" and "Méjico."

MÉXICO

MÉXICO

CAPITAL:	La Ciudad de México
POBLACIÓN:	110.000.000
GOBIERNO:	república federal
PRESIDENTE:	Felipe Calderón
DINERO ($):	peso mexicano
PRODUCTOS:	industria, petróleo, plata, telenovelas
MÚSICA, BAILE:	corridos, mariachi, rancheras
SITIOS DE INTERÉS:	Baja California, Cancún, Oaxaca, Querétaro, ruinas de los aztecas y de los mayas
COMIDA TÍPICA:	frijoles, guacamole, huevos rancheros, mole poblano, quesadillas, tacos, tamales, tequila, tortillas

MEXICANOS FAMOSOS:

Gael García Bernal (ACTOR)

Cantinflas (ACTOR)

Sor Juana Inés de la Cruz (POETA)

Salma Hayek (ACTRIZ)

Benito Juárez (HÉROE NACIONAL)

Frida Kahlo (ARTISTA)

José Clemente Orozco (MURALISTA)

Octavio Paz (POETA)

Diego Rivera (ARTISTA)

Hugo Sánchez (ATLETA)

Pancho Villa (HÉROE NACIONAL)

VOCABULARIO
LECCIÓN UNO

THEME WORDS: "PEOPLE"

la *amiga*	friend
el *amigo*	friend
el *bebé*	baby
la *chica*	girl
el *chico*	boy
el *hombre*	man
la *mujer*	woman
la *niña*	girl
el *niño*	boy

OTHER NOUNS

la *clase*	class
el *día*	day
la *escuela*	school
la *fiesta*	party
el *libro*	book
la *noche*	night
el *reloj*	clock, watch

ADJECTIVES

bueno/a	good
grande	big
guapo/a	good-looking
interesante	interesting
malo/a	bad
pequeño/a	small
rígido/a	rigid
simpático/a	nice

VERBS

admitir	to admit
aprender	to learn
bailar	to dance
beber	to drink
caminar	to walk
comer	to eat
comprar	to buy
correr	to run
enseñar	to teach
escribir	to write
ganar	to win, to earn
hablar	to talk, to speak
leer	to read
limpiar	to clean
preparar	to prepare
trabajar	to work
vender	to sell
vivir	to live

MISCELLANEOUS

a	at, to
allí	there
aquí	here
con	with
después	after
en	in, on
mucho	a lot
no	no
poco	a little
sí	yes
sin	without
también	also
y	and

LECCIÓN UNO

KEY GRAMMAR CONCEPTS 	**A) VERBS IN THE PRESENT TENSE** → *Los verbos en el presente* **B) SUBJECT PRONOUNS** → *Los pronombres pronominales* **C) INTERROGATIVES** → *Los interrogativos*

 ## A) VERBS IN THE PRESENT TENSE

Verbs are the words in a sentence that narrate the action; they tell you what is going on. Unlike in English, the letters at the end of a verb in Spanish let you know who the subject is. Once you learn these endings, you will be ready to speak complete Spanish sentences!

The infinitive of a verb is its simplest form, the starting place before it is conjugated or changed to correspond to a specific person. All Spanish infinitives end in the letters **-AR**, **-ER**, or **-IR**.

The **present tense** describes actions that are happening now, reports current conditions or traits, describes customary events, and also announces what may be happening in the immediate future.

Here are the full conjugations of three common verbs in the present tense:

	HABLAR (to speak)	**COMER** (to eat)	**VIVIR** (to live)
I	hablo	como	vivo
you (familiar)	hablas	comes	vives
he/she/you (formal)	habla	come	vive
we	hablamos	comemos	vivimos
you all (familiar)	habláis	coméis	vivís
they/you all (formal)	hablan	comen	viven

Helpful Tip: Do you notice that **-AR**, **-ER**, and **-IR** verbs share some common endings but have different ones as well? Study the <u>endings</u> of the verbs carefully. They provide a clue to help you figure out who the subject is.

✳ **EXAMPLES:** *Cristina **habla** mucho.*
　　　　　　Cristina speaks a lot.

　　　　　　***Como** chocolate en febrero.*
　　　　　　I eat chocolate in February.

　　　　　　***Vivimos** en Chihuahua, México.*
　　　　　　We live in Chihuahua, Mexico.

　　　　　　*¿**Come** Óscar de la Hoya mucha pizza?*
　　　　　　Does Óscar de la Hoya eat a lot of pizza?

　　　　　　*¿**Viven** los tigres en África?*
　　　　　　Do tigers live in Africa?

You may have noticed that the subject is sometimes mentioned *(Cristina habla . . .)* and at other times not *(Como chocolate . . .)*. Because the ending of the verb helps to identify the subject, the subject is normally only mentioned for **clarification** or **emphasis**. In a statement in which the subject is mentioned, it is usually placed before the verb; in a question, however, it will follow the verb.

The following list contains some of the most frequently used verbs in the Spanish language. All of these verbs follow the conjugation patterns presented on the previous page. Although you do not need to know the meanings of all these words just yet, you will be noticing them throughout this book. In time, they will all become old friends.

Here is a list of some "high frequency" verbs:

-AR		-ER	-IR
andar (to walk)	*estudiar* (to study)	*aprender* (to learn)	*abrir* (to open)
apagar (to turn off)	*ganar* (to earn, win)	*beber* (to drink)	*admitir* (to admit)
bailar (to dance)	*lavar* (to wash)	*comer* (to eat)	*descubrir* (to discover)
bajar (to go down)	*limpiar* (to clean)	*comprender* (to understand)	*escribir* (to write)
caminar (to walk)	*llamar* (to call)	*correr* (to run)	*ocurrir* (to occur)
cantar (to sing)	*llegar* (to arrive)	*leer* (to read)	*permitir* (to permit)
cocinar (to cook)	*llorar* (to cry)	*romper* (to break)	*subir* (to go up)
contestar (to answer)	*mirar* (to look at)	*vender* (to sell)	*vivir* (to live)
entrar (to enter)	*pasar* (to spend time)		
escapar (to escape)	*preguntar* (to ask)		
escuchar (to listen to)	*preparar* (to prepare)		
esperar (to wait for)	*trabajar* (to work)		

✳ **EXAMPLES:** *Mi papá **prepara** tacos en el restaurante.*
　　　　　　My dad prepares tacos in the restaurant.

　　　　　　*¿**Venden** los artistas mucho arte?*
　　　　　　Do the artists sell a lot of art?

*¿**Escribe** el profesor mucho en julio?*
Does the teacher write a lot in July?

Bailamos la salsa con la música de Marc Anthony.
We dance the salsa to the music of Marc Anthony.

 # PRACTICE EXERCISES

1. Conjugate these verbs fully in the present tense using the models found on page 37:

   cantar (to sing)   **vender** (to sell)   **permitir** (to permit)

   _____ _____   _____ _____   _____ _____

   _____ _____   _____ _____   _____ _____

   _____ _____   _____ _____   _____ _____

2. Now write the correct form of the indicated verb in the spaces provided:

   a. Peter Gabriel _____ la canción al final de
   Wall-E. (cantar)

   b. (We) _____ en Oaxaca, México. (Vivir)

   c. (I) _____ limonada deliciosa. (Vender)

   d. Mi mamá y mi papá _____ en un hospital. (trabajar)

   e. (You, familiar) No _____ tus errores. (admitir)

   f. (You all) _____ <u>People en español</u> en el taxi. (Leer)

   g. El actor Diego Luna _____ mucho en Hollywood.
   (aprender)

   h. Guillermo Ochoa _____ muchos trofeos de fútbol. (ganar)

   i. (I) _____ la música con mi profesora. (Practicar)

   j. (We) _____ poemas interesantes. (Escribir)

B) SUBJECT PRONOUNS

Pronouns are words that can take the place of nouns. Nouns are people, animals, places, things or ideas. A subject pronoun can serve as the main actor of a sentence. In English, we use subject pronouns all the time. In Spanish, however, **subject pronouns** are only used for emphasis or clarity.

Here are the subject pronouns in Spanish and their English equivalents:

yo →	I
tú →	you (familiar)
él →	he
ella →	she
usted (Ud.) →	you (formal)
nosotros/nosotras →	we
vosotros/vosotras* → (*used only in Spain!)	you all (familiar)
ellos →	they (masculine)
ellas →	they (feminine)
ustedes (Uds.) →	you all

Helpful Tips: **1)** You may have noticed that Spanish expresses "you" in two different ways: *tú* and *usted* (commonly abbreviated *Ud.*).
2) *Tú* is used when a person directly addresses a friend or peer. It is a familiar, friendly pronoun.
3) *Ud.* also means "you," but it is reserved for addressing a stranger, an acquaintance, someone whose title you use (Dr., Professor), or someone older than you. It is a formal, respectful greeting. When in doubt, it is wise to use *Ud.*

There are also two ways to say "you all": *vosotros/vosotras* and *ustedes (Uds.).* In most of Spain, *vosotros/vosotras* is the familiar plural form used when addressing friends. *Vosotros* is used when speaking to a group of male friends or to a group of male and female friends; *vosotras* is used only when addressing female friends. However, in all other areas of the Spanish-speaking world, *Uds.* is used to mean "you all," whether speaking to friends or strangers, to men or women.

EXAMPLES: *Yo hablo con Chayanne, pero **tú** cantas con Shakira.*
I talk with Chayanne, but you sing with Shakira.

*¿Miguel? ¿Isabel? –¡**Nosotros** estamos aquí!*
Miguel? Isabel? –We're here!

***Ellas** no comen hamburguesas en la cafetería.*
They don't eat hamburgers in the cafeteria.

Uds. no limpian el sofá.
You all don't clean the sofa.

Vosotros vivís en Guadalajara, ¿no?
You all live in Guadalajara, don't you?

Ramón y Mercedes son amigos; **él** *es de México y* **ella** *es de Venezuela.**
Ramón and Mercedes are friends; he is from Mexico, and she is from Venezuela.

Note: In this sentence, the listener would be confused without *"él"* and *"ella."*

PRACTICE EXERCISES

1. **Translate the following English pronouns into Spanish:**

   a. I _____

   b. you (familiar) _____

   c. they (feminine) _____

   d. he _____

   e. we (2 ways) _____

   f. you all (familiar) _____
   (in Spain, 2 ways)

   g. she _____

   h. you all (formal) _____

2. **The speakers of the following sentences want to emphasize the subject. Provide the proper subject pronoun. Remember, you'll know the subject by looking at the verb ending:**

   a. _____ escuchas la música de RBD.

   b. _____ aprendemos mucho en la clase de física.

   c. Marco lee día y noche; _____ es muy inteligente.

   d. Tú y _____ caminamos por el parque bonito.

   e. _____ escuchas la música de Alejandro Fernández en el autobús.

   f. Mi mamá y mi abuela enseñan español en una escuela de niñas;

   _____ son profesoras.

g. ¿Cantan _____ normalmente en la clase? –Sí, cantamos allí.

h. _____ vivís en Madrid, ¿no? –Sí, vivimos en Madrid.

i. Ana no permite distracciones; _____ es muy rígida.

j. _____ corro en el Maratón de Nueva York.

3. The following paragraph contains five verbal errors. Underline each error and write the correct word above it:

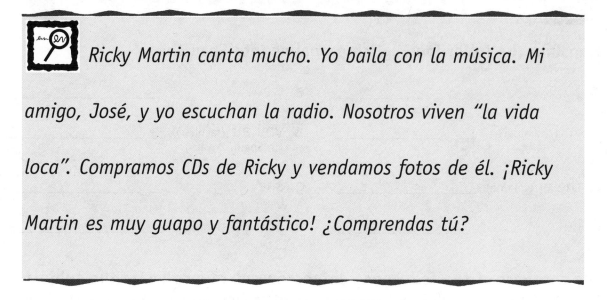

Ricky Martin canta mucho. Yo baila con la música. Mi amigo, José, y yo escuchan la radio. Nosotros viven "la vida loca". Compramos CDs de Ricky y vendamos fotos de él. ¡Ricky Martin es muy guapo y fantástico! ¿Comprendas tú?

Interrogatives are words that ask questions. These words help you zero in on the answer you want. In Spanish, these interrogative words always carry a written accent mark.

Here are the most common interrogative words:

¿Quién?/¿Quiénes? → Who?	*¿Por qué?* → Why?
¿Qué? → What?	*¿Cuándo?* → When?
¿Cuál?/¿Cuáles? → Which?/What?	*¿Cuánto?/¿Cuánta?* → How much?
¿Dónde? → Where?	*¿Cuántos?/¿Cuántas?* → How many?
	¿Cómo? → How?

¡CUIDADO! *"Porque"* means "because" when it is written as one word with no accent.

EXAMPLES: *¿Quién admite sus errores?*
Who admits errors?

¿Quiénes bailan ahora?
Who are dancing now?

¿Qué libro lees en el hotel?
What book are you reading in the hotel?

Vendo pizza y tacos. ¿Cuál compra Ud. hoy?
I sell pizza and tacos. Which are you buying today?

¿Dónde viven los chicos de RBD*?*
Where do the guys from *RBD* live?

¿Por qué no miramos Grey's Anatomy*?*
Why aren't we watching *Grey's Anatomy*?

¿Cuándo es la fiesta de San Valentín?
When is the St. Valentine's party?

¿Cuánto dinero ganan los políticos?
How much money do politicians earn?

¿Cuántos bebés hay en la familia?
How many babies are there in the family?

¿Cómo está Ud., señor Chávez? –Bien, gracias.
How are you, Mr. Chávez? –Fine, thanks.

1. Insert the appropriate interrogative word in the sentences below:

   a. ¿_____ es el examen de historia? –Mañana.

   b. ¿_____ viven los leones? –Viven en África.

   c. ¿_____ es el actor en *Spiderman III*? –Tobey Maguire.

   d. ¿_____ libro prefieres leer? –<u>Don Quijote.</u>

   e. Yo bebo mucha Coca-Cola y Pepsi. –¿_____ prefieres tú?

   f. ¿_____ no abren la puerta los niños? –Porque hace mucho frío.

   g. ¿_____ personas hay en la clase? –16.

2. The following dialogue contains four errors related to interrogative words. Underline each error and write the correct word above it:

–Hola, Marcos. ¿Quien es el chico?

–Se llama José.

–¿Cuando vive?

–Vive en Los Ángeles.

–¿Qué come José?

–Come enchiladas y tacos.

–¿Qué de los dos come más?

–José come más tacos.

–¿Cuántas tacos come?

–Come diez.

–¡Caramba!

These two sets of questions use grammatical structures and vocabulary from this lesson. Working with a partner, alternate asking and answering each question. Even though you are working with a classmate, some of the questions will use the familiar "tú" form and others will use the more formal "Ud." When you get to the bottom of each list, start over at the top, switching roles. As a variation, write out the answers in complete sentences.

A) ¿Hablas español en la clase?

¿Comes mucho chocolate?

¿Le gusta caminar en el parque?

¿Cómo se llama tu libro favorito?

¿De dónde es usted?

¿Cómo estás hoy?

¿Es grande o pequeño un bebé?

B) ¿Bailas mucho en las fiestas?

¿Dónde vives?

¿Es bueno o malo escribir en los libros?

¿Bebes Coca-Cola o Pepsi?

¿Quién trabaja en una escuela?

¿Cuándo hablas con tus amigos?

¿Cómo se llama un actor muy guapo?

The following dialogue contains grammar and vocabulary that you've seen in this lesson and in the introductory section. After listening to the CD, read this dialogue aloud, alone or with friends. Afterwards, try to answer the questions that follow either aloud or in written form.

 ## LAS AVENTURAS DE RAFAEL, ELISA Y "EL TIGRE"

ESCENA UNO

Rafael y "El Tigre" hablan en el parque. Son de Washington, D.C.

Rafael: ¿Cómo estás, Tigre?

El Tigre: Muy bien, Rafael, pero hace mucho calor hoy.

Rafael: Sí, vivimos en Washington donde siempre hace mucho calor.

El Tigre: Es verdad, pero no me gusta el calor.

Rafael: ¿Por qué no caminamos a la fiesta de mi prima?

El Tigre: ¿Quién es tu prima?

Rafael: Es Elisa . . . Elisa Montesinos.

El Tigre: Ella es muy inteligente y muy guapa. ¡Vamos! (Let's go!).

Rafael y "El Tigre" entran en la casa de Elisa.

Rafael: Hola, Elisa. Te presento a mi amigo, El Tigre.

Elisa: Hola, Tigre. Me llamo Elisa. ¿Te gusta la música?

El Tigre: Sí, mucho. Me gusta mucho el disco compacto de Carlos Santana, *Supernatural.* ¡Es lo máximo!

Elisa: Es divino. La canción *"María, María"* es sensacional.

El Tigre: ¿Bailamos un poco?

Elisa: ¿Por qué no?

Rafael come muchos Doritos y bebe Fanta de limón.

Elisa: ¡Bailas muy bien!

El Tigre: Gracias, Elisa.

Elisa: Rafael, tu amigo es muy simpático.

Rafael: Es verdad. Elisa, El Tigre y yo preparamos un viaje a Nueva York en una semana. ¿Te gusta Nueva York?

Elisa: Sí, mucho, pero mis padres son muy estrictos. No me permiten viajar.

El Tigre: No te preocupes, Elisa. Tenemos un plan excelente.

PREGUNTAS

1) ¿De dónde son Rafael y El Tigre?

_____

2) ¿Qué tiempo hace normalmente en Washington, D.C.?

_____

3) ¿Cómo se llama la prima de Rafael?

_____

4) ¿Cómo es Elisa Montesinos?

_____

5) ¿Cómo se llama el disco compacto que escuchan?

_____

6) ¿Quiénes bailan?

_____

7) ¿Qué come Rafael?

_____

8) ¿Adónde van Rafael y El Tigre en una semana?

_____

9) ¿Puede ir Elisa, también?

_____

10) ¿Cómo son los padres de Elisa?

_____

PRUEBA DE REPASO

1. Answer in complete sentences:

a. ¿Habla Ud. mucho en la clase?

_____

b. ¿Dónde lees los libros?

_____

c. ¿Come su hermano muchos tacos?

_____

d. ¿Bailan Uds. en la discoteca?

_____

e. ¿Cuándo es la clase de español?

_____

2. Conjugate the following six verbs fully in the present tense:

     hablar (to speak)   **comer** (to eat)   **vivir** (to live)

_____ _____   _____ _____   _____ _____

_____ _____   _____ _____   _____ _____

_____ _____   _____ _____   _____ _____

     limpiar (to clean)   **leer** (to read)   **admitir** (to admit)

_____ _____   _____ _____   _____ _____

_____ _____   _____ _____   _____ _____

_____ _____   _____ _____   _____ _____

3. Write the correct form of each verb in the spaces provided:

a. Yo _____ la mesa todos los días. (limpiar)

b. Nosotras _____ mucho dinero en Las Vegas. (ganar)

c. Ud. no _____ bien las lecciones. (preparar)

d. Penélope y Javier _____ a la fiesta rápidamente. (correr)

e. Tú _____ muchos productos buenos. (vender)

f. Los chicos guapos de *Linkin Park* no _____ en el parque. (trabajar)

g. Tú y ella no _____ en Cancún. (vivir)

h. La profesora de mi clase de inglés _____ muy bien la materia. (enseñar)

i. Mi primo no _____ sus errores. (admitir)

j. Ud. y yo _____ mucho en la escuela. (aprender)

4. Write all possible subject pronouns in front of each of these conjugated verbs:

a. _____ aprendes

b. _____ ganan

c. _____ leo

d. _____ preparamos

e. _____ vivís

f. _____ baila

g. _____ trabajo

h. _____ corres

i. _____ vende

5. Write an appropriate interrogative word in the spaces provided:

a. ¿_____ es la fiesta? –El viernes.

b. ¿_____ de los libros le gusta más? –Me gusta más <u>Don Quijote.</u>

c. ¿_____ es el presidente de México? –Felipe Calderón.

d. ¿_____ comes muchos tacos? –Como muchos tacos porque me gustan.

e. ¿_____ hablan español? –Hablan español en México, Colombia y Puerto Rico.

f. ¿_____ hora es? –Son las seis y media.

g. ¿_____ personas hay en la clase de español? –Veinte.

h. ¿_____ está Ud.? –Muy bien, gracias.

6. Translate the following sentences into Spanish:

a. She works with a friend in the park.

_____

b. Who is the small boy with the book?

_____

c. My brother and I run a lot, also.

_____

d. Yes, I dance with them at the party.

_____

7. The following paragraph contains seven errors. Underline each error and write the correct word above it. **¡CUIDADO!** Be on the lookout for verb errors and agreement errors:

Buenos días. Mi amiga y yo caminemos mucho en el parque. El parque no es grande; es pequeña. Después mi amiga y yo comamos en un restaurante. ¿Por que? La pizza es bueno. Los tacos son deliciosos. Mi amiga beba Sprite y yo beba té con limón. Adiós.

ESPAÑA

Océano Atlántico

FRANCIA

La Coruña

Santiago de Compostela

LA CORDILLERA CANTÁBRICA

Bilbao

LOS PIRINEOS

Valladolid

Salamanca

Zaragoza

Segovia

Barcelona

Madrid ★

RÍO TAJO

Toledo

PORTUGAL

ESPAÑA

Valencia

GOLFO DE VALENCIA

Córdoba

SIERRA MORENA

Alicante

Mar Mediterráneo

Sevilla

GOLFO DE CÁDIZ

ANDALUCÍA

Cádiz

Málaga

Granada

SIERRA NEVADA

ESPAÑOLES FAMOSOS:

Pedro Almodóvar
(DIRECTOR)

Antonio Banderas
(ACTOR)

Emilia Pardo Bazán
(ESCRITORA)

Montserrat Caballé
(CANTANTE)

Pablo Casals
(MÚSICO)

Miguel de Cervantes
(AUTOR DE DON QUIJOTE)

Penélope Cruz
(ACTRIZ)

Salvador Dalí
(ARTISTA)

Plácido Domingo
(CANTANTE)

Generalísimo
Francisco Franco
(DICTADOR)

Pau Gasol
(JUGADOR DE BALONCESTO)

Antoni Gaudí
(ARQUITECTO)

Francisco Goya
(ARTISTA)

El Greco (ARTISTA)

Miguel Induráin
(CICLISTA)

Ana María Matute
(AUTORA)

Rafael Nadal
(TENISTA)

Pablo Picasso (ARTISTA)

Andrés Segovia
(MÚSICO)

Miguel de Unamuno
(ESCRITOR Y FILÓSOFO)

Diego Velázquez
(ARTISTA)

ESPAÑA

CAPITAL: Madrid

POBLACIÓN: 40.500.000

GOBIERNO: monarquía parlamentaria

JEFE DEL ESTADO: El rey don Juan Carlos I

PRESIDENTE: José Luis Rodríguez Zapatero

DINERO ($): euro

PRODUCTOS: aceite de oliva, naranjas, vino

MÚSICA, BAILE: flamenco, sevillanas

SITIOS DE INTERÉS: Acueducto (Segovia), La Alhambra (Granada), La Mezquita (Córdoba), Museo del Prado (Madrid), Museo Guggenheim (Bilbao), Parque Güell (Barcelona)

COMIDA TÍPICA: cochinillo, cordero, gazpacho, paella, sangría, tapas, tortilla española, vino

VOCABULARIO LECCIÓN DOS

THEME WORDS: "TRANSPORTATION"

el autobús	bus
el avión	airplane
el barco	boat
la bicicleta	bicycle
el camión	truck
el coche	car
la moto(cicleta)	motorcycle
el taxi	taxi
el tren	train

OTHER NOUNS

el amor	love
la ciudad	city
la cosa	thing
el dinero	money
el disco compacto	compact disc (CD)
la fecha	date
el premio	prize
el pueblo	town, village

ADJECTIVES

alto/a	tall
atestado/a	crowded
bajo/a	short
caro/a	expensive
difícil	difficult
especial	special
fácil	easy
frío/a	cold
nuevo/a	new
pobre	poor
rico/a	rich
viejo/a	old

VERBS

abrir	to open
cerrar (ie)*	to close
comenzar (ie)	to begin
creer	to believe
jugar (ue)*	to play
llegar	to arrive
mirar	to look at
mover (ue)	to move
poder (ue)	to be able to
preferir (ie)	to prefer
recibir	to receive
recordar (ue)	to remember
servir (i)*	to serve
viajar	to travel
volver (ue)	to return

MISCELLANEOUS

ahora	now
frecuentemente	frequently
gracias	thanks
más	more
menos	less
que	that, which
siempre	always

***Note:** The letters *"ie," "ue,"* and *"i"* in parentheses will indicate a "boot" verb, explained on page 55.

LECCIÓN DOS

KEY GRAMMAR CONCEPTS

A) **"BOOT" VERBS IN THE PRESENT TENSE** → *Los verbos de "bota" en el presente*

B) **CONJUNCTIONS** → *Las conjunciones*

C) **NOUNS: SINGULAR AND PLURAL FORMS** → *Los sustantivos: las formas singulares y plurales*

D) **ADJECTIVES AND THE IDEA OF AGREEMENT** → *Los adjetivos y el concepto de concordancia*

A) "BOOT" VERBS IN THE PRESENT TENSE

The regular verbs presented in *Lección Uno* share the same stem for all six conjugations. When you conjugate certain other verbs, however, it is necessary to make changes in some of the stems, that is, in the vowel found in the next to last syllable of the infinitive. You will find three kinds of **stem changes**:

    1 e → ie

    2 o → ue

    3 e → i

These changes only take place in the singular forms and in the 3rd person plural.

Let's take a look at three model verbs that illustrate these types of stem change:

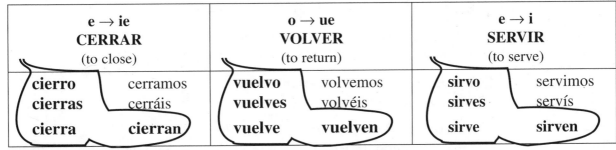

e → ie CERRAR (to close)		o → ue VOLVER (to return)		e → i SERVIR (to serve)	
cierro	cerramos	**vuelvo**	volvemos	**sirvo**	servimos
cierras	cerráis	**vuelves**	volvéis	**sirves**	servís
cierra	**cierran**	**vuelve**	**vuelven**	**sirve**	**sirven**

Helpful Tip: Can you figure out why these verbs have traditionally been called "boot" verbs? The forms that change seem to make a boot shape.

The following is a list of the most common "boot" verbs. You will notice that there are -AR, -ER, and -IR verbs represented in different categories.

Here are common "boot" verbs:

e → ie	o → ue	e → i
cerrar (to close)	*contar* (to count, to tell)	*competir* (to compete)
comenzar (to begin)	*costar* (to cost)	*conseguir*** (to obtain)
empezar (to begin)	*devolver* (to return something)	*corregir*** (to correct)
entender (to understand)	*dormir* (to sleep)	*elegir*** (to elect)
pensar (to think)	*encontrar* (to find)	*pedir* (to ask for)
perder (to lose)	*jugar** (to play)	*reír*** (to laugh)
preferir (to prefer)	*morir* (to die)	*repetir* (to repeat)
querer (to like, to want)	*mostrar* (to show)	*seguir*** (to follow)
sentar (to seat)	*mover* (to move)	*servir* (to serve)
sentir (to feel)	*poder* (to be able to)	
	recordar (to remember)	
	volver (to return)*	

*This verb is a little different:
u → ue

Note: The five asterisked verbs in this list are, in fact, "boot" verbs. In addition, however, there are some other unusual spelling changes in certain forms, which will be illustrated next lesson.

✳ **EXAMPLES:** *¿Por qué **cierras** la puerta de mi casa?*
Why are you closing the door of my house?

*Bárbara Mori no **duerme** mucho cuando viaja.*
Bárbara Mori doesn't sleep a lot when she travels.

*Los profesores **corrigen** los errores en los exámenes.*
The teachers correct the errors on the tests.

*¿Cuándo **comienza** el invierno?*
When does the winter start?

*Yo **vuelvo** con Ricky Martin a Cádiz el lunes.*
I'm returning with Ricky Martin to Cádiz on Monday.

¡CUIDADO! Remember, the changes in these "boot" verbs only occur <u>inside</u> the boot. The *nosotros/as* and *vosotros/as* forms have <u>no</u> change.

✳ **EXAMPLE:** *No **pedimos** dinero; **queremos** amor.*
We don't ask for money; we want love.

PRACTICE EXERCISES

1. Conjugate these verbs fully in the present tense using the models presented earlier on page 55:

    comenzar (to begin)   **mostrar** (to show)   **pedir** (to ask for)

_____ _____ _____ _____ _____ _____

_____ _____ _____ _____ _____ _____

_____ _____ _____ _____ _____ _____

2. In the spaces provided, conjugate the infinitives in the present tense. Be sure that the subject of the sentence agrees with the verb:

  a. Mi amigo _____ mucho en la noche. (dormir)

  b. Dara Torres siempre _____ muy bien con otras atletas profesionales. (competir)

  c. Ellos _____ que el nuevo disco compacto de Ivy Queen es fantástico. (pensar)

  d. Nosotras siempre _____ mucho dinero en Las Vegas. (perder)

  e. ¿Cuánto _____ la nueva computadora Mac? (costar)

  f. Tú y ella no _____ el día de la fiesta en el barco. (recordar)

  g. Yo _____ aprender todo el vocabulario del libro. (poder)

  h. Mis plantas _____ cuando no tienen mucho sol. (morir)

  i. Mis amigas _____ leer *El País* en el avión. (preferir)

  j. Tú no _____ los conceptos complicados de matemáticas. (entender)

  k. Mi amiga siempre _____ los libros a la biblioteca. (devolver)

3. **The following paragraph contains five verbal errors. Underline each error and write the correction above it:**

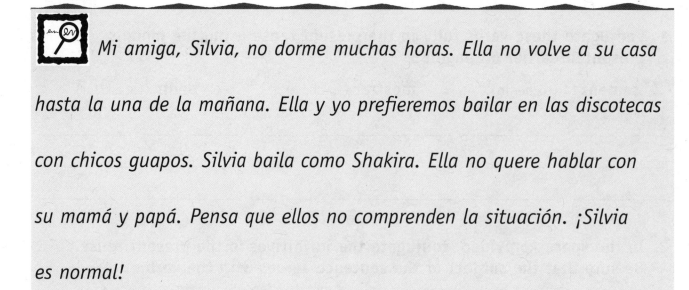

Mi amiga, Silvia, no dorme muchas horas. Ella no volve a su casa hasta la una de la mañana. Ella y yo prefieremos bailar en las discotecas con chicos guapos. Silvia baila como Shakira. Ella no quere hablar con su mamá y papá. Pensa que ellos no comprenden la situación. ¡Silvia es normal!

 B) CONJUNCTIONS

Conjunctions are words that join parts of sentences or even entire sentences. They are connecting words such as "and," "or/either," "nor/neither," "but."

Here are some common conjunctions in Spanish:

Conjunctions
$y \rightarrow$ and
$o \rightarrow$ or, either
$ni \rightarrow$ nor, neither
$pero \rightarrow$ but

 **EXAMPLES:** *Marc Anthony **y** Enrique Iglesias cantan en español.*
Marc Anthony and Enrique Iglesias sing in Spanish.

*Normalmente duermo ocho **o** nueve horas.*
I normally sleep eight or nine hours.

*No queremos **ni** pizza **ni** tamales.**
We don't want either pizza or tamales.

*Note: To avoid what is considered a "double negative" in English, we translate *"ni, ni"* in the above sentence as "either, or." Spanish sentences often have a double negative. More on this concept in a later lesson!

*José pierde mucho, **pero** yo gano frecuentemente.*
José loses a lot, but I win frequently.

*Sergio García **y** Tiger Woods compiten en el torneo de golf, **pero** yo prefiero ver* Lost.

Sergio García and Tiger Woods are competing in the golf tournament, but I prefer to watch *Lost*.

 PRACTICE EXERCISES ▶

1. Place one of these conjunctions *(y, o, ni, pero)* in the sentences below:

a. Melanie Griffith _____ Antonio Banderas trabajan en Hollywood.

b. La profesora ni repite _____ recuerda las instrucciones.

c. No puedo decidir cuál es mi número favorito: el cuatro _____ el cinco.

d. Ni John McCain _____ Nancy Pelosi son de Washington, D.C.

e. Dos _____ dos son cuatro.

f. Normalmente como dos tortillas, _____ hoy prefiero comer tres.

g. _____ Jennifer Hudson _____ David Archuleta canta en los Premios Grammy en 2010.

h. Hannah habla español, _____ Alexandra habla inglés.

i. Mi hermano juega bien al tenis, _____ ¡no es Rafael Nadal!

j. Barack _____ Hillary hablan mucho de política.

2. The following paragraph contains four errors related to conjunctions. Underline each error and write the correction above it:

Mi amigo, Diego, duerme mucho. Normalmente duerme nueve ni diez horas. Un día Diego no puede dormir. Quiere visitar el hospital, perro no puede encontrar su motocicleta. No quiere tomar ni su bicicleta o un taxi. Corre al hospital o habla con el médico. Ahora está bien.

 C) Nouns: singular and plural forms

A **noun** is a word that represents a person, place, thing, or concept.

Here is a list of some common nouns:

Common Nouns	
(la) casa → house	*(la) mesa* → table
(el) coche → car	*(el) momento* → moment
(la) lección → lesson	*(el) papel* → paper
(la) libertad → liberty	*(el) pueblo* → town
(el) libro → book	*(la) silla* → chair
(la) madre → mother	*(el) tren* → train

All of the words in the list above are singular. To make most nouns plural in Spanish, simply add an "s" if the word ends in a vowel (a, e, i, o, u). However, if the word ends in a consonant (any letter other than a, e, i, o, u), add "es."

Let's look at the plural forms of all the words listed above:

Common Nouns (plural form)	
(las) casas → houses	*(las) mesas* → tables
(los) coches → cars	*(los) momentos* → moments
(las) lecciones → lessons	*(los) papeles* → papers
(las) libertades → liberties	*(los) pueblos* → towns
(los) libros → books	*(las) sillas* → chairs
(las) madres → mothers	*(los) trenes* → trains

Helpful Tips: **1)** Did you notice that the small accent mark on the word *lección* disappeared on the plural form *lecciones*?

2) On most words that <u>end</u> with a syllable having a written accent mark, the accent mark drops off in the plural form.

3) Another example of a word like this is *huracán* (hurricane). The plural form is *huracanes* (hurricanes).

 ¡CUIDADO! There is one unusual spelling change that occurs in the plural form of some nouns (and adjectives!). If a noun (or adjective) ends with the letter "z," the "z" must become "c" when in the plural form.

 EXAMPLES: *(el) juez* (judge)   *(los) jueces* (judges)
                          (el) lápiz (pencil)   *(los) lápices* (pencils)
                          (la) nuez (nut)   *(las) nueces* (nuts)
                          (el) pez (fish)   *(los) peces* (fish)

A Special Noun Ending

The endings *"-ito"* and *"-ita"* can be used with most nouns . . . this ending may signal affection or diminutive size.

EXAMPLES: *Juan → Juanito* (Johnny)   *casa → casita* (little house)
                       perro → perrito (little dog)   *Ana → Anita* (Annie)

PRACTICE EXERCISES

1. **Write the plural forms of the following ten nouns, being careful to remember the special rules about accent marks and nouns ending with the letter "z":**

a. abrigo _____

b. pluma _____

c. papel _____

d. padre _____

e. nuez _____

f. lección _____

g. ciudad _____

h. capitán _____

i. ventana _____

j. camión _____

2. Write the *"-ito"* or *"-ita"* form of these nouns. Follow the models illustrated on the previous page.

a. papel _____

b. mesa _____

c. perro _____

d. vaso _____

e. Lola _____

f. Ana _____

D) ADJECTIVES AND THE IDEA OF AGREEMENT

An **adjective** is a word that describes a noun. Often an adjective helps to distinguish one noun from another, e.g., *tacos buenos, tacos malos* (good tacos, bad tacos).

Spanish adjectives are different from English adjectives in two important ways:

1 Spanish adjectives generally <u>follow</u> the nouns they modify.

2 Spanish adjectives must agree in gender and number with the nouns they modify.

What does this all mean? Let's look at few examples:

EXAMPLES: *libro bueno* (good book)
casa buena (good house)

chico alto (tall boy)
chica alta (tall girl)

piano nuevo (new piano)
pluma vieja (old pen)

> **Helpful Tips:** **1)** Do you notice that some of the nouns above end in "o" and some in "a"?
> **2)** In general, nouns that end in "o" are considered "masculine," and ones that end in "a" are considered "feminine."
> **3)** Do you also notice that the adjectives associated with those nouns followed the pattern (ending either with "o" or "a")?

As we learned in the previous section, nouns can also be plural. Look what happens when we make the previous nouns plural:

EXAMPLES: *libros buenos* (good books)
casas buenas (good houses)

chicos altos (tall boys)

chicas altas (tall girls)

pianos nuevos (new pianos)

plumas viejas (old pens)

As you can see, the adjectives became plural to agree with the nouns.

◆ What happens if a noun doesn't end in an *"o"* or an *"a"*? These nouns will still be either masculine or feminine; you just might not be able to know by looking at the word. You must memorize the gender (whether it's masculine or feminine) of these nouns.

Here are a few examples of nouns with modifying adjectives. You can tell if they are masculine or feminine by looking at the adjective ending:

✳ **EXAMPLES:** *leche fría* (cold milk)   *ciudad atestada* (crowded city)

hotel caro (expensive hotel)   *lápices nuevos* (new pencils)

◆ Sometimes, adjectives end with a consonant or with a vowel other than "o" or "a." These adjectives don't change endings when modifying nouns of different genders. For example, *grande* (big) can modify either *río* (river) or *casa* (house): *río grande* or *casa grande.* Here are some more examples:

✳ **EXAMPLES:** *libro fácil* (easy book)   *chica cortés* (polite girl)

prueba fácil (easy quiz)   *hombres pobres* (poor men)

chico cortés (polite boy)   *mujeres pobres* (poor women)

◆ A few adjectives ending with consonants <u>do</u> change when modifying masculine or feminine nouns. When certain adjectives of nationality end with a consonant, the letter *"a"* (or letters *"as"* for plural) is added to make the feminine form.

✳ **EXAMPLES:** *chico inglés* (English boy)

chica inglesa (English girl)

chicos ingleses (English boys)

chicas inglesas (English girls)

queso francés (French cheese)

torta francesa (French cake)

vino español (Spanish wine)

tortilla española (Spanish omelette)

coches japoneses (Japanese cars)

banderas japonesas (Japanese flags)

Helpful Tip: Do you notice that the accent mark dropped off of *inglés* and *francés* in the feminine forms *(inglesa, francesa)*?

PRACTICE EXERCISES

1. **Write the appropriate form of the adjective in parentheses to agree with each noun:**

a. silla _____ (rojo)　　**f.** diccionarios _____ (fácil)

b. guitarra _____ (eléctrico)　　**g.** novelas _____ (exótico)

c. amigos _____ (inglés)　　**h.** planta _____ (japonés)

d. padre _____ (generoso)　　**i.** oficinas _____ (grande)

e. teléfono _____ (celular)　　**j.** chicos _____ (cómico)

2. **The following paragraph contains many errors related to adjectives and nouns. Underline each error you find, and write the correction above it:**

> *Mis padres trabajan en La Casa Blanco. Preparan comida delicioso para el presidente y su familia. Cocinan tortillas españoles, tacos mexicano y ensalada francés. Ganan mucho dinero, pero prefieren tomar más días de vacaciones. Mi hermano cómica ayuda un poco en la cocina y mi hermana come los platos especialas. ¡Me gusta mucho la vida loco en la Casa Blanca!*

These two sets of questions use grammatical structures and vocabulary from this lesson. Working with a partner, alternate asking and answering each question. When you get to the bottom of each list, start over at the top, switching roles. As a variation, write out the answers in complete sentences.

A) ¿Quién cierra la puerta en la clase normalmente?

¿A qué hora vuelves a tu casa?

¿Recibes muchos discos compactos?

¿A qué hora comienza la clase de español?

¿Prefieres las ciudades grandes o los pueblos pequeños?

¿Dónde juegas al béisbol con tus amigos favoritos?

¿Es fácil o difícil recordar la fecha?

B) ¿Le gusta la comida francesa?

¿Prefiere Ud. los autobuses o los taxis? ¿Por qué?

¿Juegan Uds. (tus amigos y tú) con las bicicletas?

¿Cuánto cuesta un disco compacto nuevo?

¿Prefieres lecciones fáciles o lecciones difíciles?

¿Qué tiempo hace hoy?

¿Siempre recibes premios en la escuela?

1. Answer in complete sentences:

a. ¿Cierra Ud. la ventana en la clase?

_____

b. ¿A qué hora vuelves de la escuela?

_____

c. ¿Quién juega al tenis en esta clase?

_____

d. ¿Comes paella frecuentemente?

_____

e. ¿Mueves los brazos (your arms) cuando bailas?

_____

2. Conjugate the following six verbs fully in the present tense:

cerrar (to close)   **volver** (to return)   **servir** (to serve)

_____ _____   _____ _____   _____ _____

_____ _____   _____ _____   _____ _____

_____ _____   _____ _____   _____ _____

recordar (to remember)   **mover** (to move)   **pedir** (to ask for)

_____ _____   _____ _____   _____ _____

_____ _____   _____ _____   _____ _____

_____ _____   _____ _____   _____ _____

3. Write the correct form of each verb in the spaces provided:

a. Mi madre _____ la puerta todas las noches. (cerrar)

b. Tú y yo _____ de Sevilla el domingo. (volver)

c. Eva Longoria _____ comer la comida caliente. (preferir)

d. Tú siempre _____ qué día es hoy. (recordar)

e. Mi hermano _____ frecuentemente a mi abuela en su silla preferida. (sentar)

f. Mis amigos no _____ ver *MTV* porque sus padres prefieren un programa de Disney. (poder)

g. Rafael Nadal siempre _____ muy bien con su raqueta en Wimbledon. (competir)

h. Yo _____ la paciencia cuando camino por una ciudad atestada. (perder)

i. ¿Cuánto _____ un coche nuevo? (costar)

j. Mi madre _____ perfectamente del uno al diez en italiano. (contar)

4. In the following exercise, if a word is singular, make it plural. However, if the word is plural, make it singular:

a. casa _____

b. papel _____

c. lección _____

d. viejas _____

e. corteses _____

f. españoles _____

g. pluma _____

h. lápiz _____

i. libertades _____

5. Write an appropriate conjunction in the space provided:

a. Dos _____ dos son cuatro.

b. No puedo decidir cuál es mi sabor favorito de Ben & Jerry's: chocolate

_____ vainilla.

c. Ni mi padre _____ mi madre quieren viajar ahora a Alicante.

d. O mi madre _____ mi padre puede hablar con la profesora.

e. Normalmente me gusta escuchar la música de Shakira, _____ ahora deseo escuchar mi disco nuevo de Jaci Velásquez.

f. Marcos, Roberto _____ Elisa comienzan a estudiar en el Instituto de Segovia.

g. Mi amiga es inteligente, _____ su hermano no comprende mucho.

h. Ni Elena Ochoa _____ Sergio García juegan al golf cuando nieva.

i. En Chicago hace mucho frío _____ hace viento, también.

6. Translate the following sentences into Spanish:

a. They are returning to the city, but Johnny prefers the village.

_____

b. Ramón and Rosa always close the door.

_____

c. The Spanish kids begin the homework at three.

_____

d. Enrique Iglesias and Anna Kournikova look at the train.

_____

7. The following paragraph contains six errors. Underline each error and write the correct word above it:

Pablo conta su dinero frecuentemente. Pablo es pobre, perro no es muy pobre. Le gusta la música. Prefiere comprar discos nuevo de RBD. También, le gustan los músicos españols, especialmente Mecano, Miguel Bosé y David Bisbal. Comenza a contar el dinero a las ocho de la mañana. Es muy fácil porque sólo tiene diez dólares. Un día o su madre ni su padre compra un disco compacto muy especial para él.

COLOMBIA

COLOMBIA

CAPITAL:	Bogotá
POBLACIÓN:	45.000.000
GOBIERNO:	república
PRESIDENTE:	Álvaro Uribe Vélez
DINERO ($):	peso colombiano
PRODUCTOS:	azúcar, café, fruta, petróleo
MÚSICA, BAILE:	cumbia, influencia afro-caribeña, salsa
SITIOS DE INTERÉS:	el bosque de lluvia, Cali, Cartagena, Ciudad Perdida, Medellín, San Andrés, Villa de Leiva
COMIDA TÍPICA:	ajiaco, arroz con pollo, canasta de coco, guayaba, mazamorra, sancocho, tamales

COLOMBIANOS FAMOSOS:

Fernando Botero
(ARTISTA)

Gabriel García Márquez
(AUTOR)

Cecilia Herrera
(ARTISTA)

Juanes
(CANTANTE)

Juan Pablo Montoya
(ATLETA)

Shakira
(CANTANTE)

José Asunción Silva
(POETA)

Camilo Villegas
(ATLETA)

VOCABULARIO LECCIÓN TRES

TRACK 28 DISC 1

THEME WORDS: "BODY PARTS"

la	*boca*	mouth
el	*brazo*	arm
el	*dedo*	finger
el	*diente*	tooth
la	*mano*	hand
la	*nariz*	nose
el	*ojo*	eye
la	*oreja*	ear
el	*pelo*	hair
el	*pie*	foot
la	*pierna*	leg

OTHER NOUNS

la	*bebida*	drink
el	*cuero*	leather
la	*foto(grafía)*	photo(graph)
los	*jóvenes*	youth, youngsters
la	*luna*	moon
la	*madera*	wood
el	*plástico*	plastic
el	*problema**	problem
la	*verdad*	truth

ADJECTIVES

bonito/a	pretty
enfermo/a	sick
extraño/a (raro/a)	strange

*Although *"problema"* ends in "a", it's a <u>masculine</u> noun!

feo/a	ugly
frustrado/a	frustrated
íntimo/a	intimate, close
típico/a	typical
único/a	only, unique

VERBS

conocer	to know (a person or place)
dar	to give
decir	to say, to tell
ir	to go
odiar	to hate
oír	to hear
saber	to know (a fact)
seguir (i)	to follow
tocar	to play (an instrument), to touch
traer	to bring
ver	to see

MISCELLANEOUS

a la derecha	to the right
a la izquierda	to the left
algo	something
antes (de)	before
cerca (de)	near
después (de)	after
lejos (de)	far
nunca	never
porque	because

LECCIÓN TRES

KEY GRAMMAR CONCEPTS

A) IRREGULAR VERBS IN THE PRESENT TENSE → *Los verbos irregulares en el presente*

B) THE VERBS "SER" AND "ESTAR" → *"Ser" y "estar"*

C) DEFINITE AND INDEFINITE ARTICLES → *Los artículos definidos y indefinidos*

D) NEGATIVE SENTENCES → *Las frases negativas*

 ## A) IRREGULAR VERBS IN THE PRESENT TENSE

The following chart features verbs that are among the most common in the Spanish language. As they are used so frequently, it would be wise to master them now.

caber (to fit)		**caer** (to fall)		**coger** (to grab)		**conocer** (to know)	
quepo	cabemos	**caigo**	caemos	**cojo**	cogemos	**conozco**	conocemos
cabes	cabéis	caes	caéis	coges	cogéis	conoces	conocéis
cabe	caben	cae	caen	coge	cogen	conoce	conocen
construir (to build)		**dar** (to give)		**decir** (to say)		**estar** (to be)	
construyo	construimos	**doy**	damos	**digo**	decimos	**estoy**	estamos
construyes	construís	das	**dais**	**dices**	decís	**estás**	estáis
construye	**construyen**	da	dan	**dice**	**dicen**	**está**	**están**
hacer (to do, make)		**ir** (to go)		**oír** (to hear)		**poner** (to put)	
hago	hacemos	**voy**	**vamos**	**oigo**	**oímos**	**pongo**	ponemos
haces	hacéis	**vas**	**vais**	**oyes**	oís	pones	ponéis
hace	hacen	**va**	**van**	**oye**	**oyen**	pone	ponen
saber (to know)		**salir** (to leave)		**seguir** (to follow)		**ser** (to be)	
sé	sabemos	**salgo**	salimos	**sigo**	seguimos	**soy**	**somos**
sabes	sabéis	sales	salís	**sigues**	seguís	**eres**	**sois**
sabe	saben	sale	salen	**sigue**	**siguen**	**es**	**son**
tener (to have)		**traer** (to bring)		**valer** (to be worth)		**venir** (to come)	
tengo	tenemos	**traigo**	traemos	**valgo**	valemos	**vengo**	venimos
tienes	tenéis	traes	traéis	vales	valéis	**vienes**	venís
tiene	**tienen**	trae	traen	vale	valen	**viene**	**vienen**
ver (to see)							
veo	vemos						
ves	**veis**						
ve	ven						

Note: The forms in **boldface** indicate something a little out of the ordinary: a spelling change, a stem change, an accent mark or lack thereof.

¡CUIDADO! Some verbs have conjugations that can't be predicted easily. Some have special changes in the 1st person form only; others have special changes in every form. In this section, you will need to spend a fair amount of time memorizing the verbs presented.

Helpful Tips: **1)** You undoubtedly noticed that some verbs are irregular only in the *yo* form (e.g., *caber, caer, coger, conocer, hacer, poner, saber, salir, traer, valer*).
2) Other verbs are different only in the *yo* form and in the *vosotros/vosotras* form where there is no written accent (e.g., *dar, ver*).
3) The other verbs are irregular in more than one form.

✳ **EXAMPLES:** *Alejandro Fernández y Luis Miguel **tienen** mucho talento.*
Alejandro Fernández and Luis Miguel have a lot of talent.

*No **pongo** mis libros nuevos en la mesa.*
I don't put my new books on the table.

***Sé** que dos y dos **son** cuatro.*
I know that two and two are four.

*Mi profesora inteligente **dice** que Bogotá es bonita.*
My intelligent teacher says that Bogotá is pretty.

*Mis hermanos **construyen** casas grandes de cartón.*
My brothers are building big cardboard houses.

*Yo no **quepo** en la silla pequeña.*
I don't fit in the small seat.

*Sócrates **es** mi filósofo favorito.*
Socrates is my favorite philosopher.

***Oigo** la música, pero no **veo** la trompeta.*
I hear the music, but I don't see the trumpet.

*Mi prima **tiene** las manos pequeñas, los pies normales y una boca muy grande.*
My cousin has small hands, normal feet, and a very big mouth.

1. **Study the list of irregular verbs carefully. Now conjugate the following six verbs fully without looking at the lists. Then check your answers carefully and correct any errors:**

conocer (to know)   **decir** (to say)   **ir** (to go)

_____   _____   _____   _____   _____   _____

_____   _____   _____   _____   _____   _____

_____   _____   _____   _____   _____   _____

poner (to put)   **ser** (to be)   **ver** (to see)

_____   _____   _____   _____   _____   _____

_____   _____   _____   _____   _____   _____

_____   _____   _____   _____   _____   _____

2. **Complete the following sentences in the present tense using the correct form of the verb in parentheses:**

a. Nosotros _____ estudiantes aplicados. (ser)

b. Mi amiga, Lucía, _____ el nuevo disco de *Coldplay*. (tener)

c. Ellos no _____ la verdad. (decir)

d. Quetzal _____ el dragón en el programa de televisión, *Dragon Tales*. (ser)

e. Yo no _____ mi tarea todas las noches porque prefiero jugar con mis amigos. (hacer)

f. Mi hermana _____ los secretos íntimos de mis padres. (oír)

g. Cuando no estudias, tu mamá _____ muy frustrada. (estar)

h. Mis fotos de Elvis _____ mucho dinero. (valer)

i. Olga Tañón no _____ a ver más partidos de béisbol. (ir)

j. Mi madre coge el tren por la mañana, pero yo _____ el tren de la tarde. (coger)

3. **The following dialogue contains eight errors. Underline each error and write the correct word above it:**

Raúl:	*Vamos a salir.*
Lucía:	*No, yo no salo. No teno dinero.*
Raúl:	*Tengo diez dólares. Vamos.*
Lucía:	*Pero, yo no cabo en el taxi.*
Raúl:	*Estas loca. ¡Sí, cabes!*
Lucía:	*Pero, yo no esto contenta.*
Raúl:	*¿Por qué?*
Lucía:	*Porque yo no conoco Bogotá.*
Raúl:	*¿De dónde eres?*
Lucía:	*So de Medellín.*
Raúl:	*Caramba, ¿vienes?*
Lucía:	*Sí, vo.*

B) THE VERBS "SER" AND "ESTAR"

Spanish has two different verbs that mean "to be." Not only are their conjugations irregular, but they are also used in different situations. Here are the main uses of each verb:

1) THE USES OF "SER"

a) To identify a defining characteristic

✳ **EXAMPLES:** *Los ojos de mi hijo **son** azules.*
My son's eyes are blue.

*American Idol **es** mi programa de televisión favorito.*
American Idol is my favorite television program.

b) To tell where someone or something is from; to indicate origin

✳ **EXAMPLES:** *Camilo Villegas **es** de Colombia.*
Camilo Villegas is from Colombia.

*Mi vestido **es** de Guatemala.*
My dress is from Guatemala.

c) To tell time or give a date

✳ **EXAMPLES:** ***Son** las siete y cinco.*
It is five after seven.

*Hoy **es** el veintidós de octubre.*
Today is the twenty-second of October.

d) To indicate possession

✳ **EXAMPLES:** *La guitarra **es** de Shakira.*
The guitar is Shakira's.

*La pelota de baloncesto **es** de Marc Gasol.*
The basketball is Marc Gasol's.

e) To indicate profession, nationality, religion, or political affiliation

✳ **EXAMPLES:** *Mi abuelo **es** colombiano.*
My grandfather is Colombian.

*Bill Richardson **es** político y Geraldo Rivera **es** periodista.*
Bill Richardson is a politician, and Geraldo Rivera is a journalist.

f) To tell when or where an event is taking place

> ✳ **EXAMPLES:** *El concierto de Wisin y Yandel **es** a las seis.*
> Wisin y Yandel's concert is at six.
>
> *La fiesta de Año Nuevo **es** en Times Square.*
> The New Year's party is in Times Square.

g) To tell what something is made of

> ✳ **EXAMPLES:** *Mi casa **es** de madera.*
> My house is made out of wood.
>
> *Los pantalones de Ricky Martin **son** de cuero.*
> Ricky Martin's pants are made of leather.

h) For mathematical calculations

> ✳ **EXAMPLES:** *Tres y uno **son** cuatro.*
> Three plus one is four.
>
> *Cuatro por tres **son** doce.*
> Four times three is twelve.

2) THE USES OF "ESTAR"

a) To express a condition, as opposed to a defining characteristic

> ✳ **EXAMPLES:** ***Estoy** enferma y voy al hospital.*
> I'm sick, and I'm going to the hospital.
>
> ***Estamos** tristes porque no tenemos entradas para el concierto de Daddy Yankee.*
> We are sad because we don't have tickets for the Daddy Yankee concert.

b) To identify location (though <u>not</u> of an event!)

> ✳ **EXAMPLES:** *Mis amigos **están** en la cocina ahora.*
> My friends are in the kitchen now.
>
> *Santo Domingo **está** en la República Dominicana.*
> Santo Domingo is in the Dominican Republic.

¿ ◆ ? Did you notice that the location may be temporary or permanent?

---

c) **To indicate a change from the norm or to emphasize the special state or nature of something**

 EXAMPLES: *¡Estás muy guapo hoy!*
You look great today!

(The idea here is that you have gotten all dressed up, your hair looks great, etc. By using *estar,* the speaker emphasizes that you look <u>especially</u> good today!)

Enrique, ¡estás flaquísimo!
Enrique, you look so thin!

(The speaker is emphasizing that Enrique looks especially thin — maybe he has lost weight or his clothes make him look slimmer than usual.)

d) **To talk about certain weather conditions**

 EXAMPLES: *Está nublado ahora en Barranquilla.*
It is cloudy now in Barranquilla.

Está soleado esta tarde en la playa.
It's sunny this afternoon on the beach.

PRACTICE EXERCISES

1. **Insert the correct present tense of either the verb *"ser"* or *"estar"* in the following sentences. Write the reason (2b, 1e, etc.) in the margin to the right:**

   a. Estelle _____ muy enferma hoy y no puede cantar en el concierto. ____

   b. Nosotros _____ de Cartagena, Colombia. ____

   c. Tú _____ un profesor muy inteligente. ____

   d. Scott Gómez _____ uno de los pocos jugadores latinos de la Liga Nacional de Hockey. ____

   e. Disney World _____ en Orlando, Florida. ____

   f. _____ las cuatro de la tarde . . . ¡comienza el programa *Cristina!* ____

   g. No podemos ver la luna porque _____ muy nublado ahora. ____

   h. La guitarra bonita _____ de Carlos Ponce. ____

i. Ramona, ¡_____ muy bonita hoy . . . tu camisa es preciosa! _____

j. Los libros _____ de papel. _____

2. The following paragraph contains seven errors of *"ser"* and *"estar."* Underline each error and write the correction above it:

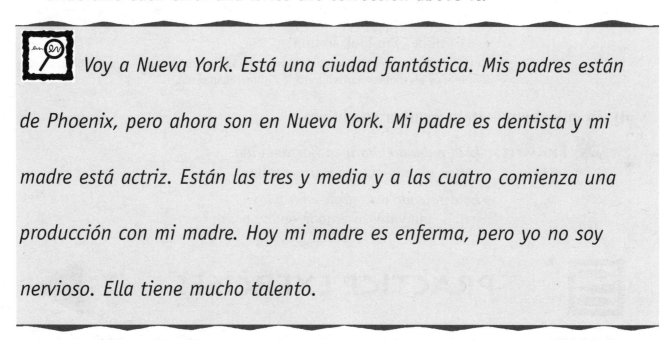

Voy a Nueva York. Está una ciudad fantástica. Mis padres están de Phoenix, pero ahora son en Nueva York. Mi padre es dentista y mi madre está actriz. Están las tres y media y a las cuatro comienza una producción con mi madre. Hoy mi madre es enferma, pero yo no soy nervioso. Ella tiene mucho talento.

C) DEFINITE AND INDEFINITE ARTICLES

Articles are adjectives that help to identify nouns. In English, we have only one **definite article** — "the," which refers to a specific thing or things, e.g., "the afternoon, the cars." We also have **indefinite articles** — "a, an," which refer to one of those things, e.g., "a car, an afternoon."

1) DEFINITE ARTICLES

Spanish has four definite articles. Remember, because they are a type of adjective, they have to agree with the masculine or feminine nouns they modify. They will also be singular or plural!

Here are the Spanish definite articles:

Definite Articles	
el (masculine, singular)	*los* (masculine, plural)
la (feminine, singular)	*las* (feminine, plural)

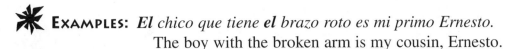

EXAMPLES: *El chico que tiene **el** brazo roto es mi primo Ernesto.*
The boy with the broken arm is my cousin, Ernesto.

*"**La** persona del siglo" es Albert Einstein, dice la revista <u>Time</u>.*
"The Person of the Century" is Albert Einstein, says <u>Time</u> Magazine.

*Como **los** chocolates en mi cama.*
I eat the chocolates in my bed.

***Las** bebidas están muy frías.*
The drinks are very cold.

2) INDEFINITE ARTICLES

Indefinite articles also have four forms, which correspond to the gender and number of the noun they modify.

Here are the Spanish indefinite articles:

Indefinite Articles	
un (masculine, singular)	***unos*** (masculine, plural)
una (feminine, singular)	***unas*** (feminine, plural)

EXAMPLES: *Normalmente leo **un** libro con mi amiga.*
I normally read a book with my friend.

*Fanny Lú es **una** cantante famosa.*
Fanny Lú is a famous singer.

*Tengo **unos** amigos que viven en Bucaramanga, Colombia.*
I have some friends who live in Bucaramanga, Colombia.

***Unas** personas misteriosas viven aquí en el hotel.*
Some mysterious people live here in the hotel.

Helpful Tip: Did you notice that both definite and indefinite articles come before the nouns that they modify? In this way, they are different from the descriptive adjectives that we saw earlier.

---

1. Fill in the blanks with the correct definite article:

a. _____ libros

b. _____ pierna

c. _____ madre

d. _____ profesores

e. _____ japonesas

f. _____ narices

g. _____ padres

h. _____ lápiz

i. _____ libertad

j. _____ cucarachas

2. Now fill in the blanks with the correct indefinite article:

a. _____ puertas

b. _____ abuelo

c. _____ guitarra

d. _____ españoles

e. _____ camisas

f. _____ dedo

g. _____ luna

h. _____ momentos

i. _____ oportunidades

j. _____ coche

3. The following paragraph contains seven errors related to definite and indefinite articles. Underline each error and write the correction above it:

 Los amigas de mi hermano Pepito están locas. Un amiga es

Natalia. Tiene una frutas en su coche. Los frutas no son buenas . . . Un

amiga es Nacha. Tiene uno guitarra eléctrica, pero su música es mala. Un

día voy a decir: "Pepito, los amigas que tienes son raras".

D) NEGATIVE SENTENCES

As you may have noticed in the **FIRST STEPS** section of this text, if you answer a question negatively, a negative word must come <u>before</u> the verb.

Here is a list of some negative words that will come in handy right now:

<table>
<tr><td colspan="2">Common Negative Words</td></tr>
<tr><td>nada →</td><td>nothing</td></tr>
<tr><td>nadie →</td><td>no one</td></tr>
<tr><td>ni →</td><td>neither, nor</td></tr>
<tr><td>no →</td><td>no, not</td></tr>
<tr><td>nunca →</td><td>never</td></tr>
</table>

EXAMPLES:
*¿Vas al concierto de Carlos Santana? –**No, no** voy.*
Are you going to the Carlos Santana concert? –No, I'm not going.

*¿Tienes mucho dinero aquí? –**No, no** tengo mucho.*
Do you have much money here? –No, I don't have much.

*¿Escuchas la música de Andrés Cabas? –**No, nunca** escucho su música. (**No, no** escucho su música **nunca**.)*
Do you listen to the music of Andrés Cabas? –I never listen to his music.

*¿Quién va a mi restaurante favorito? –**No** va **nadie**. (**Nadie** va.)*
Who is going to my favorite restaurant? –No one is going.

*¿Hay mucha comida en el refrigerador? –**No, no** hay **nada**.*
Is there a lot of food in the refrigerator? –No, there is nothing.

*¿Va Pepe o Luisa al restaurante? –**No, ni** Pepe **ni** Luisa van.*
Is Pepe or Luisa going to the restaurant? –No, neither Pepe nor Luisa is going.

*¿Tienes algo? –**No, no** tengo **nada**.**

Do you have something? –No, I don't have anything.

Note: You could <u>not</u> say: *"No, no tengo algo." Once a negative indicator is placed before the verb, words that follow <u>must</u> take a negative form.

PRACTICE EXERCISES

1. **Answer the following questions negatively, being sure to place a negative word before the verb in your answer. Use at least one of the following four negative words in each complete sentence** *(nada, nadie, nunca, ni)*:

a. ¿Tienes siempre mucha tarea en tu clase de matemáticas?

_____

b. ¿Quién va a la fiesta el sábado?

_____

c. ¿Vas frecuentemente a la discoteca con Mick Jagger?

_____

d. ¿Tienes algo?

_____

e. ¿Cuáles de tus amigos tienen dientes bonitos?

_____

f. ¿Hablas portugués, italiano y francés?

_____

g. ¿Cuándo ves *Ugly Betty* y *Lost*?

_____

2. Correct the errors that you spot in the following job interview. Be on the lookout for "negative" errors!

Sra. Ortega: Buenos días. ¿Es Ud. Roberto Gómez?

Luis Gómez: Soy no Roberto; soy Luis.

Sra.: Sí, sí. ¿Desea Ud. un trabajo?

Luis: Sí, pero tengo no experiencia.

Sra.: Pero, ¿habla Ud. bien el español?

Luis: Sí, señora.

Sra.: ¿Con quién habla Ud.?

Luis: Hablo con nadie, pero veo la televisión.

Sra.: ¿Qué programas?

Luis: American Idol y 24.

Sra.: Pero, son no programas en español.

Luis: Es verdad.

Sra.: ¿Ud. cree que soy idiota?

Luis: No . . . sí . . . no . . . no sé.

Sra.: Adiós, Sr. Gómez.

Luis: ¡Voy a volver nunca aquí!

These two sets of questions use grammatical structures and vocabulary from this lesson. Working with a partner, alternate asking and answering each question. When you get to the bottom of each list, start over at the top, switching roles. As a variation, write out the answers in complete sentences.

A) ¿Siempre dices la verdad?

¿Dónde pones los libros en la clase? (*silla* – chair, *suelo* – floor)

¿Vas a la escuela los domingos?

¿Eres americano/a?

¿Tienes muchos amigos íntimos con pelo bonito?

¿Puedes ver la luna donde vives?

¿Sabes qué hora es?

B) ¿Cómo estás hoy?

¿De qué material es tu casa? (*madera* – wood, *piedra* – stone)

¿Cuándo estás muy triste?

¿Tocas la guitarra o el piano?

¿Hay bebidas frías en la cafetería de la escuela?

¿Cuál es tu favorita banda de música?

¿Siempre escuchas la música de Enrique Iglesias?

The following dialogue contains grammar and vocabulary that you've seen in this lesson and in the introductory section. After listening to the CD, read this dialogue aloud, alone or with friends. Afterwards, try to answer the questions that follow either aloud or in written form.

 ## LAS AVENTURAS DE RAFAEL, ELISA Y "EL TIGRE"
ESCENA DOS

Rafael, "El Tigre" y Elisa hablan en un restaurante en Georgetown. Es martes.

Rafael: Sí, Tigre. No hay problema. Tengo el dinero.

El Tigre: Pero cuesta mucho viajar a Nueva York.

Rafael: Viajamos en tren, no en taxi. No cuesta mucho.

El Tigre: ¿Estás nerviosa, Elisa?

Elisa: Sí, un poco. Mis padres creen que voy a un campamento de tenis en las montañas de New Hampshire por una semana.

Rafael: Exactamente. Tus padres son muy buenos, pero un poco estúpidos.

El Tigre: Rafael, no es bueno insultar a los padres de Elisa.

Rafael: Pero, son mis tíos. ¿No recuerdas? Soy el primo de Elisa. Es mi familia. Amo muchísimo a mi tío José y a mi tía Sarita.

Entra una camarera.

Camarera: Buenas tardes.

Elisa: Hola. Para mí, un café con leche.

El Tigre: Dos, por favor.

Rafael: Prefiero una Fanta de limón.

La camarera sale y vuelve en un momento con las bebidas.

El Tigre: Muchas gracias, señorita.

Elisa: ¿A qué hora nos reunimos (do we meet) mañana en la estación de tren?

Rafael: A las nueve en punto.

El Tigre: El viaje a Nueva York sólo es de cinco horas.

Elisa: Fantástico. ¿Es posible mañana caminar un poco en el famoso Parque Central?

Rafael: Claro, Elisa. Y hay caballos para los turistas.

El Tigre: Bueno, hasta mañana, Elisa y Rafael. Vuelvo a mi casa.

Elisa: Rafael y yo volvemos a nuestras casas, también.

Rafael: Hasta mañana.

1) ¿Dónde hablan Elisa, Rafael y El Tigre?

_____

2) ¿Cómo viajan los jóvenes a Nueva York?

_____

3) ¿Está nerviosa Elisa? ¿Por qué?

_____

4) ¿Insulta Rafael a los padres de Elisa?

_____

5) ¿Qué beben los tres amigos?

_____

6) ¿Dónde se reúnen los chicos mañana?

_____

7) ¿Cuántas horas es el viaje a Nueva York?

_____

8) ¿Cómo se llama el famoso parque de Nueva York?

_____

9) ¿Qué animales hay en el parque?

_____

10) ¿Adónde van todos al final de la escena?

_____

1. Answer in complete sentences:

a. ¿Dónde estás?

_____

b. ¿Dices siempre la verdad en la clase?

_____

c. ¿A qué hora vas a la escuela?

_____

d. ¿Tienes una guitarra eléctrica?

_____

e. ¿Oyes música ahora?

_____

2. Conjugate the following six verbs fully in the present tense:

salir (to leave)   **ser** (to be)   **seguir** (to follow)

_____ _____   _____ _____   _____ _____

_____ _____   _____ _____   _____ _____

_____ _____   _____ _____   _____ _____

oír (to hear)   **estar** (to be)   **ir** (to go)

_____ _____   _____ _____   _____ _____

_____ _____   _____ _____   _____ _____

_____ _____   _____ _____   _____ _____

3. Write the correct present tense of each verb in the spaces provided:

a. Tengo los ojos cerrados. No _____ nada. (ver)

b. ¿Cuánto _____ una cámara nueva de Canon? (valer)

c. Uds. _____ de Colombia y yo soy de Uruguay. (ser)

d. Yo _____ en la clase del señor Álvarez. (estar)

e. Yo no _____ bien la ciudad de Cali. (conocer)

f. Nosotros _____ la ropa nueva en la mesa. (poner)

g. Tú no _____ la música porque hablas mucho. (oír)

h. Yo me _____ en diciembre cuando nieva mucho. (caer)

i. Yo no _____ en la silla pequeña. (caber)

j. Cristián de la Fuente dice: "Yo siempre les _____ las gracias a todos mis amigos". (dar)

4. Write the correct definite or indefinite article as indicated:

definite article	indefinite article
a. _____ madre	**a.** _____ bebida
b. _____ amigos	**b.** _____ brazo
c. _____ persona	**c.** _____ foto
d. _____ chico	**d.** _____ trenes
e. _____ trompeta	**e.** _____ jóvenes
f. _____ españoles	**f.** _____ cosa
g. _____ camisa	**g.** _____ premios
h. _____ piano	**h.** _____ bicicleta

5. Write the correct form of the present tense of *"ser"* or *"estar"*:

a. Mi tía _____ alta.

b. Nosotras _____ muy frustradas ahora.

c. _____ las siete y media.

d. _____ muy nublado ahora y no podemos ver el sol.

e. La casa _____ de madera.

f. Mi padre no _____ aquí.

g. El piano _____ de Elton John.

h. Mi abuelo _____ muy rico.

i. El concierto de Shakira _____ en Madison Square Garden.

j. ¡José, _____ muy guapo hoy! Me gusta tu camisa nueva.

k. En mi opinión, la lámpara _____ muy fea.

6. Translate the following sentences into Spanish:

a. I am from Bogotá, but I am in San Francisco.

_____

b. Alejandro is going to his uncle's school.

_____

c. We never put the old wood near the house.

_____

7. The following paragraph contains six errors related to verbs, adjectives and spelling. Underline each error and write the correction above it:

Buenos días. Están las seis de la mañana y es muy nublado.

¡Hoy no teno escuela! Mi amigo y yo vamas al parque. Vamos a comprar

comida delicioso. Posiblemente vamos a estudiar un poco las leccions en

el parque porque el lunes hay un examen, pero, primero, voy a comer

cereal y beber leche fría. Adiós.

ARGENTINA

ARGENTINA

CAPITAL: Buenos Aires

POBLACIÓN: 40.500.000

GOBIERNO: república

PRESIDENTE: Cristina Fernández de Kirchner

DINERO ($):   peso argentino

PRODUCTOS: agricultura, carne, petróleo

MÚSICA, BAILE: cumbia, tango, zamba

SITIOS DE INTERÉS: Los Andes, la Casa Rosada,
                    las Cataratas del Iguazú,
                    La Pampa, Patagonia

COMIDA TÍPICA: arroz con pollo, churrasco,
                    empanadas, locro, mate, parrillada

ARGENTINOS FAMOSOS:

Jorge Luis Borges
(ESCRITOR)

Julio Cortázar
(ESCRITOR)

Raquel Forner
(ARTISTA)

Manu Ginóbili
(ATLETA)

Diego Maradona
(FUTBOLISTA)

Juan y Evita Perón
(POLÍTICOS)

Manuel Puig
(ESCRITOR)

Gabriela Sabatini
(TENISTA)

Guillermo Vilas
(TENISTA)

VOCABULARIO LECCIÓN CUATRO

THEME WORDS: "IN TOWN"

el *aeropuerto*	airport
la *biblioteca*	library
la *calle*	street
la *cárcel*	jail
el *cine*	movie theater
la *estación de tren*	train station
la *gasolinera*	gas station
la *iglesia*	church
el *parque*	park
el *restaurante*	restaurant
la *sinagoga*	synagogue
el *supermercado*	supermarket
el *teatro*	theater
la *tienda*	store

OTHER NOUNS

el *año*	year
la *canción*	song
la *carta*	letter
el *chicle*	gum
el *continente*	continent
el *equipo*	team
la *limonada*	lemonade
el *mes*	month
la *montaña*	mountain
la *novia*	girlfriend
el *novio*	boyfriend
el *oso*	bear
el *país*	country
la *playa*	beach
el *río*	river

el *secreto*	secret
la *tarea*	homework, task
el *zapato*	shoe

ADJECTIVES

débil	weak
fuerte	strong
otro/a	another, other
pasado/a	past, last

VERBS

bajar	to go down
descubrir	to discover
elegir (i) *	to elect, to choose
llorar	to cry
necesitar	to need
subir	to go up

*This verb is conjugated: *elijo, eliges, elige, elegimos, elegís, eligen.*

MISCELLANEOUS

anoche	last night
ayer	yesterday
de la mañana	A.M. (in the morning)
de la tarde/noche	P.M. (in the afternoon/evening)
durante	during
esta mañana	this morning
esta noche	tonight
esta tarde	this afternoon
luego	later
rápidamente	quickly
¿verdad?	isn't that so?

LECCIÓN CUATRO

KEY GRAMMAR CONCEPTS

A) THE PRETERITE (PAST) TENSE OF REGULAR VERBS → *El pretérito de los verbos regulares*

B) PREPOSITIONS → *Las preposiciones*

C) PRONOUNS AFTER PREPOSITIONS → *Los pronombres después de preposiciones*

 ## A) THE PRETERITE (PAST) TENSE OF REGULAR VERBS

The **preterite** is one of many tenses used in Spanish to describe events that occurred in the past. The preterite talks about <u>completed</u> actions. These actions have a clear ending point (as opposed to habits or descriptions, which have a more ongoing, continuous feeling). The preterite emphasizes the conclusion or ending point of an event or narrative.

Here are the conjugations of three regular verbs in the preterite:

HABLAR		COMER		VIVIR	
hablé	hablamos	comí	comimos	viví	vivimos
hablaste	hablasteis	comiste	comisteis	viviste	vivisteis
habló	hablaron	comió	comieron	vivió	vivieron

Helpful Tips: **1)** Did you notice that there are accents on the *yo* and *Ud./él/ella* forms?
2) You can see that the *nosotros* form of *hablar* is *hablamos* and of *vivir* is *vivimos* — the preterite and present have identical *nosotros* forms for **-AR** and **-IR** verbs! It is only through context that you can know which tense the speaker intended.
3) Do you see the similarities between the *tú* and *vosotros/as* forms? Just add "is" to the *tú* form!

EXAMPLES: *Comí en un restaurante cubano, "Victor's Café", en Nueva York.*
I ate in a Cuban restaurant, "Victor's Café," in New York.

*Anoche **preparamos** la tarea en la biblioteca.*
We prepared the homework in the library last night.

*Coldplay **escribió** una canción excelente: "Viva la vida".*
Coldplay wrote an excellent song: *"Viva la vida."*

Vendiste el libro de español en la escuela, ¿verdad?
You sold the Spanish book in school, right?

*Mis amigos nunca **lavaron** sus abrigos de Patagonia.*
My friends never washed their Patagonia jackets.

*El año pasado, Carolina Herrera y yo **abrimos** una tienda nueva en Buenos Aires.*
Last year, Carolina Herrera and I opened a new store in Buenos Aires.

Whenever you tell how long an event lasted, you will choose the preterite tense. By saying, for example, that a person studied for a year or rested for a number of hours, you convey an ending point. This ending point, indicating a <u>completed</u> action, is a signal for the preterite.

 **EXAMPLES:** *Estudié por tres horas anoche.*
I studied last night for three hours.

Vivimos en Buenos Aires por un año.
We lived in Buenos Aires for one year.

*Esta tarde Rafael Nadal **jugó** al tenis con Roger Federer por tres horas.*
Rafael Nadal played tennis with Roger Federer for three hours this afternoon.

 PRACTICE EXERCISES ▶

1. Conjugate the following verbs fully into the preterite:

llorar (to cry)   **correr** (to run)   **permitir** (to permit)

_____ _____   _____ _____   _____ _____

_____ _____   _____ _____   _____ _____

_____ _____   _____ _____   _____ _____

esperar (to wait for)   **romper** (to break)   **escribir** (to write)

_____ _____   _____ _____   _____ _____

_____ _____   _____ _____   _____ _____

_____ _____   _____ _____   _____ _____

2. Complete the following sentences using the appropriate form of the preterite tense:

a. Speedy Gonzales _____ rápidamente al río. (correr)

b. Los Steelers de Pittsburgh _____ el Super Bowl en 2009. (ganar)

c. Thalía y Enrique Iglesias _____ juntos por unos minutos durante el programa de televisión. (bailar)

d. Rigoberta Menchú _____ el Premio Nobel de la Paz en 1992. (recibir)

e. Yo _____ la puerta grande para mi abuelo. (abrir)

f. Nosotros _____ montañas muy altas en Perú para ver Machu Picchu, la famosa ciudad de los incas. (subir)

g. La estudiante inteligente _____ muchas preguntas difíciles. (contestar)

h. No comprendo por qué tú no _____ la limonada. (beber)

i. Cuando el equipo perdió, ellas _____ por unos minutos. (llorar)

j. ¿Por qué nunca _____ Uds. chicle en la iglesia? (permitir)

k. Nosotros _____ primero a la derecha y después a la izquierda,

pero nunca _____ la calle. (caminar/encontrar)

3. The following paragraph contains five misconjugated verbs. Underline each mistaken verb and write the correct word above it:

Elián González llegió a Florida desde la isla de Cuba. Su madre y él escapieron de allí. Muchas personas desaparecieran cuando su barco se hundió en el agua. Elián vivó con familiares en Miami por muchos meses, y luego volvó a Cuba donde vive su papá. El chico es muy fuerte y a veces hay programas en la televisión sobre él.

B) PREPOSITIONS

Prepositions are words in a sentence that join with nouns and pronouns to form phrases (e.g., *in the forest; with him*). These words help to establish relationships between words.

The forms of the prepositions never change; they are the same no matter what words are nearby.

Here is a list of ten of the most common prepositions in Spanish:

Common Prepositions	
a → at, to	*en* → in, on
antes de → before	*hasta* → until
con → with	*para* → by, for, in order to
de → of, from	*por* → by, for, through
después de → after	*sin* → without

EXAMPLES: *Vamos **a** la casa de Vico C, un rapero famoso.*
We are going to the home of Vico C, a famous rapper.

*Gael García Bernal es el actor principal **en** la película* Diarios de motocicleta.
Gael García Bernal is the main actor in the movie *Motorcycle Diaries*.

*En febrero, el presidente boliviano, Evo Morales, habló **con** la presidenta chilena, Michelle Bachelet.*
In February, the Bolivian president, Evo Morales, spoke with the Chilean president, Michelle Bachelet.

*Voy a leer muchos cuentos de Jorge Luis Borges **antes de** junio.*
I'm going to read many stories by Jorge Luis Borges before June.

*Siempre dejo una carta y muchas galletas **para** Santa Claus.*
I always leave a letter and many cookies for Santa Claus.

*Hoy voy a trabajar **hasta** las diez de la noche.*
I'm going to work today until ten P.M.

The prepositions *"a"* and *"de"* form contractions when they are followed by the definite article *"el."* These two contractions are the only ones used in the Spanish language. They are obligatory! When *"a"* or *"de"* is followed by *"el,"* you <u>must</u> make the following contractions:

> *a + el = al*   *de + el = del*

Helpful Tip: Be aware that *"a"* + *él* (he, him) is not contracted!

Here are some sentences that use these contractions:

 **EXAMPLES:** *La bicicleta nueva es **del** chico, no de la chica.*
The new bicycle is the boy's, not the girl's.

*Cuando mis amigos van **al** parque, nunca me invitan.*
When my friends go to the park, they never invite me.

*Nunca vamos a revelar el secreto **del** robo nocturno.*
We will never reveal the secret of the nighttime robbery.

*Kelly Ripa y Mark Consuelos fueron primero **al** hotel y después a la playa.*
Kelly Ripa and Mark Consuelos first went to the hotel and afterwards to the beach.

¿ ◆ ? Do you notice that there are no contractions with *a la, a los, a las,* nor with *de la, de los,* or *de las*?

Certain verbs are followed by the preposition *"a"* when an infinitive follows:

aprender → to learn	*empezar (ie)* → to begin
comenzar (ie) → to begin	*ir* → to go

 EXAMPLES: *Aprendemos **a** esquiar en New Hampshire.*
We're learning to ski in New Hampshire.

*Comienzas **a** bailar.*
You are beginning to dance.

*Empiezan **a** pintar.*
They are beginning to paint.

*Voy **a** estudiar.*
I'm going to study.

PRACTICE EXERCISES

1. **Place one of these prepositions** (*a, antes de, con, de, después de, en, hasta, para, por, sin*) **in the following sentences. Make the appropriate contraction "del" or "al" when necessary. For a few sentences, there may be more than one correct answer:**

a. Mi plato favorito en este restaurante es chili _____ carne.

b. Cuando estoy en mi clase de español, siempre me siento _____ mi silla favorita.

c. No quiero ir al supermercado _____ María; ella necesita ir, también.

d. Voy _____ el hospital ahora porque mi abuelita está enferma.

e. ¡Rápido! Sólo quedan cinco minutos _____ el comienzo de la nueva película de Almodóvar, *Abrazos rotos*.

f. Si tienes tiempo, ¿quieres ir a mi casa _____ la conferencia?

g. _____ aprender a hablar bien el español, es necesario estudiar muchas horas.

h. Mi hermano siempre corre en la calle _____ llegar rápidamente; yo prefiero caminar.

i. Son las ocho _____ la noche; ahora comienza mi programa favorito, *Sábado gigante*.

j. Me gusta mucho caminar _____ la playa _____ zapatos.

2. The following letter contains six errors; a few errors are based on prepositions, the others are verbal in nature. Find them and make appropriate corrections:

Mariana:

Salí hoy de el hotel y descubré que mi novio, Jorge, salió can otra chica, Luisa. Llegaron a un restaurante a las dos de la tarde. Después de diez minutos yo entre en el restaurante. Pregunté: "Jorge, ¿vas a salir de aquí con ella o sino ella?" Jorge no es estúpido. Él saló inmediatamente con su novia favorita: yo.

Silvia

 C) PRONOUNS AFTER PREPOSITIONS

You undoubtedly remember the subject pronouns we first learned in *Lección Uno: yo, tú, él, ella, Ud., nosotros/nosotras, vosotros/vosotras, ellos, ellas,* and *Uds.* These pronouns serve as the main actors or "stars" (subjects!) of a sentence. What happens, however, when a **pronoun follows a preposition**? This lesson will teach you what to do.

Here is the list of pronouns that follow a preposition:

mí	*nosotros, nosotras*
ti	*vosotros, vosotras*
él, ella, Ud.	*ellos, ellas, Uds.*

Helpful Tips: **1)** Did you notice that this list is almost identical to the subject pronoun list? The only differences are seen in the 1st person singular *(mí)* and 2nd person singular *(ti)*.
2) *Ti* does <u>not</u> have an accent (ever!), although many beginning Spanish students can't seem to resist adding one!

✳ EXAMPLES: *Para mí, el mejor cantante es Juanes.*
For me, the best singer is Juanes.

*No vamos al concierto **sin ellos**.*
We aren't going to the concert without them.

*No sólo pienso **en mí**; pienso **en ti**, también.*
I don't only think about myself; I think of you, too.

*Podemos ir **con ella**, pero prefiero caminar sola.*
We can go with her, but I prefer to walk alone.

*Creo que Luis Miguel y Aracely Arámbula son muy guapos. ¿Qué opinión tienes **de ellos**?*
I believe that Luis Miguel and Aracely Arámbula are very good-looking. What do you think of them?

*Uds. no van a oír mucho **de mí** en el futuro porque me voy a otro país.*
You all are not going to hear much of me in the future because I am going to another country.

¡CUIDADO! After the preposition *"con,"* however, you must use these special forms:

> *conmigo* → with me
> *contigo* → with you (familiar)

✳ EXAMPLES: *Mi amiga no viene **conmigo** hoy porque sale con su novio, el gaucho.*
My friend isn't coming with me today because she is going out with her boyfriend, the cowboy.

*Mia Hamm no puede hablar **contigo** ahora porque está con Nomar Garciaparra.*
Mia Hamm can't speak with you now because she is with Nomar Garciaparra.

*No hablo con él ni con ella; hablo **contigo**.*
I'm not talking with him, nor with her; I'm talking with you.

PRACTICE EXERCISES

1. Translate the pronouns in parentheses:

a. El nuevo vídeo de Disney es para _____. (me)

b. Nunca tengo tiempo de hacer las camas para _____. (them)

c. Mi oso de peluche siempre va con_____ cuando viajo en tren. (me)

d. Jorge Campos, el futbolista, es una inspiración para _____. (us)

e. Es verdad que mis padres no saben nada de _____. (you, familiar)

f. _____ tienen mucha familia en las pampas de Argentina, ¿verdad?
(You all)

g. Voy a hablar con _____ después de clase. (you, formal)

h. ¿Qué piensas de _____? (her)

i. Esta motocicleta nueva es para _____. (him)

j. Voy a leer <u>La vida es sueño</u> con_____, mi amor. (you, familiar)

2. Try to write one long sentence that uses the following five words and phrases:

después de	*en*	*conmigo*	*de ella*	*al*

_____

_____

These two sets of questions use grammatical structures and vocabulary from this lesson. Working with a partner, alternate asking and answering each question. When you get to the bottom of each list, start over at the top, switching roles. As a variation, write out the answers in complete sentences.

A) ¿Qué comiste anoche?

¿Quién cerró la puerta en la clase hoy?

¿Escribiste una carta esta mañana?

¿Compraste zapatos nuevos en agosto?

¿Caminaron tus amigos en las montañas en el verano?

¿Preparaste una sorpresa (surprise) con tus hermanos ayer?

¿Corriste en un maratón el año pasado?

B) ¿Tienes una carta para mí?

¿Quieres oír un secreto?

¿Cuál es tu aeropuerto favorito?

¿Es muy fuerte un oso?

¿Te gusta cantar en el baño?

¿Es la limonada de la chica o del chico?

¿Vendiste tu otro coche esta tarde?

1. **Answer in complete sentences, paying close attention to whether the present or preterite is used:**

   a. ¿Hablaste mucho español ayer?

   _____

   b. ¿Escribiste muchas cartas el verano pasado?

   _____

   c. ¿Tienes información nueva para mí?

   _____

   d. ¿Estudiaron Uds. mucho el domingo?

   _____

   e. ¿Prefieres hablar conmigo o con Cristiano Ronaldo, el futbolista?

   _____

2. **Conjugate the following six verbs fully in the preterite tense:**

   hablar (to speak)   **comer** (to eat)   **vivir** (to live)

   _____   _____   _____

   _____   _____   _____

   _____   _____   _____

   necesitar (to need)   **vender** (to sell)   **escribir** (to write)

   _____   _____   _____

   _____   _____   _____

   _____   _____   _____

3. Write the correct form of the preterite in the spaces provided:

a. Sean _____ rápidamente para ganar la competición en *Survivor*. (correr)

b. Nosotros _____ hablar con el director de la escuela. (necesitar)

c. En la tienda ellos _____ chicle delicioso. (vender)

d. Diego Luna _____ con América Ferrera por cinco minutos. (hablar)

e. Uds. _____ en el restaurante cerca de la playa. (comer)

f. Mi suegra _____ en Córdoba por dos años. (vivir)

g. Antonio Banderas no _____ una carta ayer. (escribir)

h. Tú _____ una comida fantástica anoche. (cocinar)

i. Yo no _____ la silla pequeña; ¡tú y yo

_____ la silla grande! (romper/romper)

j. El sargento no _____ secretos en su clase. (permitir)

4. Write one of these prepositions in the sentences that follow (*a, antes de, con, de, después de, en, hasta, para, por, sin*)**:**

a. No voy a la playa antes de las doce; voy _____ las doce.

b. No corro con mis amigos; corro _____ ellos.

c. Voy _____ la cárcel para visitar a tus padres.

d. Vamos a estar en Los Andes _____ el fin del mes.

e. ¿Dejas muchas galletas y una carta _____ Santa Claus?

f. Hay seis gatos que viven _____ la casa.

g. "Me gustan las pizzas _____ mucho queso", confesó Peyton Manning.

h. Vamos a pasar _____ el parque ahora.

i. Primero caminamos a la tienda y después vamos _____ el banco.

j. Enero es _____ febrero.

5. Translate the pronouns in parentheses:

a. Siempre bailo el tango con_____, mi amor. (you)

b. La canción no es para _____; es para mi novio. (him)

c. ¿Qué opinión tienes de _____? (her)

d. Señor, estos platos exquisitos son para _____. (you)

e. Mis amigos no saben nada de _____. (you, familiar)

f. El equipo de fútbol no es lo suficiente fuerte para _____. (us)

g. La semana pasada mi novia necesitó hablar con_____ en la estación de tren. (me)

h. La tarea no es para _____; es para _____. (them/you, familiar)

i. Durante la fiesta, hay chicle y limonada para _____. (you all)

j. Los zapatos no son para ellos; son para _____. (me)

6. Translate the following sentences into Spanish:

a. They needed to run to the other gas station.

_____

b. The letters are for him.

_____

c. During the meeting last night, I sold my new song.

_____

7. The following paragraph contains six errors. Underline each error and write the correction above it:

Anoche una persona misteriosa llamé a la puerta. Cuando yo abrió

la puerta, la persona corró rápidamente a la calle. Grité y grité pero la

persona no hablió con mí. Hoy voy a hablar con la policía. También, voy

a vender mi casa. ¿Qué piensas de mi?

LOS ESTADOS UNIDOS

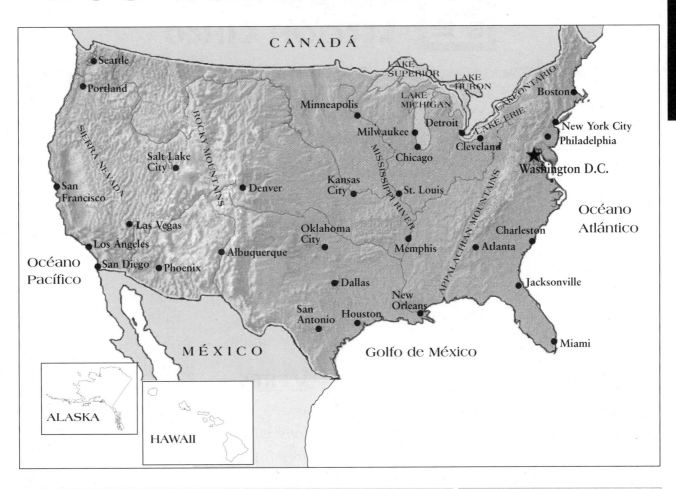

LOS ESTADOS UNIDOS

CAPITAL:	Washington, D.C.
POBLACIÓN:	304.000.000
GOBIERNO:	república constitucional
PRESIDENTE:	Barack Obama
DINERO ($):	dólar
PRODUCTOS:	agricultura, tecnología
MÚSICA, BAILE:	"bluegrass," country, jazz, rap, "square dance"
SITIOS DE INTERÉS:	las Cataratas del Niágara, el Gran Cañón del Colorado, Yosemite
COMIDA TÍPICA:	carne, hamburguesas, maíz, panqueques, pavo asado, perros calientes, pizza, tarta de manzana

ESTADOUNIDENSES FAMOSOS:

César Chávez
(ACTIVISTA)

Walt Disney
(ARTISTA)

Anna Escobedo Cabral
(TESORERA)

Scott Gómez
(ATLETA)

Ellen Ochoa
(ASTRONAUTA)

Bill Richardson
(POLÍTICO)

Loretta y Silvia Sánchez
(POLÍTICAS)

VOCABULARIO LECCIÓN CINCO

THEME WORDS: "FOOD AND DRINK"

el agua (f.)	water
el arroz	rice
el azúcar	sugar
el café	coffee
la carne	meat
la ensalada	salad
la hamburguesa	hamburger
el helado	ice cream
el huevo	egg
la mantequilla	butter
la manzana	apple
la naranja	orange
el pan	bread
el pescado	fish
el pollo	chicken
el queso	cheese
la sopa	soup
el té	tea
el tomate	tomato
el vino	wine
la zanahoria	carrot

OTHER NOUNS

el bigote	mustache
la botella	bottle
el chiste	joke
el cumpleaños	birthday
el regalo	present
la reunión	meeting, reunion
el vaso	glass

ADJECTIVES

abierto/a	open
cerrado/a	closed
eléctrico/a	electric
feliz	happy
original	original
tarde	late
temprano/a	early

VERBS

amar	to love
conseguir (i)	to get, to obtain
dormir (ue)	to sleep
esperar	to hope, to wait
insultar	to insult
llevar	to take, to carry
morir (ue)	to die
pedir (i)	to ask for, to order (food)
poner	to put
quedar	to remain
sentir (ie)	to feel, to regret

MISCELLANEOUS

a veces	at times, sometimes
aunque	although
dos veces	twice
sólo	only
una vez	once

LECCIÓN CINCO

KEY GRAMMAR CONCEPTS

A) THE PRETERITE OF "BOOT" VERBS → *El pretérito de verbos de bota*

B) DIRECT OBJECT PRONOUNS (DOPs) → *Los pronombres complementos (directos)*

C) THE PERSONAL "A" → *El uso de la "a" personal*

D) IDIOMATIC EXPRESSIONS THAT USE "TENER" → *Expresiones idiomáticas con "tener"*

A) THE PRETERITE OF "BOOT" VERBS

What happens to "boot" verbs in the preterite tense? Do all of the stem changes continue?

1) -AR AND -ER "BOOT" VERBS

There are no stem changes at all for **-AR** and **-ER** "boot" verbs! Hooray! Their preterite forms follow the exact pattern that you learned in the last lesson for regular **-AR** and **-ER** verbs.

Here are four -AR and -ER "boot" verbs in the preterite tense:

CERRAR (to close)		**PERDER** (to lose)	
cerré	cerramos	perdí	perdimos
cerraste	cerrasteis	perdiste	perdisteis
cerró	cerraron	perdió	perdieron
CONTAR (to count)		**VOLVER** (to return)	
conté	contamos	volví	volvimos
contaste	contasteis	volviste	volvisteis
contó	contaron	volvió	volvieron

Helpful Tip: As you can see, the vowels in the stem remain unchanged from the infinitive, with no variation in any form.

EXAMPLES: *Goldilocks **cerró** la puerta después de entrar en la casa de los osos.*
Goldilocks shut the door after entering the bears' house.

***Volviste** a casa muy tarde porque bailaste por tres horas.*
You returned home very late because you danced for three hours.

*Michelle Obama y yo **nos sentamos** en la misma mesa en la Casa Blanca.*
Michelle Obama and I sat down at the same table at the White House.

2) -IR "BOOT" VERBS

The **-IR** "boot" verbs, however, are different. They have a special change, found only in the 3rd person singular and 3rd person plural of the preterite: **e → i** or **o → u**. It's only the sole (bottom) of the boot that changes. It now looks more like a slipper!

Here are four -IR "boot" verbs in the preterite tense:

PEDIR (to ask for)		DORMIR (to sleep)	
pedí	pedimos	dormí	dormimos
pediste	pedisteis	dormiste	dormisteis
pidió	pidieron	durmió	durmieron
SENTIR (to feel)		MORIR (to die)	
sentí	sentimos	morí	morimos
sentiste	sentisteis	moriste	moristeis
sintió	sintieron	murió	murieron

Helpful Tip: Obviously, it is important that you remember which **-IR** verbs are stem-changers and which are not. It is a good idea to review the list of those verbs presented in *Lección Dos* (page 56).

 EXAMPLES: *Anoche Alex Rodríguez* **durmió** *nueve horas.*
Alex Rodríguez slept nine hours last night.

Mis hermanos me **pidieron** *el nuevo disco compacto de Calle 13.*
My brothers asked me for the new Calle 13 CD.

Cuando Fernando Verdasco **sirvió** *muy fuerte, tú serviste muy mal.*
When Fernando Verdasco served very strongly, you served poorly.

Celia Cruz **murió** *en 2003.*
Celia Cruz died in 2003.

Ayer mi tía **repitió** *el mismo chiste dos veces.*
My aunt repeated the same joke twice yesterday.

¿ ◆ ? Once again, did you notice that it is only the 3rd person singular and plural forms of **-IR** verbs that change in the preterite?

PRACTICE EXERCISES

1. Conjugate the following "boot" verbs fully into the preterite:

perder (to lose)	**competir** (to compete)	**morir** (to die)
_____ _____	_____ _____	_____ _____
_____ _____	_____ _____	_____ _____
_____ _____	_____ _____	_____ _____

sentar (to seat)	**pedir** (to ask for)	**dormir** (to sleep)
_____ _____	_____ _____	_____ _____
_____ _____	_____ _____	_____ _____
_____ _____	_____ _____	_____ _____

2. Complete the following sentences using the appropriate form of the preterite tense. Some, but not all, are "boot" verbs:

a. Ana Ivanovic _____ muy bien cuando ganó el Open de Francia en junio. (servir)

b. Mi hermana _____ mucho chicle para su cumpleaños. (pedir)

c. Taylor Swift _____ a Nashville después de su concierto en Dallas. (volver)

d. Tú _____ muchos regalos para tu cumpleaños. (pedir)

e. Los chicos del club _____ un nuevo presidente ayer. (elegir)

f. ¿Cuántas horas _____ el hombre anoche? (dormir)

g. Mi abuela _____ mucho dinero cuando visitó ese casino en Atlantic City. (perder)

h. Cuando ganó su primer Grammy por la canción *Believe,* Cher se

_____ muy feliz. (sentir)

i. Mis abuelos no _____ la película *Vicky Cristina Barcelona.* (entender)

j. El sargento _____ las instrucciones tres veces. (repetir)

3. **Change these verbs from the present tense to the corresponding form of the preterite:**

   a. muestra → _____   **f.** sigue → _____

   b. sirven → _____   **g.** mueren → _____

   c. pierdes → _____   **h.** muevo → _____

   d. mostramos → _____   **i.** recuerdan → _____

   e. duerme → _____   **j.** repite → _____

4. **The following letter contains seven verbal errors. Underline each mistaken verb and write the correction above it:**

 Estimado señor Presley:

   Ayer Ud. vuelvió a Memphis. Cantó muy bien en el concierto. Soy la chica con la blusa roja y la guitarra eléctrica que esperió dos horas cerca de su coche. Ud. pedió la guitarra, pero no la consiguió. No duermí bien después. Me sentí terrible. ¿Duermió Ud. bien? Mañana voy a poner mi guitarra en su coche.

                                     Silvia

B) DIRECT OBJECT PRONOUNS (DOPs)

In *Lección Uno,* we learned that pronouns can take the place of nouns. That lesson presented a list of subject pronouns that could serve as the main actor of a sentence. In *Lección Cuatro,* we learned about pronouns that followed prepositions. In this section, we will look at a special list of pronouns that have a different use.

Direct object pronouns (DOPs) are used in place of nouns that get "acted upon" by verbs directly. For example, in the sentence "Elvis found the guitar," the word "guitar" is the direct object because the guitar is what was found. In the related sentence "Elvis found it," the word "it," is the <u>direct object pronoun</u> ("it" stands for the guitar).

Let's look at another example. In the sentence "Silvia saw Elvis," "Elvis" is the direct object, because he directly received the action of the verb, i.e., <u>he</u> was seen. In the sentence, "Silvia saw him," "him" is the <u>direct object pronoun</u>.

Here is the list of direct object pronouns in Spanish:

Direct Object Pronouns	
me	*nos*
te	*os*
lo, la*	*los, las**

*Note: The object pronouns *le* and *les* are often used as masculine direct object pronouns in Spain. In this book, however, we will use *lo, la, los, las* exclusively as the direct object pronouns.

"Lo" is used in place of a singular, masculine noun, while *"la"* is used in place of a singular, feminine noun. The plural forms *"los"* and *"las"* correspond to masculine and feminine plural nouns.

WHERE DO YOU PLACE DOPs?

Direct object pronouns generally come <u>before</u> conjugated verbs in Spanish. The word order may seem peculiar to a speaker of English, who places all object pronouns after verbs. Let's look at some sentences to see these direct object pronouns in action.

 EXAMPLES: *Mi hermana comprende el libro, pero yo no **lo** comprendo.*
My sister understands the book, but I don't understand it.

*Lucía **me** ama, pero yo no **la** amo.*
Lucy loves me, but I don't love her.

*¿Los pantalones? –No **los** limpiamos.*
The pants? –We're not cleaning them.

*No **te** insulté, Rosaura; ¿no **me** crees?*
I didn't insult you, Rosaura; don't you believe me?

*No **te** oí, Lola; ¿puedes repetir las instrucciones?*
I didn't hear you, Lola; can you repeat the instructions?

*¿Tienes las botellas de Coca-Cola? –Claro, **las** tengo.*
Do you have the bottles of Coke? –Of course, I have them.

*Los Hermanos Jonas nunca **nos** ven cuando cantan.*
The Jonas Brothers never see us when they sing.

In certain cases, direct object pronouns may be <u>attached</u> to the end of a verb. For example, they may be attached to infinitives. You will see in the examples below that you may choose to put a direct object pronoun before the first verb, or attach it directly to the infinitive. In later lessons, we will also see them after affirmative commands and following present participles.

EXAMPLES: *¿La canción Not Ready to Make Nice? Las Dixie Chicks van a cantar**la** ahora. (Las Dixie Chicks **la** van a cantar ahora.)*
The song *Not Ready to Make Nice*? The Dixie Chicks are going to sing it now.

*Necesito las cartas; voy a pedir**las** en la reunión. (. . . **las** voy a pedir en la reunión).*
I need the letters; I'm going to ask for them in the meeting.

*Julia, no puedes entender**me** siempre. (Julia, no **me** puedes entender siempre.)*
Julia, you can't understand me always.

PRACTICE EXERCISES

1. Rewrite the following questions, replacing the underlined direct object with the appropriate direct object pronoun:

Example: ¿Dónde compras <u>pizza</u>? **¿Dónde la compras?**_____

a. ¿Dónde pones <u>tus libros</u>? _____

b. ¿Ves <u>muchos perros</u> en el parque? _____

c. ¿Tienes <u>la tarea</u> aquí? _____

d. ¿Comprendes <u>el cuento</u>? _____

e. ¿Vas a comprar <u>los discos compactos nuevos</u>? (two ways)

_____   _____

f. ¿Sabes hablar <u>español</u>? (two ways)

_____   _____

g. ¿Vas a repetir <u>las palabras</u>? (two ways)

_____   _____

h. ¿Quieres preparar <u>la ensalada de tomate</u>? (two ways)

_____   _____

2. **Now <u>answer</u> the following questions, replacing the underlined word(s) with the appropriate direct object pronoun:**

Example: ¿Dónde compras <u>pizza</u>? **La compro en Pizza Hut.** _____

a. ¿Dónde pones <u>tus libros</u>? _____

b. ¿<u>Me</u> amas?   _____

c. ¿<u>Te</u> entiendo siempre?   _____

d. ¿Comprendes <u>el cuento</u>? _____

e. ¿Vas a comprar <u>los discos compactos nuevos</u>? (two ways)

_____   _____

f. ¿Sabes hablar <u>italiano</u>? (two ways)

_____   _____

g. ¿Vas a repetir <u>los cuentos</u>? (two ways)

_____   _____

h. ¿Quieres cocinar <u>las hamburguesas</u>? (two ways)

_____   _____

3. Translate the following sentences into Spanish:

a. The doors? I closed them yesterday.

_____

b. The apples and oranges? I counted them with my brother.

_____

c. The test? I am going to correct it tomorrow.

_____

d. I remember you. And you, do you remember me?

_____

e. Jorge Ramos sees me, but he doesn't see you.

_____

4. The following paragraph contains five errors related to object pronouns. Underline each error and write the correction above it:

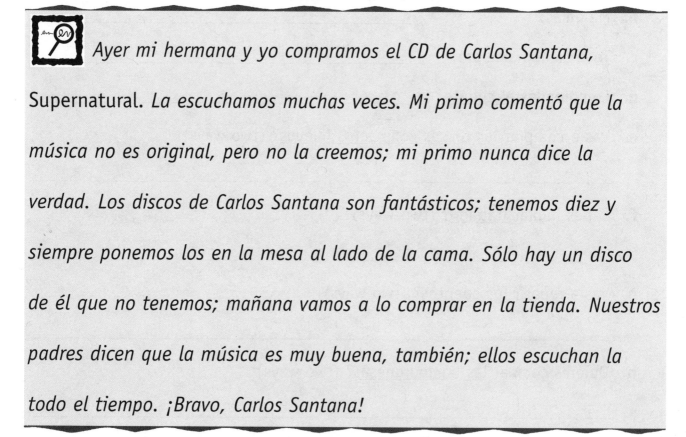

Ayer mi hermana y yo compramos el CD de Carlos Santana, Supernatural. _La escuchamos muchas veces. Mi primo comentó que la música no es original, pero no la creemos; mi primo nunca dice la verdad. Los discos de Carlos Santana son fantásticos; tenemos diez y siempre ponemos los en la mesa al lado de la cama. Sólo hay un disco de él que no tenemos; mañana vamos a lo comprar en la tienda. Nuestros padres dicen que la música es muy buena, también; ellos escuchan la todo el tiempo. ¡Bravo, Carlos Santana!_

C) THE PERSONAL "A"

In Spanish, the word *"a"* is usually placed between a verb and a direct object when that object is a person. This *"a"* does not translate into English. It's almost as if this word *"a"* protects or buffers the direct object from the force of the verb. Because we do not have anything comparable in English, it may take a little while to get the hang of this idea. Let's look at a few examples:

EXAMPLES: *Quiero **a** Lucy, pero ella no me quiere.*
I love Lucy, but she doesn't love me.

*Veo **a** dos chicos en la puerta, pero no veo mi pizza.*
(Because pizza is not a person, there is no *"a"* between it and the verb *"veo."*)
I see two boys at the door, but I don't see my pizza.

*Miramos **a** los jóvenes en la playa; ¡no llevan ropa!*
We are looking at the young people on the beach; they aren't wearing clothes!

*¿Esperas **a** tu novia otra vez? ¡Siempre llega tarde!*
Are you waiting for your girlfriend again? She always arrives late!

¡CUIDADO! After the verb *"tener,"* however, the personal *"a"* is not normally used.

EXAMPLES: *Tengo dos hermanos y una hermana.*
I have two brothers and a sister.

Tenemos una profesora de español fantástica.
We have a fantastic Spanish teacher.

 PRACTICE EXERCISE

Translate the following sentences into Spanish:

a. I see Sarita Montiel in church.

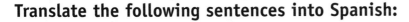

b. We have many cousins, uncles, and friends.

c. You are waiting for your teacher, right?

_____

d. They know Paz Vega very well.

_____

 D) IDIOMATIC EXPRESSIONS THAT USE "TENER"

The Spanish word _"tener,"_ meaning "to have," combines with many other words to form common expressions that you'll hear all the time. The expressions, when translated literally, may seem somewhat unusual to a speaker of English. For example, "I am thirsty" is expressed in Spanish as _"Tengo sed,"_ which literally means "I have thirst."

Here is a list of the most common _"tener"_ expressions. You will notice they are listed here in the _"yo"_ form. They, of course, can be conjugated in any form:

Common _"Tener"_ Expressions	
tengo (diez) años → I am (ten) years old	_tengo prisa_ → I am in a hurry
tengo (mucho) calor → I am (very) hot	_tengo razón_ → I am right
tengo frío → I am cold	_tengo sed_ → I am thirsty
tengo (mucha) hambre → I am (very) hungry	_tengo sueño_ → I am sleepy
tengo miedo → I am scared	_tengo suerte_ → I am lucky

All of these expressions use the Spanish word meaning "to have" along with a noun (heat, cold, hunger, fear, thirst, etc.)

There is another expression formed with a conjugation of _"tener"_ along with the word _"que"_ and an infinitive:

tengo que (bailar, dormir, estudiar, etc.) → I have to (dance, sleep, study, etc.)

Let's look at all of these *"tener"* expressions in sentences:

✳ EXAMPLES: ***Tenemos suerte;*** *la película* Wall-E *comienza en cinco minutos.*
We are lucky; the movie *Wall-E* starts in five minutes.

*Cuando **tengo sed**, siempre bebo limonada o té con hielo.*
When I'm thirsty, I always drink lemonade or iced tea.

*En verano mis abuelos siempre **tienen calor** en la playa; no sé por qué no se quedan en casa.*
In the summer, my grandparents are always hot on the beach; I don't know why they don't stay at home.

Tienes que escuchar *la canción de Carlos Santana,* Smooth. *¡Es increíble!*
You have to listen to the Carlos Santana song, *Smooth.* It's incredible!

¡Tengo razón! *Cuando nieva, todos **tienen frío** en las montañas.*
I'm right! When it snows, everyone is cold in the mountains.

*Los perros **tienen mucha hambre**; necesitan comer ahorita.*
The dogs are very hungry; they need to eat right now.

*En mi clase de español nunca **tenemos sueño** porque todo es súper-interesante.*
In my Spanish class, we are never sleepy because everything is very interesting.

*Nunca **tengo miedo** cuando camino solo en el parque; soy muy fuerte y otras personas **tienen miedo** de mí.*
I am never scared when I walk alone in the park; I am very strong, and other people are afraid of me.

*Michael Jordan **tiene cuarenta y seis años**.*
Michael Jordan is forty-six years old.

*"**¡Tengo prisa!*** *El tren sale a las ocho", dijo Gael García Bernal.*
"I'm in a hurry! The train leaves at eight," said Gael García Bernal.

Tengo que estudiar *mucho porque del examen mañana.*
I have to study a lot because of the test tomorrow.

1. Fill in the following spaces with a *"tener"* expression from page 120, being certain to conjugate *"tener"* properly to agree with the subject:

a. LeBron James no _____ de nadie; es muy inteligente y muy fuerte.

b. Cuando mis padres _____, siempre van o a Burger King para comer un Whopper o a Ben y Jerry's para tomar un helado.

c. Yo _____ ahora; necesito dormir dos o tres horas más.

d. En el espacio los astronautas nunca _____ porque tienen ropa muy especial.

e. ¡Yo _____ aquí! Hace mucho sol y el acondicionador de aire no funciona bien.

f. Cuando mi tío va a Las Vegas, nunca _____; siempre pierde todo el dinero.

g. El embajador _____ ir hoy a Bolivia para hablar con el nuevo presidente.

h. Es bueno beber mucha agua si tú _____ durante un maratón.

i. Mi padre duerme en el sofá cuando _____.

j. No hace sol y nieva mucho ahora; por eso, yo _____.

2. Translate the following sentences into Spanish, being certain to use a *"tener"* expression:

a. She is sleepy because she slept only three hours last night.

_____

b. My uncle normally isn't lucky, but he won a lot of money in November.

_____

c. We have to buy a new chair because the old chair is ugly.

_____

d. I'm hungry, thirsty and cold. Where is there a Taco Bell?

_____

e. David Ortiz is never scared when he plays baseball.

_____

3. **The following paragraph contains six errors in total: two preterite errors, two direct object pronoun errors, and two mistakes related to _"tener"_ expressions. Find each error and correct it:**

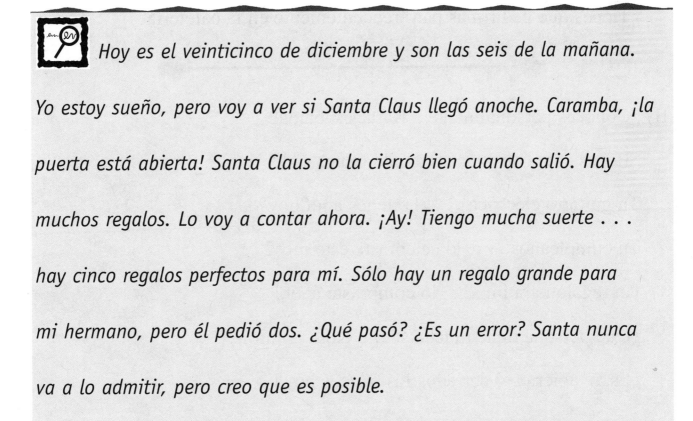

Hoy es el veinticinco de diciembre y son las seis de la mañana.

Yo estoy sueño, pero voy a ver si Santa Claus llegó anoche. Caramba, ¡la

puerta está abierta! Santa Claus no la cierró bien cuando salió. Hay

muchos regalos. Lo voy a contar ahora. ¡Ay! Tiengo mucha suerte . . .

hay cinco regalos perfectos para mí. Sólo hay un regalo grande para

mi hermano, pero él pedió dos. ¿Qué pasó? ¿Es un error? Santa nunca

va a lo admitir, pero creo que es posible.

These two sets of questions use grammatical structures and vocabulary from this lesson. Working with a partner, alternate asking and answering each question. When you get to the bottom of each list, start over at the top, switching roles. As a variation, write out the answers in complete sentences.

A) ¿A qué hora volviste a casa anoche?

¿Quién cerró la puerta de tu casa hoy?

¿Cuántas horas durmió tu amigo anoche?

¿Qué persona famosa murió recientemente?

¿Normalmente insultas a tus amigos?

¿Compras pantalones nuevos una vez o dos veces al año?

¿Tienes que pedir más pan frecuentemente en la cafetería?

B) ¿Conoces personalmente a Barack Obama?

¿Bebes café con azúcar cuando tienes sed?

Tu guitarra eléctrica . . . ¿la tienes aquí hoy?

Tu cumpleaños . . . ¿lo celebraste este mes?

Un regalo para mí . . . ¿lo compraste ayer?

¿Qué persona tiene mucha suerte en tu opinión?

¿Están abiertos o cerrados los bancos hoy?

DIALOGUE

The following dialogue contains grammar and vocabulary that you've seen in this lesson and in the introductory section. After listening to the CD, read this dialogue aloud, alone or with friends. Afterwards, try to answer the questions that follow either aloud or in written form.

 ## LAS AVENTURAS DE RAFAEL, ELISA Y "EL TIGRE"

ESCENA TRES

Rafael, "El Tigre", y Elisa están en un tren de Amtrak. Sus mochilas están a sus pies y los tres jóvenes hablan animadamente.

El Tigre:	¿Cuándo vamos a llegar a Nueva York, Rafael?
Rafael:	En quince minutos, Tigre. ¡No te preocupes!
El Tigre:	Es un viaje bien largo.
Rafael:	Tranquilo, miren; ¿pueden Uds. ver los edificios muy altos a la distancia?
El Tigre:	Yo no veo nada.
Rafael:	Abre los ojos, Tigre, ¿no ves el Empire State Building allí?
El Tigre:	Sí, ahora yo lo veo. Elisa, no dices nada. ¿Por qué?
Elisa:	Pues, estoy muy emocionada. Y muy nerviosa. Y me siento culpable (guilty) también. Mis padres creen que estoy en New Hampshire ahora. Voy a llamarlos esta noche con mi teléfono celular. ¡No van a saber que estoy en Nueva York!

Un hombre alto y misterioso pasa por el vagón (train car). *Tiene bigote y lleva una chaqueta que dice "NY Mets". No dice nada mientras pasa cerca de ellos.*

Rafael:	Pronto llegamos a Penn Station. Tomamos un taxi a Central Park. Tengo un amigo, Javier, que vive muy cerca. Podemos pasar la noche en su apartamento.
El Tigre:	Pero un taxi cuesta muchísimo dinero. Yo prefiero caminar.
Elisa:	Yo, también. Rafael, ¿es simpático tu amigo?
Rafael:	Claro, es súper-simpático. Y sus padres no están en casa hoy porque están de viaje. Su prima, Marisela, se queda en casa con él. Ella sólo tiene veintitrés años y es muy simpática.
Elisa:	Me alegro. Y otra chica es buena para nuestro grupo. Pero tengo hambre. ¿Tienes más chicle, Tigre?
El Tigre:	Claro.

"El Tigre" busca su mochila. Mira debajo de los asientos, encima de ellos y por todos lados.

Rafael: Llegamos ya. Aquí estamos.

El tren se detiene (stops). *Se oye un anuncio* (An announcement is heard).

Voz: Llegamos ahora a Penn Station en la ciudad de Nueva York. Todos los pasajeros tienen que bajar aquí. Gracias.

El Tigre: ¡Caramba! Elisa, Rafael. ¿Dónde está mi mochila?

Elisa: No sé. ¿No está debajo del asiento?

El Tigre: No, no está.

Rafael: Siempre pierdes tus cosas, Tigre.

Elisa: Pero, un momento. ¿De qué color es tu mochila?

El Tigre: Verde.

Elisa: Claro. No recuerdas, ese hombre con el bigote. Creo que ahora él tiene tu mochila.

Rafael: ¡Miren! Creo que lo veo en el andén. ¡Vamos!

Elisa: ¡Vamos!

El Tigre: ¡Vamos!

Los tres amigos salen rápidamente. Hay muchas personas y es muy difícil ver. En la distancia, una mujer vestida de blanco observa la escena con un telescopio.

PREGUNTAS

1) ¿Qué tipo de transportación usan los jóvenes en su viaje a Nueva York?

_____

2) ¿Qué edificio famoso ven a la distancia?

_____

3) ¿Cómo se siente Elisa ahora?

_____

4) ¿Qué palabras tiene el hombre misterioso en su chaqueta?

_____

5) ¿Dónde van a pasar la noche los tres amigos?

_____

6) ¿Por qué está alegre Elisa con la noticia sobre Marisela?

_____

7) ¿Qué quiere Elisa? ¿Por qué?

_____

8) ¿Qué busca El Tigre?

_____

9) ¿Quién tiene probablemente la mochila?

_____

10) ¿Quién observa la escena al final?

_____

1. Answer in complete sentences:

a. ¿Durmió Ud. bien o mal anoche?

_____

b. ¿Quién sirvió la comida anoche en tu casa?

_____

c. ¿Conoces a Antonio Villaraigosa, el alcalde de Los Ángeles?

_____

d. ¿Qué cantante famoso/a murió recientemente?

_____

e. ¿Pidieron Uds. muchos favores esta semana?

_____

2. Conjugate the following six verbs fully in the preterite tense:

    cerrar (to close)   **volver** (to return)   **pedir** (to ask for)

_____ _____   _____ _____   _____ _____

_____ _____   _____ _____   _____ _____

_____ _____   _____ _____   _____ _____

    contar (to count)   **entender** (to understand)   **dormir** (to sleep)

_____ _____   _____ _____   _____ _____

_____ _____   _____ _____   _____ _____

_____ _____   _____ _____   _____ _____

3. **Write the correct form of the preterite in the spaces provided:**

   a. Los chicos _____ del uno al diez y después corrieron a la reunión. (contar)

   b. Mis amigos _____ tres pizzas con salchicha y tres botellas grandes de Coca-Cola. (pedir)

   c. Alejandro Sanz _____ a su amiga en la primera fila del concierto. (sentar)

   d. Óscar de la Hoya no se _____ muy bien cuando perdió la corona contra Manny Pacquiao. (sentir)

   e. Los chicos con los ojos rojos no _____ bien anoche. (dormir)

   f. Tito Puente _____ su talento cuando presentó las nominaciones a los Grammy Latinos. (mostrar)

   g. Mi nieta _____ no hablar conmigo después del incidente. (preferir)

   h. Andrés Galarraga _____ que el clima de Atlanta era magnífico. (pensar)

   i. Aunque Mike Huckabee _____ las elecciones, ganó muchos votos. (perder)

   j. Los perros me _____ de la playa a mi casa. (seguir)

4. **Answer the following questions, replacing the underlined words with the correct direct object pronoun** (me, te, lo, la, nos, os, los, las):

   a. ¿Compraste la botella de vino aquí?

   _____

   b. ¿Comió tu amigo una hamburguesa hoy?

   _____

c. ¿Dónde compró Ricky Martin <u>sus pantalones de cuero nuevos</u>?

_____

d. ¿Comiste <u>pavo asado</u> la semana pasada?

_____

e. ¿Puedes poner <u>los papeles</u> en la mesa? (two ways)

_____   _____

f. ¿Vas a limpiar <u>las blusas nuevas</u>? (two ways)

_____   _____

g. ¿Vas a comprar <u>los regalos</u> en la tienda? (two ways)

_____   _____

h. ¿Insultaste a <u>María</u>?

_____

5. Insert a personal _"a"_ in the following sentences when needed:

a. Amo mucho _____ mi novia porque es muy cariñosa.

b. Queremos _____ los libros nuevos de Julia Álvarez.

c. Nunca veo _____ Lili Estefan en la televisión.

d. Tengo _____ tres primos y cinco sobrinos.

e. Esperamos _____ Fernando Colunga; siempre llega tarde.

6. Insert a common _"tener"_ expression into the following spaces:

a. Yo _____ en Las Vegas porque siempre gano dinero.

b. Nosotros _____; vamos a beber muchísima agua.

c. Cuando nieva y no tengo mi ropa caliente, yo _____.

d. Cuando mi hermana ve películas de terror siempre _____.

e. Tú _____, ¿verdad? ¿No quieres comer más pescado, una ensalada con queso o una tarta de manzana con helado?

7. **Find the errors in the following list of things to do. There's one error in each line:**

1) Tengo que lavo la ropa.

2) Tengo que invitar mi primo Lorenzo a la fiesta.

3) Los regalos — tengo que los comprar en la tienda.

4) Tengo que correr en el parque con mis amigos favorito.

5) Las chicas durmieron en casa anoche.

6) ¿La sopa? No lo comí ayer.

7) No veo a la zanahoria en la ensalada.

8) Tengo muy frío en diciembre.

ECUADOR & PERÚ

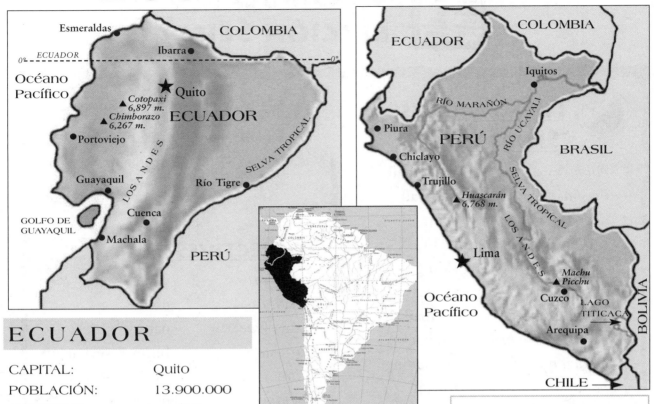

ECUADOR

CAPITAL:	Quito
POBLACIÓN:	13.900.000
GOBIERNO:	república
PRESIDENTE:	Rafael Correa
DINERO ($):	dólar (EEUU), sucre
PRODUCTOS:	bananas, gambas, madera, petróleo
MÚSICA, BAILE:	cachullape, salsa, sanjuanes
SITIOS DE INTERÉS:	Chimborazo, Islas Galápagos
COMIDA TÍPICA:	caldo de patas, ceviche, llapingachos (cheese and potato cakes), locro, patacones

PERÚ

CAPITAL:	Lima
POBLACIÓN:	29.000.000
GOBIERNO:	república constitucional
PRESIDENTE:	Alan García Pérez
DINERO ($):	nuevo sol
PRODUCTOS:	algodón, azúcar, metales, pescado
MÚSICA, BAILE:	"El cóndor pasa", huaylas, marinera norteña, zampoña
SITIOS DE INTERÉS:	Arequipa, Cuzco, lago Titicaca, Machu Picchu (templo de los incas), Parque Nacional del Manu
COMIDA TÍPICA:	ceviche, mazamorra morada, papas a la huancaína, pisco

ECUATORIANOS FAMOSOS:

Eugenio Espejo
(ESCRITOR, MÉDICO)

Oswaldo Guayasamín
(PINTOR)

Jefferson Pérez
(ATLETA)

PERUANOS FAMOSOS:

Eva Ayllón
(CANTANTE)

Chabuca Granda
(CANTANTE)

Javier Pérez de Cuéllar
(DIPLOMÁTICO)

César Vallejo
(POETA)

Mario Vargas Llosa
(ESCRITOR)

VOCABULARIO LECCIÓN SEIS

THEME WORDS: "SPORTS"

el	baloncesto	basketball
el	béisbol	baseball
el	deporte	sport
el	equipo	team
el	esquí	skiing
el	fútbol	soccer
el	fútbol americano	football
el	hockey sobre hielo	ice hockey
la	natación	swimming
el	remo	rowing
el	tenis	tennis
la	vela	sailing

OTHER NOUNS

el	buzón	mailbox
el/la	camarero/a (mesero/a)	waiter
el	cartel	poster
el	clima	climate
la	cuenta	bill
el	cuento	story, tale
la	década	decade
el	empleo	job
la	entrevista	interview
la	misa	mass, church service
la	película	film (used in a camera), movie

el	precio	price
el	recibo	receipt
la	revista	magazine
la	sorpresa	surprise
la	toalla	towel

ADJECTIVES

ancho/a	wide
divino/a	divine
estrecho/a	narrow
furioso/a	furious, very mad
libre	free
mejor	better, best
orgulloso/a	proud
peor	worse, worst

VERBS

besar	to kiss
caber	to fit
cambiar	to change
detener	to detain, to stop
gritar	to shout
pagar	to pay
susurrar	to whisper

MISCELLANEOUS

como	as, since, like
en voz alta	aloud
enfrente de	in front of
ir de compras	to go shopping
sobre	over, about

LECCIÓN SEIS

KEY GRAMMAR CONCEPTS

A) THE PRETERITE OF IRREGULAR VERBS → *El pretérito de verbos irregulares*

B) POSSESSIVE ADJECTIVES → *Los adjetivos posesivos*

C) INDIRECT OBJECT PRONOUNS (IDOPs) → *Los pronombres complementos (indirectos)*

D) THE VERB "GUSTAR" → *El verbo "gustar"*

A) THE PRETERITE OF IRREGULAR VERBS

In *Lección Cuatro,* we saw the preterite conjugations for regular verbs in Spanish.

In *Lección Cinco,* we learned that **-AR** and **-ER** stem-changing verbs are also regular in the preterite, while the **-IR** verbs have a special vowel change in the 3rd person singular and plural.

This lesson will take a final look at preterite verbs. The eighteen verbs that you will see on the following page are <u>irregular</u> in the preterite. They have conjugations that you simply must memorize. Because these verbs are among the most commonly used in the Spanish language, you should be sure to study them thoroughly.

You will notice a number of interesting features of these conjugations:

◆ There are no written accents marks in any form!

◆ Once you memorize the *"yo"* form for each verb, the rest of the conjugations will follow a familiar pattern.

◆ The letter *"i"* drops out after the *"j"* in the 3rd person singular and plural of verbs that end with *"-cir"* (e.g., *conducir, decir, producir*) as well as in the verb *"traer."*

◆ You will see that the conjugations of *"ir"* and *"ser"* are absolutely identical in the preterite. Because of this fact, you will need to rely on the context of the sentence to know which verb the speaker is using.

andar (to walk)		**caber** (to fit)		**conducir** (to drive)	
anduve	anduvimos	cupe	cupimos	conduje	condujimos
anduviste	anduvisteis	cupiste	cupisteis	condujiste	condujisteis
anduvo	anduvieron	cupo	cupieron	condujo	condujeron

dar (to give)		**decir** (to say, to tell)		**estar** (to be)	
di	dimos	dije	dijimos	estuve	estuvimos
diste	disteis	dijiste	dijisteis	estuviste	estuvisteis
dio	dieron	dijo	dijeron	estuvo	estuvieron

hacer (to do, to make)		**ir** (to go)		**poder** (to be able to)	
hice	hicimos	fui	fuimos	pude	pudimos
hiciste	hicisteis	fuiste	fuisteis	pudiste	pudisteis
hizo	hicieron	fue	fueron	pudo	pudieron

poner (to put)		**producir** (to produce)		**querer** (to want, to wish)	
puse	pusimos	produje	produjimos	quise	quisimos
pusiste	pusisteis	produjiste	produjisteis	quisiste	quisisteis
puso	pusieron	produjo	produjeron	quiso	quisieron

saber (to know)		**ser** (to be)		**tener** (to have)	
supe	supimos	fui	fuimos	tuve	tuvimos
supiste	supisteis	fuiste	fuisteis	tuviste	tuvisteis
supo	supieron	fue	fueron	tuvo	tuvieron

traer (to bring)		**venir** (to come)		**ver** (to see)	
traje	trajimos	vine	vinimos	vi	vimos
trajiste	trajisteis	viniste	vinisteis	viste	visteis
trajo	trajeron	vino	vinieron	vio	vieron

Let's take a look at a number of these verbs in the preterite:

 EXAMPLES: *Anduve a la escuela esta mañana porque me gusta el aire fresco.*
I walked to school this morning because I like fresh air.

*Mi amiga **dijo** que Alfredo Palacio ya no es el presidente de Ecuador.*
My friend said that Alfredo Palacio is no longer the president of Ecuador.

*Cuando **pusiste** la rana en la silla de la profesora, ella comenzó a gritar.*
When you put the frog on the teacher's chair, she began to scream.

*Salma Hayek **vino** con Francois-Henri Pinault a la fiesta en Soho.*
Salma Hayek came with Francois-Henri Pinault to the party in Soho.

*Cuando el profesor nos **vio** en la cafetería, **tuvimos** que salir.*
When the teacher saw us in the cafeteria, we had to leave.

*Mis amigas **fueron** al concierto de* Tommy Torres.
My friends went to the *Tommy Torres* concert.

***Conduje** el coche muy rápidamente y ahora estoy en la cárcel.*
I drove the car very fast, and now I'm in jail.

*Mi amiga me **trajo** un cartel de David Bisbal.*
My friend brought me a David Bisbal poster.

*Anoche nadie **pudo** ir al partido de baloncesto para ver a Manu Ginóbili por el examen de hoy.*
No one could go to the basketball game last night to see Manu Ginóbili because of the test today.

There are also some verbs that are irregular in a few conjugations only. The irregularities are found in consonants and in vowels, which change or are added to preserve a sound that is found in the infinitive. We'll fully conjugate four such verbs here, but you will also see some additional infinitives in parentheses that follow the same pattern.

COMENZAR (empezar) (to begin/to begin)		LEER (creer) (to read/to believe)	
comencé	comenzamos	leí	leímos
comenzaste	comenzasteis	leíste	leísteis
comenzó	comenzaron	**leyó**	**leyeron**
PAGAR (colgar, llegar) (to pay/to hang up/to arrive)		TOCAR (buscar, sacar) (to play/to look for/to take out)	
pagué	pagamos	**toqué**	tocamos
pagaste	pagasteis	tocaste	tocasteis
pagó	pagaron	tocó	tocaron

In the verbs above, the special changes have been highlighted in **boldface**. Unlike the other irregular verbs in this section, only one or two of the forms are irregular.

EXAMPLES: *Cuando yo **pagué** la cuenta, mi papá dijo: "Gracias".*
When I paid the bill, my dad said: "Thanks."

*Yo **toqué** el piano por cinco minutos, pero Elton John tocó por una hora.*
I played the piano for five minutes, but Elton John played for an hour.

*Mis amigos **leyeron** un artículo interesante sobre el actor Edward James Olmos en una revista.*
My friends read an interesting article about the actor Edward James Olmos in a magazine.

*Cuando **comencé** a lavar los platos, mi madre me dio un beso.*
When I began to wash the dishes, my mom kissed me.

1. Conjugate the following verbs fully into the preterite:

      estar (to be)   **ser** (to be)   **decir** (to say)

_____

_____

_____

      venir (to come)   **comenzar** (to begin)   **pagar** (to pay)

_____

_____

_____

2. Now change each of the following verbs from the present tense to the corresponding form of the preterite:

    Examples: van → **fueron**_____   puede → **pudo**_____

    a. dice   → _____   **f.** hacéis → _____

    b. estás   → _____   **g.** cabe → _____

    c. comienzo → _____   **h.** hago → _____

    d. traemos → _____   **i.** tienes → _____

    e. andan → _____   **j.** vienen → _____

3. Complete the following sentences using the appropriate form of the preterite tense:

    a. Jennifer López no _____ anoche, y por eso canté yo. (venir)

    b. Antonio Banderas _____ a la playa solo. (andar)

c. Ayer mis primos _____ el coche nuevo de mi tía. (conducir)

d. Nosotros _____ la guitarra enfrente de la casa. (poner)

e. Benjamín Bratt y Talisa Soto _____ sólo unos minutos en el restaurante peruano. (estar)

f. Tú _____ a Machu Picchu sin mí el verano pasado. (ir)

g. Como mi amigo nunca tiene dinero, yo _____ la cuenta en el restaurante anoche. (pagar)

h. Mi novia dijo que ella comenzó la discusión, pero no es verdad — yo la

_____. (comenzar)

i. El pobre elefante no _____ en el cuarto estrecho. (caber)

j. "No robé el banco", _____ en voz alta cuando la policía me detuvo. (decir)

4. The following paragraph contains seven errors related to preterite verbs. Underline each error and write the correct word above it:

Mi hermano condució su moto a la playa. Estoy furioso porque yo andé solo con todas las toallas y bebidas. Cuando llegé, vi a mi hermano, Raúl, con sus amigos. Él me vió, pero no hició nada. Vi la pizza en las manos de sus amigos, pero ellos no me daron nada. Lloré por unos minutos, y luego yo fue a casa en la moto que tomé de mi hermano.

¡Y me llevé todas las toallas y bebidas!

Possessive adjectives are words that let people know to whom or to what something belongs. Unlike most other adjectives, possessive adjectives are placed <u>before</u> the nouns they modify. Remember, because these words are adjectives, they must correspond in gender and number to the nouns they describe.

Here are the Spanish possessive adjectives:

mi/mis	*nuestro/nuestra/nuestros/nuestras*
tu/tus	*vuestro/vuestra/vuestros/vuestras*
su/sus	*su/sus*

Here are their equivalents in English:

my	our
your (familiar)	your all's (familiar)
his, her, your (formal)	their, your all's (formal)

 **EXAMPLES:** *"**Mi** bisabuela es 'La Catrina'"*, *dijo Jamie González.*
"My great-grandmother is 'La Catrina,'" said Jamie González.

*Slumdog Millionaire es **nuestra** película favorita del año.*
Slumdog Millionaire is our favorite movie of the year.

*Mis amigos me informaron que Cuzco es **su** ciudad favorita.*
My friends informed me that Cuzco is their favorite city.

*"**Vuestro** tío os ama mucho", repitió **nuestro** tío Cristóbal.*
"Your uncle loves you all a lot," repeated our Uncle Cristóbal.

*Siempre voy de compras a Sears porque **sus** precios son bajos.*
I always go shopping at Sears because their prices are low.

*"**Tu** voz es divina", gritó un aficionado en el concierto de Shakira.*
"Your voice is divine," shouted a fan at the Shakira concert.

*"No veo **sus** recibos", me informó el inspector.*
"I don't see your receipts," the inspector informed me.

*Meryl Streep hace muchas películas; **su** película más reciente fue* Doubt.
Meryl Streep makes many movies; her most recent movie was *Doubt*.

Keep these things in mind as you put these possessive adjectives to use:

1 These adjectives agree with what is <u>possessed</u>, not the <u>possessor</u>!

> my books = **mis** *libros*
> their chair = **su** *silla*
> our computer = **nuestra** *computadora*
> your (fam.) grandparents = **tus** *abuelos*

2 Because *"su"* or *"sus"* can mean "his," "her," "your," "their," or "your all's," the context of the sentence is quite important. To avoid confusion, you can choose an alternate construction that uses the preposition *"de"* with a pronoun that follows a preposition.

EXAMPLES:

su primo =	*el primo* **de él**	his cousin
	el primo **de ella**	her cousin
	el primo **de Ud.**	your cousin
	el primo **de ellos**	their cousin
	el primo **de ellas**	their cousin
	el primo **de Uds.**	your (pl.) cousin
sus primos =	*los primos* **de él**	his cousins
	los primos **de ella**	her cousins
	los primos **de Ud.**	your cousins
	los primos **de ellos**	their cousins
	los primos **de ellas**	their cousins
	los primos **de Uds.**	your (pl.) cousins

1. Translate the following into Spanish:

a. my papers _____

b. our grandmother _____

c. their salad (two ways)

_____   _____

d. her movie (two ways)

_____   _____

e. his glass of water (two ways)

_____   _____

f. your all's table (two ways)

_____   _____

g. my mosquito _____

h. our tomatoes _____

2. Complete the following sentences by translating the possessive adjective in parentheses into the appropriate form:

a. Cuando _____ guitarrista no llegó, yo acompañé a Alexandre Pires. (his)

b. Tenemos muy buenos recuerdos de _____ vacaciones en las Islas Galápagos. (our)

c. De todos los éxitos *(hits)* de los BeeGees, *Saturday Night Fever* fue

_____ disco más popular. (their)

d. _____ amigos comieron todos los Doritos, y por eso tuve que volver a la tienda. (my)

e. Vosotros no tenéis _____ raquetas de tenis hoy; ¿preferís jugar al fútbol? (your)

f. _____ amigas nunca recuerdan _____ aniversario. (her/her)

g. "_____ suerte va a cambiar pronto", me susurró la mujer después de leerme la mano. (your, familiar)

h. El colombiano Juanes tiene mucho talento; _____ álbum, *La vida . . . Es un ratico,* es un gran éxito. (their)

i. "_____ perro, Pal, es mi mejor amigo", dice Arthur. (my)

j. "Tenemos mucha confianza en _____ alumnos", dijo el maestro cuando habló con el periodista. (our)

3. The following paragraph contains six errors. Underline each error and write the correct word above it:

> Mi hermanos organizaron una fiesta de sorpresa. Todos nuestro amigos recibieron invitaciones, pero yo no. Mi invitación no llegó nunca. Todos gritaron mis nombre cuando volví a casa. Carla y Miguel decoraron las tortas; comí la torta bonita de Carla, no la torta feo de Miguel. Dije: "¡Muchas gracias por todo sus trabajo!". Mis amigos y mis hermanos son fantásticos. ¿Cómo son tu amigos?

Lección Cinco introduced direct object pronouns (*me, te, lo, la, nos, os, los, las*). These pronouns took the place of nouns that took a "direct hit" from a verb (*¿El dinero? Bonnie y Clyde lo robaron*).

This lesson introduces another type of object pronoun. **Indirect object pronouns (IDOPs)** take the place of nouns that receive an action <u>indirectly</u>.

In the sentence, "I wrote Elvis a letter," the word "letter" clearly is the direct object — the letter is what was written. "Elvis," however, is the <u>indirect object</u>. He is connected to the action of writing because he will receive the letter, but because he is not the letter, he is not the direct object.

In the sentence "I wrote him a letter," "him" is the <u>indirect object pronoun</u> that stands for Elvis.

Let's look at another example. In the sentence "Elvis told me a secret," "a secret" is the direct object. Elvis told what? A secret. The word "me" is the indirect object pronoun because Elvis told the secret **to** me.

Here are the indirect object pronouns (IDOPs) in Spanish:

Indirect Object Pronouns	
me	*nos*
te	*os*
le	*les*

Helpful Tip: Did you notice that *"me, te, nos, os"* are the exact same forms you used for DOPs — direct object pronouns?

 **EXAMPLES:** *Siempre **le** digo "gracias" al camarero cuando **me** trae la comida.*
I always say "thanks" to the waiter when he brings me the food.

*Cuando los turistas comenzaron a sacar fotos en la iglesia, la guía **les** gritó: "¡Señores, por favor, no se permite!"*
When the tourists began to take pictures in the church, the guide shouted at them: "Please, it isn't allowed!"

***Le** debo mucho dinero a mi amigo; tengo que conseguir otro empleo.*
I owe a lot of money to my friend; I have to get another job.

***Os** digo que Alex Rodríguez y Carlos Beltrán hablaron anoche por teléfono.*
I'm telling you all that Alex Rodríguez and Carlos Beltrán talked last night by phone.

*No **te** pido mucho; simplemente **me** vas a dar tu coche y me voy en seguida.*
I'm not asking you for much; you simply are going to give me your car, and I'll leave at once.

To clarify or to emphasize one of these indirect object pronouns, you may choose to add the following words to a sentence:

a mí	*a nosotros, a nosotras*
a ti	*a vosotros, a vosotras*
a él	*a ellos*
a ella	*a ellas*
a Ud.	*a Uds.*

Sometimes this indirect object pronoun may seem redundant to a speaker of English. For example, in *"Le digo 'hola' a Jose,"* *"le"* and *"a José"* both refer to the same person! But this practice adds clarity or emphasis: *¡Te voy a llamar a ti primero!* (I'm going to call you first!)

 EXAMPLES: *Te doy los libros **a ti**, no a Nacha.*
I'm giving the books to you, not to Nacha.

*Hugh Jackman **nos** informó primero **a nosotros** que iba a hacer el programa de los Oscar.*
Hugh Jackman informed us first that he was going to do the Oscars this year.

In all of the examples above, the indirect object pronouns came directly before the verb. However, just like direct object pronouns, the IDOPs sometimes are attached to verbs. For example, they may be attached to infinitives.

You will see in the examples below that you may choose to put an <u>indirect</u> object pronoun before the first verb, or attach it directly to the infinitive. In later lessons, we will also see DOPs and IDOPs placed after affirmative commands and present participles.

 EXAMPLES: *Tengo que informar**te** que no puedo ir al club contigo.*
I have to inform you that I can't go with you to the club.

*Voy a dar**le** a Ud. (**Le** voy a dar a Ud.) la oportunidad de ganar un viaje a Machu Picchu.*
I'm going to give you a chance to win a trip to Machu Picchu.

*Necesitamos reservar**les** (**Les** necesitamos reservar)* una habitación doble.*
We need to reserve you all (them) a double room.

*Note: Do you remember how to clarify the meaning of *"les"*? Simply add *"a ellos"* or *"a ellas"* or *"a Uds."*: *Les necesitamos reservar una habitacíon **a ellos/ellas/Uds**.*

1. **Write the appropriate indirect object pronoun in the spaces provided:**

a. Hace unos años Nicole Kidman ganó un Óscar; _____ dio el trofeo a su hijo.

b. Este año Brad Pitt no ganó un Óscar; no _____ dio un trofeo a sus hijos.

c. El guitarrista Paco de Lucía no _____ dedicó a mí una canción; estoy muy triste.

d. "Siempre _____ doy muchos besos", _____ dijo la madre a su hijo.

e. Cher _____ ofrece música nueva a nosotros cada década.

f. Siempre _____ digo muchos secretos a mis amigas.

g. "_____ voy a llamar mañana después de la entrevista", _____ comentó Matt Damon a su mejor amigo, Ben Affleck.

2. **Insert the correct indirect object pronoun** *(me, te, le, nos, os, les)* **or direct object pronoun** *(me, te, lo, la, nos, os, los, las)* **into the following letter:**

Paco:

Cuando _____ escribí una carta a Marisela, no _____
        (to her)   (me)

contestó. Voy a escribir_____ otra vez. ¿Recuerdas que
                          (to her)

_____ dije que ella no _____ ama? ¡Es verdad! Tiene otro
   (you)   (me)

novio. ¿Su nombre? _____ sé. Se llama Paco y vive en la Calle
                    (it)

Ocho. ¿_____ conoces? Vive en tu calle, el mismo número.
(him)

Marisela dice que va a llamar_____ luego.
(us)

Hasta luego,

Javier

3. **There is one error in each of the following five sentences. Underline each error and write the correction above it:**

1) "No debo nada", les dijo el hombre orgulloso al

   presidente del banco.

2) Tienes que llamarme a mi después de recibir tu premio.

3) "Pronto voy a les tocar el Concierto de Aranjuez", les

   prometió Paco de Lucía a los invitados.

4) "Siempre lo digo la verdad a la policía", dice el ladrón.

5) Un día Britney Spears va a nos decir exactamente qué

   pasó aquella noche en Las Vegas cuando se casó con

   su amigo Jason.

D) THE VERB "GUSTAR"

Back in the **FIRST STEPS** section of this text, you had the chance to practice a little with the verb *"gustar."* You learned that *"me gusta"* is usually translated as "I like" in Spanish. In fact, the literal translation of *"me gusta"* is not "I like"; it actually means "it is pleasing to me."

"Gustar" is one of a number of Spanish verbs that always use indirect object pronouns. The construction of a sentence with *"gustar"* places an indirect object first, then a form of *"gustar"* and, finally, the subject:

Indirect Object Pronoun		Form of "Gustar"		Subject
(me, te, le, nos, os, les)	**+**	(usually *gusta, gustan*)	**+**	

Because the subject is most often an object or some objects, the form of *"gustar"* will normally be in the 3rd person singular or 3rd person plural.

EXAMPLES: *Me gusta el clima de Guayaquil en primavera.*
I like the climate in Guayaquil in the spring (The climate in Guayaquil is pleasing to me in the spring).

Nos gusta la Casa Rosada en Buenos Aires.
We like the Pink House in Buenos Aires.

¿Te gustan los trajes de baño que llevan los chicos?
Do you like the bathing suits that the boys are wearing?

Os gustan los equipos de fútbol que hacen muchos goles.
You all like soccer teams that score a lot of goals.

Me gustan los vídeos que tienen en Netflix.
I like the videos that they have in Netflix.

A ella le gustó el mes que pasó en Ibarra.
She liked the month that she spent in Ibarra.

¿Les gusta a Uds. la nueva novela de Isabel Allende?
Do you all like the new novel of Isabel Allende?

Helpful Tips: **1)** Did you notice that in the last two sentences above, the speaker added some additional words to emphasize or make clear who received the indirect action of the verb?
2) For example, in the sentence, *"A ella le gustó el mes que pasó en Ibarra,"* the words *"a ella"* make it clear that the month was pleasing to her rather than to him or to you (formal).
3) Similarly, in *"¿Les gusta a Uds. la nueva novela de Isabel Allende?"*, the words *"a Uds."* inform the listeners that the speaker wanted to know if the novel is pleasing to you all, rather than to them.

What happens if an infinitive is the subject of one of these sentences? Will the verb be singular or plural? The answer — singular!

 EXAMPLES: *Me **gusta** leer en la cama.*
I like to read in bed (Reading in bed pleases me).

*Nos **gusta** poner las cartas en el buzón.*
We like to put the letters in the mailbox.

What happens if there are multiple infinitives? Will the form of *"gustar"* still be singular? The answer — yes!

 EXAMPLES: *Te **gusta** leer y escribir poesía en el parque.*
You like to read and write poetry in the park (Reading and writing poetry in the park pleases you).

*A mis amigos les **gusta** bailar y cantar en la playa.*
My friends like to dance and sing on the beach.

 # PRACTICE EXERCISES

1. In the sentences below, insert the correct form of the verb *"gustar"*:

a. Nos _____ la lluvia en la primavera.

b. Me _____ más los equipos de hockey que los de fútbol americano.

c. Te _____ cantar en la casa cuando no hay nadie.

d. A mi prima le _____ las noches románticas de Lima.

e. A nuestro abuelo le _____ beber vino bueno y comprar coches viejos.

f. Cuando Eva Longoria tiene mucho tiempo libre, le _____ visitar a su familia en México.

g. A nosotros nos _____ las canciones de Alejandro Sanz y las de Luis Miguel — son fantásticas.

h. No me _____ la carne que me sirvieron anoche en el restaurante.

2. Choose an indirect object pronoun (IDOP) *(me, te, le, nos, os, les)* **for each of the following sentences:**

a. A nosotras no _____ gusta el frío en diciembre.

b. Siempre _____ escribimos muchas cartas a mi abuela.

c. A mí _____ gustan los precios en la tienda.

d. ¡_____ voy a llamar a ti primero!

e. ¡_____ voy a escribir a ellos luego!

f. _____ digo a vosotros otra vez: ¡No!

3. Now translate these sentences into Spanish, always being certain to use a form of *"gustar"*:

a. We like tacos with cheese; they are delicious.

_____

_____

b. I like to listen to classical music; Bach and Beethoven are great!

_____

_____

c. My teachers like the truth.

_____

_____

d. She likes to talk and walk; I like dogs and cats.

_____

_____

These two sets of questions use grammatical structures and vocabulary from this lesson. Working with a partner, alternate asking and answering each question. When you get to the bottom of each list, start over at the top, switching roles. As a variation, write out the answers in complete sentences.

 A) ¿Anduviste hoy a la escuela o tomaste el autobús?

¿Tuviste una entrevista ayer con un representante de la universidad?

¿Viste el cartel para el concierto el sábado?

¿Te gusta besar una rana?

¿Es mejor susurrar o gritar en la biblioteca?

¿Les escribes muchas cartas a tus padres?

¿Dónde pusiste los libros esta mañana?

B) ¿Fuiste de compras con tu mamá recientemente?

A tus amigos, ¿les gusta más la natación o el remo?

A ti, ¿te gustan las zanahorias?

¿Tienes mucho tiempo libre en un día típico?

¿Es mejor contar o escuchar un cuento?

¿Quién te dijo "hola" hoy?

¿A quién le dijiste "hola" hoy?

PRUEBA DE REPASO

1. Answer in complete sentences:

a. ¿A qué hora hiciste la tarea anoche?

_____

b. ¿Viniste a la escuela el domingo?

_____

c. A ti, ¿te gustan las toallas nuevas o las toallas viejas?

_____

d. ¿Trajiste hoy un buen libro a la playa?

_____

e. ¿Estás orgulloso/a de tu familia?

_____

2. Conjugate the following six verbs fully in the preterite tense. Check your answers by looking at the charts on pages 136 and 137:

tener (to have)   **decir** (to say)   **dar** (to give)

_____ _____   _____ _____   _____ _____

_____ _____   _____ _____   _____ _____

_____ _____   _____ _____   _____ _____

leer (to read)   **andar** (to walk)   **poder** (to be able to)

_____ _____   _____ _____   _____ _____

_____ _____   _____ _____   _____ _____

_____ _____   _____ _____   _____ _____

3. Conjugate each verb in the appropriate form of the preterite:

a. Mi amiga _____ rápidamente para llegar a tiempo al concierto de Carlos Vives. (conducir)

b. Yo no _____ dormir en la cama de mi abuelita porque es muy pequeña. (poder)

c. Ud. no _____ nada anoche . . . ¿por qué no trabaja Ud. más? (hacer)

d. Mi abuelo _____ muchas millas en el parque para mejorar la salud. (andar)

e. Luis Miguel _____ en Nueva York ayer para promocionar su nuevo álbum *Cómplices*. (estar)

f. Cameron Díaz no _____ a la fiesta la semana pasada porque fue a Hawaii con su amiga Drew Barrymore. (ir)

g. El camarero nos _____ la cuenta a la mesa. (traer)

h. Ellos nunca me _____ cerca del buzón. (ver)

i. Ya te _____ que me gusta mucho el programa de George López. (decir)

j. Mi amiga _____ en una revista que Óscar de la Hoya tiene muchos problemas ahora. (leer)

4. Write the correct form of the possessive adjectives in the spaces provided:

a. _____ iglesia (our)

b. _____ empleos (their)

c. _____ traje de baño (her)

d. _____ bebida (their)

e. _____ escuelas (our)

f. _____ precio (your all's)

g. _____ toallas (his)

h. _____ toallas (my)

i. _____ revistas (your, formal)

j. _____ camarero (her)

5. Fill in the blanks with either the correct form of *"gustar"* or the proper indirect object pronoun *(me, te, le, nos, os, les)*:

a. A nosotros nos _____ las zanahorias.

b. A ella _____ gusta gritar en la iglesia.

c. A ti no te _____ esquiar por el frío.

d. A él _____ gustó besar a su novia enfrente de sus amigos.

e. Me _____ las calles estrechas.

f. Nos _____ escuchar la música de Willy Chirino.

6. Translate the following sentences into Spanish:

a. You like to read and write romantic books.

_____

b. She said: "I like my school, my church and my family."

_____

c. I gave a lot of money to my best friend. ¡CUIDADO! (Don't forget an indirect object pronoun!)

_____

7. Underline and correct the five errors in the following paragraph:

Estoy furiosa. No hay mucha cartas en el buzón hoy. ¿No tuvieran tiempo María y Claudia para escribirme la semana pasada? Mis amigas nunca escriben me. No me gusto mis amigas. Como soy muy orgullosa, no voy a les decir nada. En el futuro, nunca voy a ir al parque con ellas en mi tiempo libre.

VENEZUELA

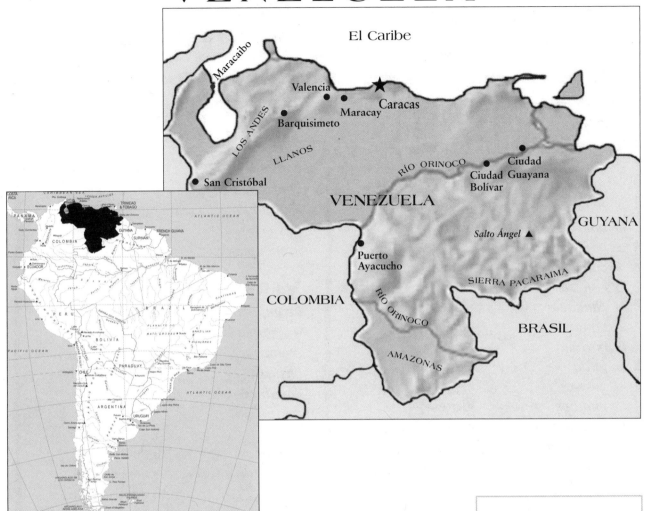

VENEZUELA

CAPITAL:	Caracas
POBLACIÓN:	26.400.000
GOBIERNO:	república federal
PRESIDENTE:	Hugo Chávez
DINERO ($):	bolívar
PRODUCTOS:	arroz, café, petróleo
MÚSICA, BAILE:	boleros, joropo, salsa
SITIOS DE INTERÉS:	Gran Sabana, Llanos, Mérida, Parque Central (Caracas), Río Orinoco, Salto del Ángel (highest waterfall in world), San Juan
COMIDA TÍPICA:	arepas, cachapas, empanadas, hallaca, merengada, pabellón criollo, sancocho

VENEZOLANOS FAMOSOS:

Baruj Benacerraf
(CIENTÍFICO)

Simón Bolívar
(GENERAL, "EL LIBERTADOR")

Miguel Cabrera
(BEISBOLISTA)

Rómulo Gallegos
(ESCRITOR)

Mercedes Pardo
(ARTISTA)

Teresa de la Parra
(ESCRITORA)

VOCABULARIO LECCIÓN SIETE

THEME WORDS: "CLOTHES"

el	abrigo	coat
el	arete	earring
la	blusa	blouse
la	bota	boot
la	bufanda	scarf
los	calcetines	socks
la	camisa	shirt
la	chaqueta	jacket
el	cinturón	belt
la	corbata	tie
la	falda	skirt
la	gorra	cap, hat
los	guantes	gloves
los	pantalones	pants
el	pendiente	earring
la	ropa	clothes
el	sombrero	hat
el	suéter	sweater
el	traje de baño	swimsuit
el	vestido	dress
los	zapatos	shoes

OTHER NOUNS

el	asiento	seat
la	billetera	wallet
la	entrada	admission ticket, entrance
la	milla	mile
la	palabra	word
el	teléfono	telephone
la	vaca	cow

ADJECTIVES

alegre	happy
atlético/a	athletic
caliente	warm, hot
cansado/a	tired
estúpido/a	stupid
misterioso/a	mysterious
preocupado/a	upset

VERBS

acompañar	to accompany
acostarse (ue)	to go to bed
afeitar(se)	to shave (oneself)
casarse	to get married
cepillarse	to brush one's (hair, teeth)
crear	to create, to make
decidir	to decide
despertarse (ie)	to wake up
hacer	to do, to make
lavarse	to wash oneself
levantarse	to get up
llamar	to call
ocurrir	to occur, to happen
peinarse	to comb one's hair
ponerse	to put on
reírse (i)	to laugh
sentar (ie)	to seat (someone)
sentarse (ie)	to sit down
volar (ue)	to fly

MISCELLANEOUS

de nuevo	again
despacio	slowly
por eso	therefore
si	if

LECCIÓN SIETE

KEY GRAMMAR
CONCEPTS

A) THE IMPERFECT TENSE → *El imperfecto*

B) REFLEXIVE OBJECT PRONOUNS (ROPs) → *Los pronombres reflexivos*

C) ADVERBS → *Los adverbios*

D) TALKING ABOUT THE WEATHER → *¿Qué tiempo hace hoy?*

 A) THE IMPERFECT TENSE

The **imperfect** is another verb tense used to describe action from the past. It differs from the preterite in a number of ways and is used in different situations.

Let's first take a look at the conjugations of the regular verbs. The good news is that there are only three irregular verbs in Spanish: *"ir," "ser,"* and *"ver"*! All of these irregular conjugations will be covered in *Lección Ocho*.

All other verbs in Spanish are <u>completely</u> regular: there are no stem-changing forms or any special spelling changes. For this reason, the imperfect tense is often a favorite among Spanish students.

Here are the regular forms of the imperfect tense:

HABLAR		COMER		VIVIR	
hablaba	hablábamos	comía	comíamos	vivía	vivíamos
hablabas	hablabais	comías	comíais	vivías	vivíais
hablaba	hablaban	comía	comían	vivía	vivían

Helpful Tips: **1)** Did you notice that there are accents only on the *nosotros/nosotras* form of **-AR** verbs *(hablar)* and on every form of the **-ER** and **-IR** verbs *(comer, vivir)*? **2)** Did you also notice that **-ER** and **-IR** endings are identical?

The three verbs on the next page are representative of those that are irregular in the present. You will recall that *cerrar* and *pedir* are "boot" verbs, while *conocer* has a spelling change in the *"yo"* form. You will notice, however, that these verbs are completely normal in the imperfect!

Here are two "boot" verbs and one "spelling-changer" in the imperfect:

CERRAR		CONOCER		PEDIR	
cerraba	cerrábamos	conocía	conocíamos	pedía	pedíamos
cerrabas	cerrabais	conocías	conocíais	pedías	pedíais
cerraba	cerraban	conocía	conocían	pedía	pedían

WHEN IS THE IMPERFECT USED?

1) INCOMPLETE ACTIONS — ACTIONS IN PROGRESS

Unlike the preterite, which describes completed action, the imperfect can describe action that hadn't been completed yet or that was ongoing.

✴ **EXAMPLES:** *Leíamos el libro cuando el teléfono sonó.*
We were reading the book when the phone rang.

Dorina jugaba a las cartas cuando su amigo, el chico del pendiente, llegó.
Dorina was playing cards when her friend, the boy with the earring, arrived.

Nadie quería ir al parque; por eso todos se quedaron a la mesa.
No one wanted to go to the park; therefore, everyone stayed at the table.

Mark Teixera dijo que iba a marcar un jonrón en Nueva York anoche, pero no lo hizo.
Mark Teixera said that he was going to hit a homerun in New York last night, but he didn't do it.

Helpful Tip: In all of the examples above, did you notice that the verb in the imperfect tense described actions that <u>hadn't</u> been completed (We were in the middle of reading the book; Dorina was in the middle of a card game; No one was interested in going to the park; Manny Ramírez was planning to hit a homerun)?

2) DESCRIPTION

The imperfect is used for descriptions in the past. This use really makes a lot of sense. When you describe someone as tall or clever, for example, these descriptions are clearly not completed actions. The ongoing nature of a description, with no clear ending point, is a good clue for the imperfect.

✴ **EXAMPLES:** *La mujer misteriosa del sombrero tenía ojos azules.*
The mysterious woman with the hat had blue eyes.

¡La sopa de tomate estaba muy caliente!
The tomato soup was very hot!

La nueva película de Alejandro Amenábar, Agora, **parecía**
fantástica.
The new Alejandro Amenábar movie, *Agora*, seemed fantastic.

Después de correr diez millas, **estábamos** *muy cansados.*
After running ten miles, we were very tired.

3) TELLING TIME

A special use of the imperfect is for telling time in the past. Now is the time to memorize the two irregular forms of the imperfect of *"ser"* used below *(era, eran)*. The rest of the irregular forms will be covered in *Lección Ocho*.

 EXAMPLES: *Eran las diez de la noche cuando me dormí.*
It was ten at night when I fell asleep.

Era la una de la mañana cuando descubrí que no tenía mi billetera, ni mi suéter, ni mi chaqueta.
It was one A.M. when I discovered that I didn't have my wallet, sweater or jacket.

4) HABITUAL ACTIONS

The imperfect is also used to describe habitual actions in the past. Anything that a person used to do regularly calls for the imperfect.

 EXAMPLES: *Cuando tenía diez años,* **comía** *Frosted Flakes cada mañana con mis hermanos.*
When I was ten years old, I used to eat Frosted Flakes every morning with my brothers.

Mi amigo Nick **contaba** *los mejores chistes; todos* **se reían** *mucho.*
My friend Nick used to tell the best jokes; everyone used to laugh a lot.

Mis amigos y yo **leíamos** <u>The Boxcar Children</u> *durante la siesta; nuestra historia favorita se* **llamaba** <u>The Yellow House Mystery</u>.
My friends and I used to read <u>The Boxcar Children</u> series during rest time; our favorite was called <u>The Yellow House Mystery</u>.

Antes siempre me **invitabas** *a las fiestas; ¿por qué nunca me llamas ahora?*
In the past you always used to invite me to parties; why don't you ever call me now?

PRACTICE EXERCISES

1. Conjugate the following verbs fully into the imperfect:

andar (to walk)   **comprender** (to understand)

_____ _____   _____ _____

_____ _____   _____ _____

_____ _____   _____ _____

escribir (to write)   **comenzar** (to begin)

_____ _____   _____ _____

_____ _____   _____ _____

_____ _____   _____ _____

escoger (to choose)   **repetir** (to repeat)

_____ _____   _____ _____

_____ _____   _____ _____

_____ _____   _____ _____

2. Now change each of the following verbs from the present or preterite tense to the corresponding form of the imperfect. Also, add all possible subject pronouns:

Examples: tienen → <u>(ellos, ellas, Uds.) tenían</u>   compraste → <u>(tú) comprabas</u>

a. comienza → _____   **f.** pedí → _____

b. pierdes → _____   **g.** cupo → _____

c. bebemos → _____   **h.** pintaste → _____

d. admite → _____   **i.** vienen → _____

e. limpian → _____   **j.** estuvimos → _____

3. Complete the following sentences using the appropriate form of the imperfect tense:

a. Yo nunca _____ a mis profesores en las clases de español; por eso, no sé hablar bien el español. (escuchar)

b. Rob Thomas _____ la letra de la canción *"Smooth"* mientras Carlos Santana tocaba la guitarra. (cantar)

c. El ladrón del abrigo gris _____ la puerta del banco cuando un coche de la policía llegó a la escena. (abrir)

d. Nuestros amigos siempre hacían excursiones con la familia a Caracas; mis hermanos y yo siempre _____ acompañarlos. (querer)

e. Penélope Cruz y Antonio Banderas _____ muy contentos cuando anunciaron que Pedro Almodóvar ganó un Óscar. (parecer)

f. Cuando García Márquez tenía cinco años, _____ en Aracataca, un pueblo de Colombia. (vivir)

g. Todos _____ sorprendidos cuando vieron el vestido verde que llevaba Jennifer López en los Grammys. (estar)

h. Nosotros siempre _____ los discos nuevos de Led Zeppelin cuando vivíamos en Ohio. (comprar)

i. De niño, Jim Carrey siempre _____ cuentos cómicos . . . de adulto hizo una película cómica extraordinaria: *Liar, Liar.* (escribir)

j. _____ las once y media de la noche cuando Danica Patrick me llamó para hablar de NASCAR. (Ser)

4. The following paragraph contains six errors. The preterite has been used in some instances where the imperfect was a better choice, and there are some spelling problems with a couple of imperfect verb forms.

 Esta tarde jugué al tenis cuando comenzó a llover. Fueron las tres de la tarde. El cielo estuvo muy gris cuando mi amigo me dijo: "Vamos. Llueve mucho". Mi amigo pareció agitado, y yo le dije: "Bueno, vamos". Vuelvíamos a casa cuando el sol apareció. Decidimos jugar más. Mi amigo y yo estabamos muy contentos.

🔑 B) REFLEXIVE OBJECT PRONOUNS (ROPs)

So far we have learned two categories of object pronouns:
  1) Direct Object Pronouns *(me, te, lo, la, nos, os, los, las)*
  2) Indirect Object Pronouns *(me, te, le, nos, os, les)*.

A speaker chooses between these pronouns depending on whether the noun being replaced is the direct object or the indirect object of the verb.

This lesson presents a final list of pronouns that are associated with verbs. These pronouns are **reflexive**.

In the sentence: "I see myself in the mirror," the word "myself" is the reflexive object pronoun. This type of pronoun can easily be identified because the subject of the verb is also an object of the verb. Whom do I see in the mirror? I see myself!

In the sentence: "Daniel bought himself a new computer," "himself" is the reflexive object pronoun. The subject, "Daniel," bought something to give to himself.

Reflexive Object Pronouns	
me	*nos*
te	*os*
se	*se*

Helpful Tip: Once again, *"me, te, nos, os"* should look familiar. They also serve as DOPs (direct object pronouns) and IDOPs (indirect object pronouns).

 **EXAMPLES:** *Me llamo Julia García, no Julio García.*
My name is (I call myself) Julia García, not Julio García.

Nos lavamos las manos antes de comer.
We wash our hands before eating. (In this sentence, we are clearly washing ourselves . . . *"las manos"* identifies what part of our body we are washing. In a reflexive sentence, a definite article, rather than a possessive adjective, is used in Spanish with body parts and articles of clothing.)

Mi amigo se pone los pantalones y la corbata muy despacio.
My friend puts on his pants and tie very slowly.

Tú te consideras muy guapo, ¿verdad?
You consider yourself very good-looking, don't you?

Os ponéis en una buena posición otra vez.
You all are putting yourselves in a good position again.

Esos músicos se llaman Beyoncé y Jay-Z.
Those musicians are named (call themselves) Beyoncé and Jay-Z.

Mi hermano se acuesta a las diez.
My brother goes (puts himself) to bed at ten o'clock.

Mi papá se sienta en la silla cómoda.
My dad sits down in the comfortable chair.

To clarify or to emphasize one of these reflexive object pronouns, you may choose to add the following words:

a mí (mismo, misma, etc.)	*a nosotros, a nosotras*
a ti	*a vosotros, a vosotras*
a sí	*a sí*

To add even extra emphasis, the words *"mismo, misma, mismos, mismas"* can follow any of the words above. You simply choose the form that agrees with the subject.

 **EXAMPLES:** *Muchas veces me digo a mí misma que tengo mucho talento.*
Many times I tell <u>myself</u> that I have a lot of talent.

Nos miramos a nosotras mismas en el espejo antes de salir para la escuela.
We look at <u>ourselves</u> in the mirror before leaving for school.

No necesitas admirtirme a mí que no eres perfecto; necesitas admitirte a ti mismo que no eres perfecto.
You don't have to admit to me that you aren't perfect; you need to admit to <u>yourself</u> that you are not perfect.

Si ellas quieren recibir una carta, ¡tienen que escribirse a sí mismas!
If they want to receive a letter, they have to write to themselves!

1. **Complete the following sentences using the appropriate reflexive object pronoun** *(me, te, se, nos, os, se)*:

   a. _____ siento en mi silla favorita cuando estoy muy cansado.

   b. El álbum más romántico de Miguel Bosé _____ llama *"Papito"*.

   c. _____ lavamos la cara y las manos cuando vamos a misa.

   d. _____ dices que nunca vas a comer en ese restaurante otra vez.

   e. Mi amiga _____ cepilla los dientes con Crest.

   f. ¿Por qué _____ comprasteis un regalo para Navidad?

   g. Cuando nadie me llama por teléfono, _____ pregunto: ¿Por qué no tengo amigos?

2. **Now add the following words** *(a mí, a ti, a sí, a nosotros/nosotras, a vosotros/ vosotras, a sí)* **to emphasize the reflexive pronoun found in each sentence. Add** *"mismo, misma, mismos, mismas"* **to at least a few of the sentences:**

   a. Me digo _____ que necesito encontrar otro trabajo.

   b. Mi padre siempre se dice _____: "De tal palo, tal astilla *(Like father, like son)*".

   c. Ellos se consideran _____ los chicos más atléticos del universo.

   d. Mi vecina se miente _____ cuando dice que no tiene muchos zapatos.

   e. ¿Por qué os dais _____ los mejores asientos?

   f. Mi hermana se conoce muy bien _____; nunca trata de hacer nada si está cansada.

C) ADVERBS

Adverbs are words that are used to modify or qualify verbs, adjectives, or other adverbs. These words tell how, when, where, or with what intensity something is done.

In the sentence **"I stupidly bought a car last year that was so poorly made,"** there are a number of adverbs:

◆ **"stupidly"** is an adverb that qualifies the verb "bought."

◆ **"last year"** is an adverbial phrase which modifies the verb "bought," telling the listener when the action was done.

◆ **"so"** is an adverb because it lets us know how poorly the car was made; it modifies the adverb "poorly."

◆ **"poorly"** is also an adverb which modifies "made"; it tells us how the car was made.

In Spanish, adverbs are commonly placed <u>after</u> verbs and <u>before</u> adjectives or other adverbs.

Here is a list of twenty common adverbs in Spanish:

Common Adverbs			
allí	→ there	*muy*	→ very
antes	→ before	*nunca*	→ never
aquí	→ here	*poco*	→ a little
ayer	→ yesterday	*pronto*	→ soon
bien	→ fine	*siempre*	→ always
después	→ after	*también*	→ also
hoy	→ today	*tan*	→ so
mal	→ poorly	*tanto*	→ so much
mañana	→ tomorrow	*tarde*	→ late
mucho	→ a lot	*temprano*	→ early

Helpful Tips: **1)** Be aware that some of these words have more than one grammatical use. For example, *"ayer"* and *"hoy"* are both nouns in this sentence: *"Ayer fue martes, pero hoy es miércoles,"* but they are adverbs in this one: *"Comí en McDonald's ayer, pero como en Taco Bell hoy."*
2) In the following sentence, *"mucho"* and *"poco"* are adjectives: *"Tengo mucho talento y poco dinero,"* but in this one they are adverbs: *"Bailamos mucho, pero estudiamos poco."*
3) As adverbs, *"mucho"* and *"poco"* have <u>one</u> form. As adjectives, they have <u>four</u>: *mucho, mucha, muchos, muchas; poco, poca, pocos, pocas.*

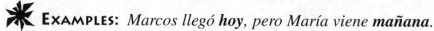

Examples: *Marcos llegó **hoy**, pero María viene **mañana**.*
Marcos arrived today, but María is coming tomorrow.

*Mi amigo es **tan** estúpido que cree que las vacas pueden volar.*
My friend is so stupid that he thinks cows can fly.

*Luis Miguel está **muy** enfermo; no puede cantar **bien** ahora.*
Luis Miguel is very sick; he can't sing well now.

*Siempre compro las entradas **temprano** porque el espectáculo es popular.*
I always buy the tickets early because the show is popular.

*La Universidad de Florida tiene un equipo de baloncesto **muy** bueno, y la Universidad de Connecticut, **también**.*
The University of Florida has a very good basketball team, and the University of Connecticut, too.

*Carolina Herrera trabaja **mucho** en la industria de la moda; **pronto** va a venderle ropa a todo el mundo.*
Carolina Herrera works a lot in the fashion industry; soon she is going to sell clothes to the whole world.

*"**Más** vale **tarde** que **nunca**" es un refrán **muy** común en español.*
"Better late than never" is a very common saying in Spanish.

 # PRACTICE EXERCISES ▶

1. **Complete the following sentences using any adverb from this list that makes sense** (*allí, antes, aquí, ayer, bien, después, hoy, mal, mañana, mucho, muy, nunca, poco, pronto, siempre, también, tan, tanto, tarde, temprano*). **A number of sentences may have more than one correct answer:**

a. Paul McCartney todavía es _____ popular que es difícil conseguir una entrada para sus conciertos.

b. Marcos no llegó ni _____, ni hoy; va a llegar mañana.

c. Estoy _____ cansada y no me siento _____; voy a acostarme después de las clases.

d. Mi hermana es una fanática; siempre se cepilla los dientes por la mañana,

pero yo _____ lo hago.

e. "Uds. necesitan sentarse _____ en las sillas y comenzar a estudiar", les dijo la profesora a los alumnos.

f. _____ yo siempre bebía café con leche, pero ahora prefiero tomar té con limón.

g. Mis primos, Luis, Dalia, Domingo y Loli vienen a la fiesta . . . y, claro,

Roberto viene, _____.

h. Raúl de Molina, el periodista en *El Gordo y La Flaca*, come _____; por eso, se llama "El Gordo".

i. No tienes que preocuparte — mi padre viene con el coche en dos minutos;

sí, viene muy _____.

j. No me gusta ir _____ al cine porque no deseo perderme ni un minuto de la película.

2. Now write your own original sentences using the following adverbs. In some sentences, you will be asked to incorporate more than one adverb into the sentence:

a. temprano

_____

b. hoy; mañana

_____

c. mal

_____

d. antes; pronto

_____

e. también

_____

Talking about the weather is a common topic of conversation in almost every culture. At the beginning of this book, you learned a few expressions to describe the weather. In this section, you will find even more ways to do so. Now that you understand more about the various parts of speech, you will see that the constructions themselves differ in English and Spanish.

Here is a good list of expanded vocabulary for talking about the weather:

¿Qué tiempo hace hoy?	How's the weather today? (Literally: What weather is it doing/making today?)
Hace frío. Hace mucho frío.	It's cold. It's very cold. (Literally: It's making cold. It's making a lot of cold.)
Hace calor. Hace mucho calor.	It's hot. It's very hot. (Literally: It's making heat. It's making a lot of heat.)
Hace sol. Hace mucho sol.	It's sunny. It's very sunny. (Literally: It's making sun. It's making a lot of sun.)
Llueve. Llueve un poco.	It's raining. It's raining a little.
Nieva.	It's snowing.
Está nublado.	It's cloudy.
Está soleado.	It's sunny.
Graniza.	It's hailing.
Hace (mucho) viento.	It's (very) windy. (Literally: It's making [a lot of] wind.)
Hay (mucha) niebla.	It's (very) foggy. (Literally: There is [a lot of] fog.)

PRACTICE EXERCISES

1. **Using the weather vocabulary that you just learned, write an appropriate expression that you associate with each picture:**

a. _____

b. _____

c. _____

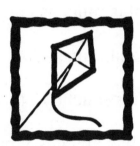

d. _____

2. **Pretend that you have just been hired at your local television station as the new meteorologist. Prepare a script for a telecast which describes not only the current weather in your area, but also the national forecast. Be certain that there are a number of different weather patterns in play across the country:**

_____

_____

_____

_____

_____

_____

These two sets of questions use grammatical structures and vocabulary from this lesson. Working with a partner, alternate asking and answering each question. When you get to the bottom of each list, start over at the top, switching roles. As a variation, write out the answers in complete sentences.

 A) Cuando tenías ocho años:

¿dónde vivías?

¿bebías más jugo de naranja o jugo de tomate?

¿cómo se llamaba tu mejor amigo?

¿recibías muchas cartas de tus abuelos?

¿hablaban tus padres por teléfono durante la comida?

¿te reías mucho con tus amigos?

¿llevabas guantes y bufanda cuando nevaba?

B) ¿Te sientes alegre hoy?

¿Te compraste una entrada para la nueva exposición en el museo?

¿Te preguntas por qué no vuelan las vacas?

¿Normalmente hablas despacio o rápidamente?

¿Puedes decirme un buen chiste ahora?

¿Prefieres llegar tarde o temprano a una película?

¿Estás alegre cuando hace mucho viento?

DIALOGUE

The following dialogue contains grammar and vocabulary that you've seen in this lesson and in the introductory section. After listening to the CD, read this dialogue aloud, alone or with friends. Afterwards, try to answer the questions that follow either aloud or in written form.

 ## LAS AVENTURAS DE RAFAEL, ELISA Y "EL TIGRE"

ESCENA CUATRO

Rafael, "El Tigre", y Elisa duermen tranquilamente en un apartamento en Nueva York. A las ocho en punto, Marisela, la prima de Javier (el amigo de Rafael), los llama.

Marisela:	Buenos días. Buenos días. ¡Levántense Uds.!
El Tigre:	¿Qué hora es, Marisela?
Marisela:	Son las ocho de la mañana. Es hora de desayunar. En unos minutos tenemos que ir a la comisaría (police station) para ver si tienen información sobre tu mochila.
Rafael:	Buenos días. Tengo hambre, Javier y Marisela. ¿Qué hay de comer?
Javier:	Cereal, tostadas, jugo, Pop-Tarts y café.
El Tigre:	Oye, Marisela, tomé una decisión anoche. No importa la mochila. Puedo comprar más ropa hoy. Y todavía tengo dinero en la billetera.
Javier:	Te puedo prestar mi ropa vieja, Tigre. Creo que usamos la misma talla (size) más o menos.
Elisa:	Rafael, tus amigos son simpáticos. ¡Tenemos mucha suerte!
Rafael:	Gracias. Pero ese hombre que robó la mochila . . . soñé con él (I dreamt about him) anoche. Creo que lo conozco.
Elisa:	No pienses en eso. Todo va bien ahora. Hablé con mis padres anoche y estaban muy felices. Les dije que el campamento de tenis es bonito y que tenía muchas ganas de practicar el tenis. Mi padre estaba muy contento.

Suena el teléfono. Javier lo contesta.

Javier:	Aló. Aló.

Javier cuelga el teléfono.

Javier:	¡Qué extraño! No habla nadie.
Marisela:	Pues, ¿quién sabe? A lo mejor (probably) un número equivocado. Pero, vamos, chicos. Tengo un día fantástico para Uds. Primero vamos al Museo Metropolitano de Arte para ver una exposición de Frida Kahlo y Diego Rivera, y después vamos a almorzar en mi favorito restaurante cubano, "Victor's Café".

Rafael:	Javier me dijo que Uds. vieron a Elvis Crespo en "Victor's Café" la semana pasada. ¿Es verdad?
Javier:	Claro, chico. Es toda la verdad.
Elisa:	Elvis canta muy bien y es muy guapo, también. Me encanta la canción *"Suavemente"*.

Los chicos se preparan para el día. Se duchan, se peinan y se visten.

Javier:	¿Es verdad que Uds. tienen que irse mañana? Nueva York es tan grande y hay tanto que hacer.
Marisela:	Es verdad. Esta tarde filman una película de Spike Lee en Central Park. Si hay tiempo después de almorzar, vamos a ver si podemos ver un poquito.
El Tigre:	Spike Lee es fantástico. Me gustaría mucho.
Javier:	¿Saben Uds. que Nueva York es el sitio más popular en la historia del cine? ¿Se dan cuenta (Do you realize?) de todas las películas que filmaron aquí?
El Tigre:	Pues, *King Kong* es una.
Javier:	También *West Side Story, Kramer vs. Kramer, When Harry Met Sally, Serpico, Fame, Sleepless in Seattle, Breakfast at Tiffany's, Taxi Driver* y *Saturday Night Fever.*
Elisa:	¡Es increíble! Vamos.
El Tigre:	Si hay tiempo esta tarde, ¿podemos comer un helado en "Serendipity"? Rafael me dijo que tienen una bebida de chocolate fantástica.
Marisela:	Sí, chico. Te prometo que vamos por allí.

Elisa, "El Tigre", Rafael, Javier y Marisela salen del apartamento. Al salir, el teléfono suena de nuevo. Javier decide no contestarlo.

PREGUNTAS

1) **¿Dónde duermen Rafael, Elisa y El Tigre?**

   _____

2) **¿A qué hora se levantaron?**

   _____

3) **¿Qué van a comer para el desayuno?**

   _____

4) **¿Por qué no van a la comisaría (police station)?**

   _____

5) **¿Por qué no necesita comprar ropa nueva El Tigre?**

   _____

6) **¿Qué exposición especial hay en el Museo Metropolitano de Arte?**

   _____

7) **¿Dónde van a almorzar?**

   _____

8) **¿Qué cantante famoso comió recientemente en ese restaurante?**

   _____

9) **¿Cómo se llaman tres películas famosas que fueron filmadas en Nueva York?**

   _____

10) **¿Qué problema hay con el teléfono en esta escena?**

   _____

1. Answer in complete sentences:

a. ¿Qué tiempo hace hoy en Caracas, Venezuela?

_____

b. Cuando tenías dos años, ¿hablabas español?

_____

c. Cuando tenías diez años, ¿comías más carne o más pescado?

_____

d. ¿Te lavas las manos siempre antes de comer?

_____

e. ¿Adónde vas después de clase hoy?

_____

2. Conjugate the following six verbs fully in the imperfect tense:

hablar (to talk)   **comer** (to eat)   **vivir** (to live)

_____ _____   _____ _____   _____ _____

_____ _____   _____ _____   _____ _____

_____ _____   _____ _____   _____ _____

cerrar (to close)   **volver** (to return)   **pedir** (to ask for)

_____ _____   _____ _____   _____ _____

_____ _____   _____ _____   _____ _____

_____ _____   _____ _____   _____ _____

3. Conjugate each verb into the appropriate form of the imperfect:

a. Mis padres me _____ a la tienda cuando me perdí en las calles atestadas de Nueva York. (acompañar)

b. Cuando tenía ocho años, yo _____ frecuentemente la casa de mis abuelos cerca del Salto de Ángel. (visitar)

c. ¿Qué tiempo _____ ayer en las montañas de Chile? (hacer)

d. Normalmente mi papá no _____ nada; era mi madre que siempre tomaba todas las decisiones. (decidir)

e. Cuando mi tío _____ de Fenway Park, Julio Lugo marcó otro jonrón. (salir)

f. ¿Cómo _____ esa famosa cocinera que murió en 2004? –Julia Child. (llamarse)

g. Los padres de Robin Williams siempre _____ cuando él, de niño, les contaba chistes. (reírse)

h. Mi hijo, Jamie, siempre _____ ranas en el río cerca de nuestra casa. (encontrar)

i. Nosotros no _____ nada hasta que el profesor nos lo explicó todo. (entender)

j. En mi barrio todos _____ agitados debido al *(due to the)* misterioso robo en la iglesia. (estar)

4. Complete the following sentences with one of the following reflexive object pronouns *(me, te, se, nos, os, se)***:**

a. _____ llamo Óscar de la Hoya y soy boxeador y cantante.

b. El álbum que más me gusta de los Red Hot Chili Peppers _____ llama *Stadium Arcadium*.

c. Mis hijos nunca _____ cepillaban los dientes cuando eran pequeños.

d. Nunca _____ admites los problemas que tienes . . . ¿por qué no puedes ser más honesto contigo mismo?

e. Vosotros _____ laváis las manos antes de comer.

f. _____ dije que soy atlética y que puedo correr veintiséis millas.

g. Ellos no _____ conocen muy bien a sí mismos; por eso, no pueden estar siempre alegres.

h. Mis abuelos _____ prepararon una comida exquisita con empanadas, ceviche y frutas tropicales.

5. Write the "opposite" of the following adverbs:

a. bien _____

b. poco _____

c. nunca _____

d. tarde _____

e. mañana _____

f. aquí _____

g. después _____

6. Translate the following sentences into Spanish:

a. It's hailing, and we are very upset.

_____

b. She always used to call her friends after each party.

_____

c. Paco laughs so much during math class!

_____

7. The following postcard contains six errors. Underline each error and write the correction above it:

Hola Chita:

Estoy en San Cristóbal, Venezuela. Llueva mucho hoy, pero estoy alegre. Ayer en el hotel, yo duermía a las siete de la mañana cuando alguien entró en mi habitación. Un señor anunció: "Es miércoles. El hotel está cerrada hoy". Yo estabo muy confundida. Decidí irme de allí. Primero lavé me la cara y me cepillé el pelo. Me puse una falda nueva y una camisa blanca. Tomé las maletas y pagé la cuenta. ¡Nunca voy a volver al "Hotel California"!

Muchos besos,

Consuelo

BOLIVIA & CHILE

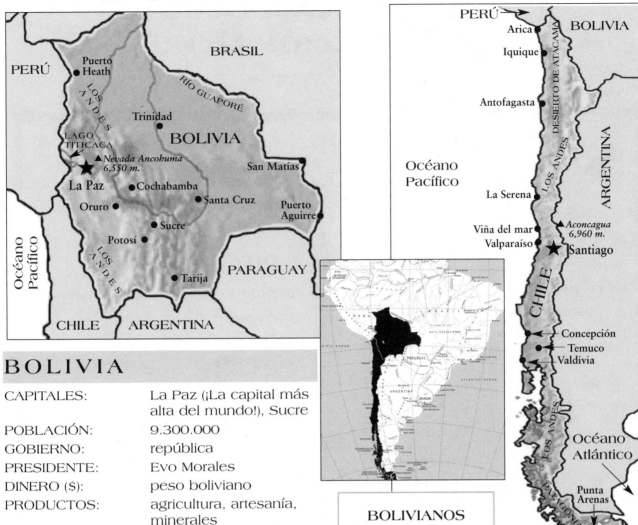

BOLIVIA

CAPITALES:	La Paz (¡La capital más alta del mundo!), Sucre
POBLACIÓN:	9.300.000
GOBIERNO:	república
PRESIDENTE:	Evo Morales
DINERO ($):	peso boliviano
PRODUCTOS:	agricultura, artesanía, minerales
MÚSICA, BAILE:	auqui-auqui, cueca, tinku
SITIOS DE INTERÉS:	El lago Titicaca, Parque Nacional, Salar de Uyuni
COMIDA TÍPICA:	empanadas, humitas, marraqueta (pan), salsa picante

CHILE

CAPITAL:	Santiago
POBLACIÓN:	16.500.000
GOBIERNO:	república
PRESIDENTA:	Michelle Bachelet
DINERO ($):	peso chileno
PRODUCTOS:	agricultura, cobre, vino
MÚSICA, BAILE:	costillar, cueca, refalosa
SITIOS DE INTERÉS:	Los Andes, desierto de Atacama, Isla de Pascua, Tierra del Fuego, Valle de la Luna
COMIDA TÍPICA:	cazuela de ave, empanadas, parrillada de mariscos, pastel de chocho, sopaipillas, vino

BOLIVIANOS FAMOSOS:

Marina Núñez del Prado
(ESCULTORA)

Víctor Paz
(POLÍTICO)

Edmundo Paz Soldán
(ESCRITOR)

Javier Taborga
(ATLETA)

CHILENOS FAMOSOS:

Isabel Allende
(NOVELISTA)

Salvador Allende
(POLÍTICO)

Gabriela Mistral
(POETA)

Pablo Neruda
(POETA)

Bernardo O'Higgins
(HÉROE NACIONAL)

181

VOCABULARIO LECCIÓN OCHO

THEME WORDS: "AT HOME"

la	alfombra	carpet, rug
el	armario	closet
la	bañera	tub
las	cortinas	curtains
el	(cuarto de) baño	bathroom
la	cuchara	spoon
el	cuchillo	knife
la	ducha	shower
las	escaleras	stairs
la	escoba	broom
el	fregadero	sink (in kitchen)
el	lavabo	sink (in bathroom)
el	plato	plate, dish
el	sofá	sofa
el	tenedor	fork

OTHER NOUNS

el	accidente	accident
el/la	asistente/a de vuelo	flight attendant
el	boleto	ticket
el	enemigo	enemy
el	lago	lake

el	pastel	cake
la	torta	cake
el	tostador	toaster

ADJECTIVES

cariñoso/a	affectionate
generoso/a	generous
mayor	older
menor	younger
sabroso/a	tasty, delicious
solo/a	alone

VERBS

cortar	to cut
desear	to desire
mostrar (ue)	to show
prestar	to lend
repetir (i)	to repeat
sonar (ue)	to ring

MISCELLANEOUS

todavía	still
todavía no	not yet

LECCIÓN OCHO

KEY GRAMMAR CONCEPTS

A) IRREGULAR VERBS IN THE IMPERFECT TENSE → *Los verbos irregulares en el imperfecto*

B) DOUBLE OBJECT PRONOUNS → *Cuando hay dos pronombres complementos*

C) ADVERBS THAT END WITH "-MENTE" → *Los adverbios que terminan con "-mente"*

 A) IRREGULAR VERBS IN THE IMPERFECT TENSE

As you learned in the last lesson, there are only three irregular verbs in the imperfect tense: *"ir,"* *"ser,"* and *"ver."* Every other verb is completely regular — no stem changes, no strange spelling, no tricks.

Here are the three verbs that are irregular in the imperfect:

IR		SER		VER	
iba	íbamos	era	éramos	veía	veíamos
ibas	ibais	eras	erais	veías	veíais
iba	iban	era	eran	veía	veían

¡CUIDADO! At first glance, some students wonder why *"ver"* is irregular. If it were regular, however, the conjugations would be: **vía, vías, vía,* etc., and not *veía, veías,* and *veía,* etc.

Let's look at these common verbs in action:

EXAMPLES: *Eran las diez de la noche cuando me dormí.*
It was ten P.M. when I fell asleep.

*Mientras **íbamos** a la casa de la abuela, tuvimos un accidente.*
When we were going to Grandma's house, we had an accident.

*Yo siempre **veía** a mi tío cuando vivía en La Paz.*
I always used to see my uncle when I lived in La Paz.

*Mi profesora de inglés **era** una mujer alta.*
My English teacher was a tall woman.

*Taylor Swift **iba** a cantar en Central Park el año pasado.*
Taylor Swift was going to sing in Central Park last year.

*Cuando **éramos** niños, **veíamos** el programa* I Love Lucy *porque Desi Arnaz fue uno de los primeros actores cubanos en la televisión.*

> When we were kids, we used to watch the show *I Love Lucy* because Desi Arnaz was one of the first Cuban actors on television.

***Era** la una y media de la mañana cuando mi hermano mayor volvió a casa; mis padres estaban furiosos.*

> It was one-thirty in the morning when my older brother returned home; my parents were furious.

 ## PRACTICE EXERCISES

1. **Now change each of the following verbs from either the present or preterite tense to the corresponding form of the imperfect:**

Example: vas → <u>**ibas**</u>

a. soy → _____

b. viste → _____

c. sois → _____

d. vieron → _____

e. van → _____

f. vamos → _____

g. ven → _____

h. somos → _____

i. veo → _____

j. fue → _____

2. **Complete the following sentences using the appropriate form of the imperfect tense:**

a. _____ las diez de la noche cuando comenzó mi programa favorito de WWF. (ser)

b. Mi hermana nunca _____ conmigo a un restaurante; prefería la comida sabrosa de mi mamá. (ir)

c. Anoche nosotros _____ *Desperate Housewives* en la sala cuando sonó el teléfono. (ver)

d. Uds. siempre _____ a sus amigos cuando iban al lago durante el verano. (ver)

e. Cuando mi padre _____ al trabajo, vio a Lance Armstrong enfrente del hotel. (ir)

f. Mi mejor amigo nunca _____ cómico; siempre tomaba todo en serio. (ser)

3. In the following "family tale," fill in the blanks with the appropriate imperfect form of "ir," "ser," or "ver":

Cuando mi abuelo _____ niño, siempre _____ a la casa de mi

abuela. Como vivían en la misma calle, él la _____ todas las tardes. Se

sentaban en un sofá grande. Mi abuela _____ mayor que él, pero eso no

_____ importante para mi abuelo. Un día anunció que _____ a casarse

con ella. Y _____ la verdad. Ahora hace cincuenta años que están casados.

B) DOUBLE OBJECT PRONOUNS

Do you remember all of the object pronouns we have studied thus far?

Here is a review of object pronouns:

Reflexive Object Pronouns (ROPs)		Indirect Object Pronouns (IDOPs)		Direct Object Pronouns (DOPs)	
me	*nos*	*me*	*nos*	*me*	*nos*
te	*os*	*te*	*os*	*te*	*os*
se	*se*	*le*	*les*	*lo, la*	*los, las*

Oftentimes, a speaker will choose to use two object pronouns in the same sentence. The nouns for which these pronouns stand will already have been made clear to the listener or reader.

For example, the English sentence "I gave a present to my sister" could be rewritten: "I gave it to her," which uses both a direct object pronoun (DOP) — "it" — and an indirect object pronoun (IDOP) — "her."

Similarly, the sentence "My aunt sang some lullabies to herself" could be rewritten: "My aunt sang them to herself," which uses both a DOP — "them" — and a reflexive object pronoun (ROP) — "herself."

ARE THERE SPECIAL RULES ABOUT USING MULTIPLE OBJECT PRONOUNS?

Yes, indeed! Here are some things to keep in mind when using multiple object pronouns.

1) ORDER OF THESE PRONOUNS: "RID"

The order for these pronouns is always reflexive object pronoun first, then indirect object pronoun, and finally direct object pronoun. By memorizing the word "**RID**," (**R**eflexive, **I**ndirect, and **D**irect), you should be able to keep the order straight. Let's look at a few sample sentences:

> ❋ **EXAMPLES:** *¿El plato? Mi hermana **me lo** dio.*
> The plate? My sister gave it to me.
> (**Note:** In this sentence, *"me"* is the IDOP and *"lo"* is the DOP.)
>
> *¿Las manos? **Nos las** lavamos antes de comer.*
> Our hands? We wash them before eating.
> (**Note:** In this sentence, *"nos"* is the ROP, and *"las"* is the DOP.)
>
> *¿Las palabras? **Me las** repito cada día.*
> The words? I am repeating them to myself every day.
>
> *Angélica me compró el nuevo disco compacto de Kanye West. **Te lo** toco mañana.*
> Angélica bought me the new Kanye West CD. I'll play it for you tomorrow.

Helpful Tip: Do you notice that these object pronouns are placed directly <u>before</u> the conjugated verb?

---

2) THE USE OF "SE" TO REPLACE "LE" OR "LES"

There is a special case in Spanish in which the 3rd person <u>indirect</u> object pronoun *le* or *les* is replaced by the word *se*. This change occurs when *le* or *les* is followed by any 3rd person <u>direct object</u> pronoun: *lo, la, los,* or *las*.

What was the thinking behind this rule? Probably to avoid putting two short words next to each other that begin with "l," e.g., *"le lo" or "les la." It is easier for the ear to distinguish these words when the first word is changed to *se*:

> *Se*
> *¿La pizza? Le la doy a mi amigo.*

> ❋ **EXAMPLES:** *¿El secreto del enemigo? **Se lo** dije al coronel.*
> The enemy's secret? I told it to the colonel.
> (**Note:** In this sentence, *"le"* meaning "to him" was replaced by the word *"se."*)

*¿La revista nueva? **Se la** llevo a mi madre.*
The new magazine? I'm taking it to my mother.
(**Note:** In this sentence, *"le"* meaning "to her" was replaced by the word *"se."*)

*¿Los regalos que están en la mesa? **Se los** doy a mis mejores amigos.*
The presents on the table? I'm giving them to my best friends.
(**Note:** In this sentence, *"les"* meaning "to them" was replaced by the word *"se."*)

*¿Las instrucciones para operar el tostador? **Se las** dejé a mi hermano.*
The instructions for operating the toaster? I left them for my brother.
(**Note:** In this sentence, *"le"* meaning "to him" was replaced by the word *"se."*)

¿Las palabras de la canción Louie, Louie*? **Se las** repetí a mi madre, pero no las entendió.*
The words to *Louie, Louie?* I repeated them to my mom, but she didn't understand them.
(**Note:** In this sentence, *"le"* meaning "to her" was replaced by the word *"se."*)

*El futbolista chileno Gary Medel me prestó una camisa amarilla, pero nunca **se la** devolví.*
The Chilean soccer player Gary Medel lent me a yellow shirt, but I never returned it to him.
(**Note:** In this sentence, *"le"* meaning "to him" was replaced by the word *"se."*)

3) VERB FOLLOWED BY AN INFINITIVE

When one verb is followed by an infinitive, you may choose to put these multiple object pronouns before the first verb, or you may attach them to the infinitive. You may not separate them, however, by putting one object pronoun before the first verb and attaching the second to the infinitive!

EXAMPLES: *¿La invitación? Voy a dár**tela** a ti (**Te la** voy a dar a ti).*
The invitation? I'm going to give it to you.

*¿Los vasos de cristal? **Se los** tengo que comprar a mi amiga (Tengo que comprár**selos** a mi amiga).*
The crystal glasses? I need to buy them for my friend.

*Manolo me escribe cartas a mí, pero no **se las** quiere escribir a su mamá (. . . no quiere escribír**selas** a su mamá).*
Manolo writes letters to me, but he doesn't want to write them to his mother.

Helpful Tip: You may have noticed that when you add two object pronouns to an infinitive, it is necessary to place a written accent mark on the third syllable from the end of the new word created (e.g., *dártela . . . comprárselos . . . escribírselas*).

---

1. Rewrite the following sentences, by substituting an object pronoun for the underlined words. Remember to replace "le/les" with "se":

a. Roberto me compra <u>la alfombra</u> mañana.

_____

b. Luis Miguel le dedica <u>muchas canciones</u> a su familia.

_____

c. Nuestros abuelos nos regalaron <u>la nueva revista de Oprah Winfrey</u>.

_____

d. Te voy a sacar <u>muchas fotos</u> mañana durante el viaje a la Isla de Pascua.

_____

e. Necesitamos mostrarles <u>los pasaportes</u> a los guardias.

_____

f. Iba a confesarte <u>un secreto importante</u>.

_____

g. Los incas nos enseñaron <u>lecciones importantes de agricultura</u>.

_____

h. Mis primos les dieron <u>botellas de vino chileno</u> a sus amigos para la fiesta.

_____

i. Mi hermana mayor es fantástica. Nos va a limpiar <u>la ducha y la bañera</u>.

_____

2. **In the following sentences, write the appropriate double object pronouns in the space provided. Add an accent mark when necessary:**

   a. ¿La nueva película de Diego Luna? Voy a mostrar_____ a mi amiga.

   b. ¿Los pasaportes? _____ necesito mostrar al asistente de vuelo.

   c. ¿Las baladas de Mariah Carey? Ella _____ va a cantar a nosotros.

   d. ¿El teléfono? Mi madre _____ va a contestar (a mí).

   e. ¿Una torta de cumpleaños? Mi abuela desea hacer_____ a mi hermana.

3. **The following paragraph contains six object pronoun errors. Underline each error and write the correction above it:**

   El día de mi cumpleaños, mi abuela quería me hacer una torta.

   Me preparó la por la mañana. Era de chocolate. Cuando mis amigos

   llegaron, mi abuela la quería darles a ellos, también. Ella siempre

   era muy generosa. Pero la torta era para mí. Yo no quería se la dar a mis

   amigos porque sabía que iban a comer mucho. Pero, ¡qué sorpresa! Mi

   abuela me hizo dos tortas. Por eso, la primera les la di a mis amigos,

   y la otra la me comí yo solito.

C) ADVERBS THAT END WITH "-MENTE"

Last lesson you learned how adverbs modify verbs, adjectives, and other adverbs. The adverbs presented helped to tell how, when, where, or how intensely something was done. This lesson will present other adverbs, all of which end with "*-mente*." This ending is equivalent to the "-ly" ending in English (e.g., quickly, patiently, stubbornly, etc.).

Here is a simple formula for transforming most adjectives into adverbs:

◆ Take the feminine form of an adjective and add *"-mente"*:

Masculine Adjective		Feminine Adjective		Adverb	English Equivalent
rápido	→	*rápida*	→	*rápida**mente***	quickly
loco	→	*loca*	→	*loca**mente***	crazily
intenso	→	*intensa*	→	*intensa**mente***	intensely

◆ As adjectives that end in a vowel other than *"o"* or *"a"* are already both feminine and masculine, there is no need to change them at all!

fuerte	→	***fuertemente*** (strongly)
alegre	→	***alegremente*** (happily)

◆ Add *"-mente"* to adjectives that end in a consonant.

leal	→	***lealmente*** (loyally)
cortés	→	***cortésmente*** (courteously)

PRACTICE EXERCISES

1. Convert the following adjectives into adverbs by adding *"–mente,"* remembering the instructions presented in this section:

Example: lento → **lentamente**

a. rápido → _____

b. feliz → _____

c. cordial → _____

d. triste → _____

e. alegre → _____

f. ruidoso → _____

g. paciente → _____   i. general → _____

h. contento → _____   j. extraño → _____

2. Translate the following sentences into Spanish, using the adverbial construction found in this section:

a. The boys ran quickly to the bathroom when the class ended.

_____

_____

b. José Feliciano sang the song intensely.

_____

_____

c. Consuelo said sadly that her friend was sick.

_____

_____

3. Identify and correct the four errors in this list of things to do:

 Para hacer mañana:

1) Cortar el césped cuidadosomente

2) Hablar con mi mamá cariñosamente

3) Llegar a la clase puntualamente

4) Lavar los tenedores, cucharas y cuchillos rápidomente en el fregadero

5) Entregar la tarea alegramente

These two sets of questions use grammatical structures and vocabulary from this lesson. Working with a partner, alternate asking and answering each question. When you get to the bottom of each list, start over at the top, switching roles. As a variation, write out the answers in complete sentences.

A) ¿Eras un/una niño/niña muy alto/alta?

¿Ibas de viaje frecuentemente con tus padres?

¿Te gustaba nadar en el agua fría?

¿Veías mucho la televisión cuando eras niño/niña?

¿Cuántos años tenían tus padres cuando se casaron?

A ti, ¿te gusta cortar el césped?

¿Escribes las composiciones alegremente?

B) Un chiste . . . ¿vas a decírmelo ahora?

Unas Coca-Colas . . . ¿vas a comprármelas luego?

Los regalos . . . ¿quieres mostrármelos ahora?

Las fotos . . . ¿deseas prestármelas esta noche?

¿Todavía tienes muchos enemigos?

¿Haces la tarea intensamente?

¿Hablas con los adultos cordialmente?

PRUEBA DE REPASO

1. Answer in complete sentences:

a. ¿Adónde ibas de vacaciones cuando eras más joven?

_____

b. ¿Siempre deseabas estudiar español?

_____

c. ¿Prefieres las tortas de chocolate o las de vainilla?

_____

d. ¿Limpias las escaleras alegremente o tristemente?

_____

e. El secreto . . . ¿vas a decírmelo ahora?

_____

2. Conjugate the following three verbs fully in the imperfect tense:

    ir (to go)   **ser** (to be)   **ver** (to see)

_____ _____   _____ _____   _____ _____

_____ _____   _____ _____   _____ _____

_____ _____   _____ _____   _____ _____

3. Conjugate each verb into the appropriate form of the imperfect:

a. _____ las siete y media de la noche cuando Lucero me llamó por teléfono. (ser)

b. Yo _____ a comprar el nuevo disco de _Los Tigres del Norte,_ pero descubrí que no tenía dinero. (ir)

c. Yo siempre _____ a mi abuela cuando vivíamos en Santa Cruz. (ver)

d. Nosotros nunca _____ la televisión cuando estábamos de vacaciones cerca del lago Titicaca. (ver)

e. Cuando mis padres _____ a Chile en avión, los asistentes de vuelo nunca los atendían. (ir)

f. José _____ mi vecino cuando era niño. (ser)

g. Mi esposa y yo _____ a la playa cuando comenzó a llover fuertemente. (ir)

h. Ricardo Montalbán _____ mi actor favorito cuando era niña. (ser)

4. Rewrite the following sentences, replacing the underlined words with an appropriate object pronoun:

a. Mi tío me dio <u>un regalo</u> para mi cumpleaños.

_____

b. Te voy a sacar <u>una foto</u> en unos minutos.

_____

c. Siempre le decía <u>los secretos</u> a mi mejor amiga.

_____

d. Les voy a repetir <u>las palabras</u> a los profesores.

_____

e. Mis primos nunca me mostraban <u>el armario secreto</u>.

_____

f. Uds. quieren prestarme <u>un teléfono</u>, ¿verdad?

_____

5. Convert the following adjectives into adverbs:

a. cariñoso → _____   e. general → _____

b. generoso → _____   f. obvio → _____

c. leal → _____   g. sincero → _____

d. fuerte → _____   h. elegante → _____

6. Translate the following sentences into Spanish. Pay close attention to the verbs: one is in the present, two are in the preterite, and two more are in the imperfect.

a. Before, I used to work intensely; now I sleep day and night.

_____

b. The lawn? I cut it for you yesterday.

_____

c. It was eight o'clock when the accident happened in the dining room.

_____

7. Find and correct the five errors in this diary entry:

11 de febrero

Hacían mucho frío hoy. Era las seis de la mañana cuando comenzó a nevar. Le escribí una carta a mi novia. Era una carta muy negativa y decidí no enviárlela. Todavía quiero Raquela, pero no me trata tan cariñosomente como antes. Creo que la lluvia es el problema. Voy a dormir un poco más.

NICARAGUA

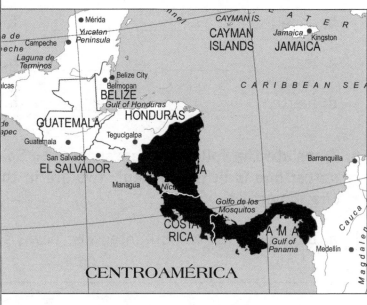

COSTA RICA

PANAMÁ

NICARAGUA, COSTA RICA & PANAMÁ

NICARAGUA

CAPITAL:	Managua
POBLACIÓN:	5.800.000
GOBIERNO:	república
PRESIDENTE:	Daniel Ortega Saavedra
DINERO ($):	córdoba
PRODUCTOS:	algodón, café, fruta, petróleo, plátano
MÚSICA, BAILE:	bamba, rumba
SITIOS DE INTERÉS:	La Flor, las huellas de Acahualinc, El lago de Nicaragua
COMIDA TÍPICA:	baho, gallo pinto, nacatamales

NICARAGÜENSES FAMOSOS:

Violeta Barrios de Chamorro (POLÍTICA)

Ernesto Cardenal (POLÍTICO)

Rubén Darío (POETA)

COSTA RICA

CAPITAL:	San José
POBLACIÓN:	4.200.000
GOBIERNO:	república democrática
PRESIDENTE:	Óscar Arias Sánchez
DINERO ($):	colón costarricense
PRODUCTOS:	azúcar, bananas, café, melón, muebles, piña
MÚSICA, BAILE:	merengue, punto guanacasteco, salsa
SITIOS DE INTERÉS:	Monte Verde, Parques Nacionales Tortuguero y Corcovado, Volcán Arenal, Volcán Irazú
COMIDA TÍPICA:	casado, gallo pinto, gallos (filled tortillas), olla de carne, pan de yuca, sopa negra

COSTARRICENSES FAMOSOS:

Franklin Chang (ASTRONAUTA)

Editus (CONJUNTO MUSICAL)

Claudia Poll (ATLETA)

Silvia Poll (ATLETA)

PANAMÁ

CAPITAL:	La Ciudad de Panamá
POBLACIÓN:	3.300.000
GOBIERNO:	democracia constitucional
PRESIDENTE:	Martín Torrijos Espino
DINERO ($):	balboa, dólar
PRODUCTOS:	cacao, petróleo, piña, plátano
MÚSICA, BAILE:	afro-caribeña
SITIOS DE INTERÉS:	Archipiélago de San Blas, El canal de Panamá, Península Azuero, Volcán Barú
COMIDA TÍPICA:	arroz con coco, ceviche, chicha dulce, corvina, ropa vieja, sancocho de gallina, saos

PANAMEÑOS FAMOSOS:

Rubén Blades (MÚSICO)

Roberto Durán (BOXEADOR)

Mireya Moscoso (POLÍTICA)

Mariano Rivera (BEISBOLISTA)

VOCABULARIO
LECCIÓN NUEVE

TRACK 13 DISC 2

THEME WORDS: "AT SCHOOL"

la	bandera	flag
el	calendario	calendar
la	campana	bell
el	escritorio	desk
el	examen	test
el	**mapa**	map
la	mochila	backpack
la	oficina	office
la	pizarra	blackboard
el/la	profesor/a	teacher
la	prueba	proof, quiz, test
el	pupitre	student desk
la	tiza	chalk
la	universidad	university

OTHER NOUNS

el	acondicionador de aire	air conditioner
el	beso	kiss
el	campeonato	championship
el	código postal	zip code
la	libra	pound
la	lotería	lottery
la	llegada	arrival
el	meteorólogo	meteorologist

la	tempestad	storm
la	tormenta	storm
el/la	vecino/a	neighbor

ADJECTIVES

barato/a	cheap
corto/a	short
demasiado/a	too much (pl., too many)
emocionado/a	excited
largo/a	long
próximo/a	next

VERBS

colgar (ue)	to hang (up)
enojarse	to become angry
graduarse	to graduate
mudarse	to move (relocate)
negar (ie)	to deny
probar (ue)	to taste, to try

MISCELLANEOUS

montar en bicicleta	to ride a bicycle
por fin	finally
por supuesto	of course
saber de memoria	to know by heart
tranquilamente	calmly

LECCIÓN NUEVE

KEY GRAMMAR CONCEPTS

A) Choosing between the preterite and imperfect → *¿El pretérito o el imperfecto?*

B) Choosing between "saber" and "conocer" → *"Saber" vs. "conocer"*

C) Special expressions with "hacer" → *Expresiones con "hacer"*

D) The construction with "acabar de" — Talking about what you've just done → *"Acabar de"*

 ## A) Choosing between the preterite and imperfect

The ability to **choose wisely between the preterite and imperfect** is a sign of a good Spanish speaker. Oftentimes, sentences can make perfect sense using either the preterite or imperfect; however, the meaning of each sentence may be quite different.

Let's first review the key concepts of each of these past tenses:

Preterite	Imperfect
◆ Single, complete event	◆ Incomplete, ongoing event
◆ The beginning or ending point of an action	◆ Description
	◆ Telling time in the past
◆ When you tell how long an action lasted	◆ Habitual actions

Let's take a look at a number of sentences that contain both a preterite and imperfect verb. Try to figure out why the speaker has chosen each tense.

 Examples: *Eran las once de la noche cuando mi hermano **volvió** a casa.*
It was eleven at night when my brother returned home.

*Comíamos en el restaurante cuando Wilmer Valderrama **entró**.*
We were eating in the restaurant when Wilmer Valderrama entered.

*En el pasado, Ricky Martin siempre **cantaba** "Livin' la Vida Loca" durante los conciertos, pero anoche no la **cantó**.*
In the past, Ricky Martin always used to sing *"Livin' la Vida Loca"* during his concerts, but last night he didn't sing it.

*Aunque el atleta **era** muy fuerte, ayer sólo **levantó** doscientas libras.*
Although the athlete was very strong, he only lifted two hundred pounds yesterday.

Mientras veía el programa Cristina *anoche,* **descubrí** *que Fernando Colunga* **era** *muy guapo.*

> While I was watching the program *Cristina* last night, I discovered that Fernando Colunga was very good-looking.

Estuve *en San José sólo tres días porque siempre* **hacía** *muchísimo calor durante el verano.*

> I was in San José for only three days because it always was so hot during the summer.

Mi perrito **estaba** *tan cansado que por fin se* **durmió** *en el sofá.*

> My little dog was so tired that he finally fell asleep on the sofa.

Mi hermana menor normalmente no **comía** *hamburguesas, pero un día* **tenía** *muchísima hambre y las* **probó**.

> My little sister normally didn't eat hamburgers, but one day she was very hungry and she tried them.

Los campistas **esperaban** *en las montañas cuando* **comenzó** *a nevar.*

> The campers were waiting in the mountains when it began to snow.

In the above sentences, the contrast between the preterite and imperfect is striking. Did you notice the following?

◆ The descriptive use of the imperfect (*Mi perrito* **estaba** *cansado . . .; . . . el atleta* **era** *muy fuerte . . .*)

◆ The habitual use of the imperfect (*. . . normalmente no* **comía** *hamburguesas . . .; . . . siempre cantaba* "Livin' la Vida Loca" *. . .*)

◆ The use of the imperfect to tell time (**Eran** *las once de la noche . . .*)

◆ An incomplete event is "interrupted" by a preterite action (**Comíamos** *en el restaurante cuando Wilmer Valderrama* **entró***; Mientras* **veía** *el programa* Cristina *anoche,* **descubrí** *que Fernando Colunga . . .*)

◆ When the speaker tells how long an event lasted, the preterite was used (**Estuve** *en San José sólo tres días . . .*)

◆ If there was no clear ending point, the imperfect was chosen (*Los campistas* **esperaban** *en las montañas . . .*)

As you work through the practice exercises on the next page, try to ask yourself what the speaker is intending.

◆¿◆ ◆?◆ Is there a clear ending point of a completed action? If so, use the preterite. If not, you will likely choose the imperfect.

PRACTICE EXERCISES

1. **In the following paragraphs, choose between the preterite and imperfect. Try to pick the tense that you think best captures the feel of the narrative:**

a. Cuando yo _____ (ser) joven, vivía en Chicago. Nuestra familia

_____ (tener) una casa bonita cerca de un parque. Un día

_____ (hacer) mucho calor. Mi mamá _____ (decir) que los

meteorólogos _____ en la televisión (anunciar) que

_____ (ir) a llover mucho esa noche. _____ (Ser) las siete

de la noche cuando _____ (comenzar) la tempestad. Mis hermanos

y yo _____ (tener) mucho miedo. _____

(Llover) fuertemente por doce horas. Por la mañana por fin _____

(salir) el sol. Mis hermanos y yo _____ (decir): "¡Bravo!"

b. Yo _____ (leer) una revista tranquilamente en casa anoche cuando

_____ (sonar) el teléfono. Lo _____ (contestar) y un

hombre _____ (decir): "¡Felicidades! Ud. _____ (ganar) la

lotería". No _____ (saber) qué hacer. _____ (Estar) muy

contenta y emocionada. _____ (Colgar) el receptor (*receiver*) y

_____ (comenzar) a buscar el boleto. _____

(Buscar) y _____ (buscar), pero no lo _____ (poder)

encontrar. ¿Dónde _____ (estar)? Unos momentos más tarde, mi perro,

Eugenio, _____ (entrar) en el cuarto. _____ (Tener) el

boleto en la boca. Lo _____ (tomar) y le _____ (dar)

un beso muy grande a Eugenio.

B) CHOOSING BETWEEN "SABER" AND "CONOCER"

Spanish has two ways to say "to know": "*saber*" and "*conocer.*"

1 *"Saber"* **is used when a person is speaking about a fact or giving information, something that usually could be articulated easily.**

For example, if you were to ask: "Do you know where I live?", you would use the verb *"saber,"* because the answer is a fact: *¿Sabes dónde vivo? –Sí, lo sé . . . Calle Mango 129.*

If a person says that he or she knows how to do something, (e.g., dance the cha-cha), that speaker will also use *"saber."* (*María sabe bailar el chachachá* — Mary knows how to dance the cha-cha. The steps of the cha-cha can be explained or diagrammed.

Note: You <u>don't</u> need the word *"como"* meaning "how."

2 *"Conocer"* **conveys the idea of being acquainted with a person or place.**

For example, if you want to say that Lola knows Lili, you say *"Lola conoce a Lili."* Remember, *"saber"* is used with facts; clearly a person is not a fact. A person cannot be easily articulated, explained or diagrammed!

If you wanted to ask someone if he or she knows the city of Lima well, you choose *"conocer."* *¿Conoces Managua? –Sí, la conozco.* A city, of course, is not something that can be articulated.

If, however, you wanted to know the <u>name</u> of a city, you would ask: *¿Sabes la capital de Nicaragua? –Sí, lo sé; es Managua.*

The following sentences highlight the differences between *"saber"* and *"conocer."*

EXAMPLES: *¿Sabe Ud. si llueve ahora? –No, no lo sé.*
Do you know if it's raining now? –No, I don't know.

Conozco a muchas personas de Nicaragua.
I know many people from Nicaragua.

¿Conoces bien la Ciudad de Panamá?
Do you know Panama City well?

Sabemos que no hay muchos restaurantes buenos por aquí.
We know that there aren't many good restaurants around here.

¿Sabes la hora? –Por supuesto, son las seis y media.
Do you know what time it is? –Of course, it's six-thirty.

Hoy en día es muy importante conocer bien a los vecinos.
Nowadays it's very important to know one's neighbors well.

Como no sabes bailar bien, prefiero no ir al baile contigo.
Since you don't know how to dance well, I prefer not to go to the dance with you.

Sé de memoria todas las palabras del poema "Lola".
I know by heart all the words of the poem "*Lola.*"

¿Conoces a mi primo Charlie? Es alto, moreno y muy atlético.
Do you know my cousin, Charlie? He is tall, dark and very athletic.

¡CUIDADO! Pay attention to the special uses of *"saber"* and *"conocer"* in the preterite and imperfect tenses. When you decide that you want to use a past tense of *"saber"* and *"conocer,"* you should know that the translations in English are a little different.

	Preterite	**Imperfect**
saber	*supe* → I found out (a fact)	*sabía* → I knew, I used to know (a fact)
conocer	*conocí* → I met (a person)	*conocía* → I knew, I used to know (a person, a place)

Let's look at a few examples of these sentences:

✹ **EXAMPLES:** *Anoche **conocí** a un hombre muy guapo . . . se llama Iván.*
   Last night I met a very good-looking man . . . his name is Ivan.

*Cuando era joven, **conocía** a muchas personas que jugaban al baloncesto.*
   When I was young, I knew (used to know) a lot of people who played basketball.

*Mi bisabuela **conoció** a una mujer que sobrevivió el hundimiento del Titanic.*
   My great-grandmother met a woman who survived the sinking of the Titanic.

***Conocíamos** muchos restaurantes baratos en Heredia, Costa Rica.*
   We used to know a lot of inexpensive restaurants in Heredia, Costa Rica.

*Anoche **supe** que mi novia tiene otro novio.*
   Last night I found out that my girlfriend has another boyfriend.

*Todo el mundo **sabía** que la profesora era muy difícil.*
   Everyone knew that the teacher was very hard.

*Cuando mis padres **supieron** que yo no tenía el coche, se enojaron muchísimo.*
   When my parents found out that I didn't have the car, they got very mad.

*No **sabía** que Libertad Lamarque era una actriz tan famosa.*
   I didn't know that Libertad Lamarque was such a famous actress.

PRACTICE EXERCISES

1. **Write the correct form of the present tense of *"saber"* or *"conocer"* in the following sentences:**

   a. Yo no _____ bien a la profesora de inglés en esta escuela.

   b. Nadie _____ si hay un buen restaurante cerca de la playa.

   c. ¿_____ (tú) dónde viven los nuevos vecinos?

   d. Nosotras _____ que es peligroso montar en bicicleta sin casco.

   e. Mi prima _____ bien la ciudad de Granada; hace mucho tiempo que vive allí.

   f. Penélope Casas y Ferrán Adria _____ preparar muchos platos riquísimos.

   g. Yo _____ una tienda donde hay mochilas, banderas y campanas.

   h. Ellos _____ que no puedo ir a la fiesta esta tarde por el examen de mañana.

   i. ¿_____ Uds. la música nueva de Adele? –Sí, la _____, pero no nos gusta.

   j. Mis padres _____ que no me gusta volver a casa antes de la medianoche.

2. In this paragraph, you will once again decide between *"saber"* and *"conocer."* This paragraph, however, was written in the past, so you will also have to decide between the preterite and imperfect.

Mi primo Eduardo _____ a Nomar Garciaparra un día en

Los Ángeles. Eduardo _____ que Nomar iba a salir por la

puerta de atrás. También _____ personalmente a un policía

que trabajaba en Los Ángeles. Cuando yo _____ que Eduardo

tenía el autógrafo de Nomar, estaba muy celoso. ¿Por qué no fui con él al partido?

C) SPECIAL EXPRESSIONS WITH "HACER"

You have seen the word *"hacer"* throughout this text. As you remember, it is commonly used to mean "to do" or "to make." You also know that *"hacer"* is used when talking about the weather. This section presents a number of expressions or constructions that use the word *"hacer."*

Here are a number of expressions or constructions that use the word *"hacer"*:

hacerse amigos →	to become friends
hacer caso a →	to pay attention to
hacer cola →	to stand in line
hacer frente a →	to face up to
hacer frío, calor, etc. →	to be cold, hot, etc. (outside)
hacer la maleta →	to pack one's suitcase
hacer las paces →	to make up (to make peace)
hacer una pregunta →	to ask a question

Let's look at these expressions used in sentences:

EXAMPLES: *Primero Eva Longoria y Tony Parker **se hicieron** muy buenos amigos y después se casaron en París.*
First Eva Longoria and Tony Parker became very good friends, and afterwards they got married in Paris.

*Nunca les **hago caso** a mis padres cuando me gritan.*
I never pay attention to my parents when they shout at me.

*Como no me gusta **hacer cola**, nunca voy a los estrenos de las nuevas películas.*

Because I don't like to stand in line, I never go to the premieres of new movies.

*Tienes que **hacer frente** al hecho de que no tienes muchos amigos.*

You have to face up to the fact that you don't have many friends.

*¿Te puedo **hacer una pregunta**? ¿Por qué **hace muchísimo frío** en Patagonia?*

May I ask you a question? Why is it very cold in Patagonia?

*Marco **hace la maleta** porque va de viaje a Costa Rica.*

Marco is packing his bag because he is going on a trip to Costa Rica.

*Cuando peleo con mis hermanas, siempre me gusta **hacer las paces** rápidamente.*

When I fight with my sisters, I always like to make up quickly.

There is also a special construction using "*hacer*" that describes something that began in the past and continues into the present.

"*Hace*" + X + *que* + Verb = I have been doing something for X.
(period of time)   (in present tense)   (period of time)

✳ EXAMPLES: *Hace mucho tiempo que Gloria Estefan vive en Miami.*

Gloria Estefan has been living in Miami for a long time.

Hace dos años que trabajo en el restaurante.

I have been working in the restaurant for two years.

¿Cuánto tiempo hace que tú tienes tu propio televisor? –Hace seis años que lo tengo.

How long have you had your own television set? –I've had it for six years.

Hace dos horas que leo este libro nuevo de Julia Álvarez.

I have been reading this new book of Julia Álvarez for two hours.

PRACTICE EXERCISES

1. Complete the following sentences by using the correct form of one of the following expressions using "hacer" *(hacerse amigos, hacer caso a, hacer cola, hacer frente, hacer frío, calor, etc., hacer la maleta, hacer las paces, hacer una pregunta).* **Use each expression just once:**

a. ¿Te puedo _____? ¿Dónde está San José?

b. ¡Qué pena! Hay demasiada gente aquí que quiere ver la película de Kate Winslet, *The Reader*. Como nunca me gusta _____, voy a ver otra película.

c. Cuando mi amiga _____, ¡siempre coge demasiada ropa!

d. El profesor anunció: "En esta clase es esencial _____ todo lo que digo".

e. Cuando era más joven, nunca me gustaba _____ con mi hermana; prefería estar enojada con ella todo el tiempo.

f. Mi hijo y el niño del nuevo vecino _____ muy rápidamente; ahora juegan juntos a menudo.

g. Necesito comprar un acondicionador de aire porque _____ en esta casa.

h. Muchas personas no pueden _____ a sus problemas; necesitan negar la realidad.

2. Now complete these sentences by conjugating the following infinitives in the present tense. Then translate the sentences into English:

a. Hace dos horas que yo _____ en este avión. (estar)

_____

b. Hace muchas semanas que ellos _____ el programa *Prison Break* en la tele. (ver)

_____

c. Hace un año que nosotros _____ en Nueva York. (vivir)

_____

d. Hace muchos años que los Chicago Cubs no _____ un campeonato de béisbol. (ganar)

_____

e. Hace muchos meses que mi tío no _____ trabajo. (tener)

_____

3. Finally, translate the following sentences into Spanish, using the new construction with *"hacer"*:

Example: I've been studying for ten minutes.
Hace diez minutos que estudio. _____

a. I've been speaking Spanish for one year.

_____

b. Alejandro Fernández has been singing for many years.

_____

c. I have been studying the map for twenty minutes.

_____

d. We have been living in San José for fifteen months.

_____

e. I haven't seen you for a long time.

_____

D) THE CONSTRUCTION WITH "ACABAR DE"

Spanish has a very useful construction for describing events that just took place. For example, if you want to say "I just arrived," you say *"Acabo de llegar."* This construction makes use of the present tense of *"acabar,"* which means "to end," along with the preposition *"de"* and an infinitive.

Here is the formula for saying that something just happened:

> **The present tense of** *"acabar"* **+** *"de"* **+ Infinitive**

Let's take a look at some more sentences with this handy construction:

 EXAMPLES: *Javier Bardem y Penélope Cruz **acaban de salir**.*
Javier Bardem and Penélope Cruz just left.

***Acabo de ver** la película de Sean Penn, Milk.*
I've just seen the Sean Penn movie, *Milk*.

*Tú **acabas de mentir**.*
You just lied.

***Acabamos de oír** que va a llover mañana.*
We just heard that it is going to rain tomorrow.

*Mi amiga **acaba de comprar** entradas para el próximo concierto de Kanye West.*
My friend just bought tickets for the next concert of Kanye West.

***Acabo de contestar** el teléfono . . . mi abogada me llamó otra vez.*
I just answered the phone . . . my lawyer called me again.

1. **Write the appropriate form of** *"acabar"* **in the following sentences:**

   a. Tú _____ de escribir tu código postal.

   b. Nosotras _____ de ver una película muy aburrida.

   c. Alguien _____ de entrar por la puerta de atrás.

   d. Mis padres _____ de escribirme una carta muy bonita.

   e. Muchos de mis amigos _____ de graduarse de la universidad.

2. **Now translate the following sentences into Spanish:**

   a. I just bought a new desk.

   _____

   b. They just woke up.

   _____

   c. My friend just asked me a question.

   _____

   d. He just tasted the rice with coconut.

   _____

   e. We just discovered that our crazy neighbor wants to sell her house.

   _____

These two sets of questions use grammatical structures and vocabulary from this lesson. Working with a partner, alternate asking and answering each question. When you get to the bottom of each list, start over at the top, switching roles. As a variation, write out the answers in complete sentences.

A) ¿En cuántos años vas a graduarte de la universidad?

Cuando eras niño/niña, ¿te enojabas frecuentemente?

¿Montabas mucho en bicicleta durante los veranos?

¿Cuál es tu código postal?

¿Tienes una mochila para tus libros?

¿Escribes con tiza en la pizarra?

¿Bailabas frecuentemente con tus amigos cuando eras más joven?

B) ¿Conoces bien la ciudad de Lima?

¿Sabes dónde podemos comprar boletos de lotería?

¿Conoces personalmente a los padres de nuestro/a profesor/a de español?

¿Sabes de memoria todas las capitales de los países de Centroamérica?

¿Acabas de comer antes de llegar a clase?

¿Con quién acabas de hablar?

¿Cuánto tiempo hace que vives en tu casa?

The following dialogue contains grammar and vocabulary that you've seen in this lesson and in the introductory section. After listening to the CD, read this dialogue aloud, alone or with friends. Afterwards, try to answer the questions that follow either aloud or in written form.

 ## LAS AVENTURAS DE RAFAEL, ELISA Y "EL TIGRE"

ESCENA CINCO

Son las nueve de la noche. Rafael, "El Tigre", Elisa, Javier y Marisela caminan por la Tercera Avenida en Nueva York. Deciden tomar un café en una cafetería llamada "E.J.'s".

Rafael: ¡Qué día más increíble!

Elisa: Rafael tiene razón. Los cuadros que vimos de Kahlo en el museo eran impresionantes.

Javier: A mí me gustaron más los murales de Rivera.

El Tigre: Para decirles la verdad, el chocolate caliente en "Serendipity" fue lo que a mí más me gustó.

Rafael: Siempre piensas en la comida. Pues, la película de Spike Lee en Central Park fue fantástica, también. No sabía cuánto trabajo es necesario para filmar sólo unos minutos de acción.

Elisa: ¿Reconocieron Uds. a algunos actores conocidos?

Javier: Yo, sí. Creo que vi a Javier Bardem; oí que tiene un papel (role) importante en la película. Me gusta mucho Javier porque su nombre es tan distinguido.

Una camarera llega a la mesa.

Camarera: Buenas noches. ¿Les gustaría tomar algo?

Marisela: Un café con leche, por favor.

Elisa: Para mí, una Coca-Cola.

Javier: Un café solo.

Rafael: Y yo, una Coca-Cola, también.

El Tigre: Para mí, una Coca-Cola y un pedazo de torta de chocolate, con cinco tenedores, por favor.

Los chicos se ríen. En este momento un hombre con bigote y una mujer vestida de blanco llegan y se sientan en una mesa al fondo de la cafetería. Los chicos no los ven, pero el hombre y la mujer los miran cuidadosamente.

Javier: ¡Qué pena que Uds. tengan que (What a shame that you all have . . .) irse mañana!

Marisela: Es verdad. Todavía hay tanto que hacer.

Rafael: Uds. son tan generosos. Pero tenemos la idea loca de ir también a Chicago. Creo que podemos llegar allí en veinticuatro horas por tren. Vamos a pasar un día allá y volver a Washington para este fin de semana.

La camarera vuelve a la mesa con las bebidas y la torta de chocolate.

Elisa: Es una idea loca. Uds. nunca me dijeron que pensaban hacer eso.

El Tigre: Pues, ¿no te encantan las sorpresas?

Elisa: Pues, sí, pero pensaba que íbamos a pasar tres o cuatro días aquí.

Rafael: Pero, tenemos que ver el mundo. ¡Somos jóvenes!

Javier y Marisela se susurran algo al oído.

Javier: Y tengo una sorpresa para Uds. ¡Marisela y yo vamos con Uds. a Chicago!

Elisa: Fantástico. Pero, ¿y tus padres? ¿No vuelven esta noche?

Javier: Decidieron quedarse unos días más en Dallas. Marisela les dijo que íbamos a pasar unos días en su apartamento en Greenwich Village.

Rafael: Es una idea fenomenal. Todos vamos juntos a Chicago. Pero vamos al apartamento ahora. Tenemos que acostarnos temprano. El tren sale a las seis de la mañana.

El Tigre: Un momento. Tengo que comer más torta.

Todos se ríen. Elisa, "El Tigre", Rafael, Javier y Marisela se levantan, pagan la cuenta y salen de la cafetería. El hombre del bigote y la mujer vestida de blanco los siguen a la calle.

PREGUNTAS

1) ¿Dónde están los jóvenes cuando la escena comienza?

_____

2) ¿Qué parte del día les gustó más a Elisa y a Rafael?

_____

3) ¿Cuál fue la mejor parte del día según El Tigre?

_____

4) ¿A qué actor famoso vio Javier?

_____

5) ¿Qué bebidas pidieron los jóvenes en la cafetería?

_____

6) ¿Quiénes entran ahora al restaurante?

_____

7) ¿Qué ciudad famosa piensan visitar los chicos?

_____

8) ¿Quiénes van también?

_____

9) ¿A qué hora sale el tren por la mañana?

_____

10) ¿Quiénes siguen a los jóvenes a la calle?

_____

1. Answer in complete sentences:

a. ¿Ibas frecuentemente a la playa cuando eras joven?

_____

b. ¿Conoces a mis mejores amigos?

_____

c. ¿En dónde tienes que hacer cola muchas veces?

_____

d. ¿Siempre les haces caso a todos los profesores?

_____

e. ¿Qué lección de este libro acabas de estudiar?

_____

2. Conjugate each verb fully first in the preterite AND then in the imperfect tense:

cerrar (to close)   **vender** (to sell)   **ir** (to go)

_____ _____   _____ _____   _____ _____

_____ _____   _____ _____   _____ _____

_____ _____   _____ _____   _____ _____

_____ _____   _____ _____   _____ _____

_____ _____   _____ _____   _____ _____

_____ _____   _____ _____   _____ _____

3. In the following paragraph, conjugate each verb into the proper form of either the preterite or imperfect tense:

Cuando mis abuelos _____ (ser) jóvenes, _____

(vivir) en Managua, Nicaragua. En 1943, ellos _____ (casarse)

y _____ (mudarse) a Nueva York. La vida en Nueva York no

_____ (ser) fácil, pero mi abuelo _____

(conseguir) un buen trabajo en una fábrica de Long Island. Mi abuela

_____ (aprender) a hablar inglés primero, pero mi abuelo

_____ (tardar) muchos años en dominar la lengua. Cuando mi

padre _____ (nacer) en 1951, mis abuelos _____

(estar) muy orgullosos. Mi padre _____ (graduarse) de la

Universidad de Nueva York en 1972 y ahora es profesor de español.

4. Fill in the following sentences with the correct form of the verb *"saber"* or *"conocer"*:

a. Estoy muy emocionado porque acabo de _____ a Juan Soler.

b. Mi abuela _____ el secreto íntimo de la vecina.

c. Nosotros no _____ a qué hora nos va a decir el pronóstico del tiempo el meteorólogo.

d. Mi tía _____ muy bien el pueblo de León.

e. ¿_____ Ud. cuánto cuesta una libra de tomates?

f. Yo _____ personalmente a Emilio Estévez y a su hermano Martin Sheen.

5. Match the following *"hacer"* expressions with their English equivalent:

a) *hacer cola*   1) to face up to

b) *hacer una pregunta*   2) to make up

c) *hacer la maleta*   3) to pack

d) *hacerse amigos*   4) to ask a question

e) *hacer las paces*   5) to stand in line

f) *hacer frente a*   6) to become friends

6. Translate the following sentences into Spanish:

a. My friend just met the Mexican actor Gael García Bernal.

_____

_____

b. I just bought an air conditioner because it's hot in our house.

_____

_____

c. Our uncle has lived in Panama City for two years. (Use an *"hacer"* expression.)

_____

_____

d. He packed his luggage, he stood in line, and he finally left on the airplane.

_____

_____

7. The following newspaper account contains five errors. Underline each error and write the correction above it:

Julio Iglesias acabba de grabar otro disco nuevo

El famoso cantante español presentó hoy en una reunión

en Madrid su nuevo álbum, titulado "Romantic Classics".

Canta música muy romántica, ideal para hacer las pazes

con un viejo amigo o hacerse amigos de alguien nuevo.

Todos conocen que Julio tiene talento, pero nadie lo sabe

personalmente. Sólo sus hijos, Enrique y Julio, Jr., lo

conocen bien. En la reunión de ayer, Julio dijio que

este álbum es el mejor de su carrera. ¡Adelante, Julio!

Te queremos.

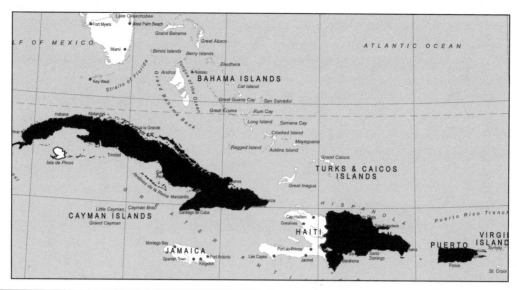

CUBA

Golfo de México

Océano Atlántico

La Habana

Pinar del Rio

Matanzas

Santa Clara

Cienfuegos

Sancti-Spiritus

CUBA

Isla de la Juventud

El Caribe

Nuevitas

Camagüey

Holguín

GOLFO DE GUACANA YOBO

SIERRA MAESTRA

Santiago de Cuba

Guantánamo

LA REPÚBLICA DOMINICANA

Puerto Plata

Océano Atlántico

Santiago de Caballeros

La Vega

HAITI

LA REPÚBLICA DOMINICANA

CORDILLERA CENTRAL

San Pedro de Macorís

Santo Domingo

Barahona

El Caribe

PUERTO RICO

San Juan

Océano Atlántico

Arecibo

Bayamón

Carolina

CORDILLERA CENTRAL

PUERTO RICO

Mayagüez

Ponce

Isla de Vieques

El Caribe

CUBA, LA REPÚBLICA DOMINICANA & PUERTO RICO

CUBA

CAPITAL:	La Habana
POBLACIÓN:	11.400.000
GOBIERNO:	república socialista
PRIMER MINISTRO:	Raúl Castro
DINERO ($):	peso cubano
PRODUCTOS:	azúcar, minerales, tabaco
MÚSICA, BAILE:	habanera, jazz, mambo, rumba, son
SITIOS DE INTERÉS:	Castillo del Morro
COMIDA TÍPICA:	congris, fruta, moros y cristianos, plátanos

CUBANOS FAMOSOS:

José Capablanca (AJEDRECISTA)

Celia Cruz (CANTANTE)

Gloria Estefan (CANTANTE)

José Martí (POETA)

LA REPÚBLICA DOMINICANA

CAPITAL:	Santo Domingo
POBLACIÓN:	9.500.000
GOBIERNO:	democracia representativa
PRESIDENTE:	Leonel Fernández Reyna
DINERO ($):	peso dominicano
PRODUCTOS:	azúcar, cacao, carne, fruta, minerales, tabaco
MÚSICA, BAILE:	bachata, marimba, merengue
SITIOS DE INTERÉS:	Lago Enriquillo, Pico Duarte
COMIDA TÍPICA:	chivo asado, comida criolla, mondongo, sancocho

DOMINICANOS FAMOSOS:

Julia Álvarez (ESCRITORA)

Francisco Casanova (CANTANTE)

Alex Rodríguez (BEISBOLISTA)

Manny Ramírez (BEISBOLISTA)

PUERTO RICO

CAPITAL:	San Juan
POBLACIÓN:	4.000.000
GOBIERNO:	estado libre asociado (commonwealth)
GOBERNADOR:	Luis Fortuño Burset
DINERO ($):	dólar americano
PRODUCTOS:	agricultura, azúcar, café, piña, ron, tabaco
MÚSICA, BAILE:	bomba, salsa
SITIOS DE INTERÉS:	Isla Mona, Ponce, El Yunque
COMIDA TÍPICA:	arroz con habichuelas, asopao, empanadillas, mofongo, pollo frito con tostones

PUERTORRIQUEÑOS FAMOSOS:

Roberto Clemente (BEISBOLISTA)

José Feliciano (MÚSICO)

José Ferrer (ACTOR)

Ricky Martin (CANTANTE)

Concha Meléndez (ESCRITORA)

Rita Moreno (ACTRIZ)

Chichi Rodríguez (GOLFISTA)

VOCABULARIO LECCIÓN DIEZ

THEME WORDS: "OUTDOORS"

el *árbol*	tree
el *arbusto*	bush
el *césped*	lawn
el *cielo*	sky
la *estrella*	star
la *flor*	flower
la *hierba*	grass
el *jardín*	garden
la *luna*	moon
la *pala*	shovel
la *piscina*	swimming pool
la *puesta del sol*	sunset
la *rosa*	rose
la *salida del sol*	sunrise
la *tierra*	soil, earth
el *tulipán*	tulip

OTHER NOUNS

la *fila*	row
la *luna de miel*	honeymoon
el *resultado*	result
el *vídeo*	VCR, video

ADJECTIVES

humilde	humble
pelirrojo/a	red-headed

VERBS

bañarse	to take a bath
caer	to fall
casarse con	to get married to
charlar	to chat
compartir	to share
conducir	to drive
ducharse	to shower
equivocarse	to make a mistake
felicitar	to congratulate
freír (i)	to fry
nadar	to swim

MISCELLANEOUS

este	east
norte	north
oeste	west
sur	south
ya	already
ya no	no longer, anymore

LECCIÓN DIEZ

KEY GRAMMAR CONCEPTS

A) THE PROGRESSIVE TENSE → *El progresivo*

B) REFLEXIVE AND RECIPROCAL CONSTRUCTIONS → *Las construcciones reflexivas y las construcciones recíprocas*

C) EQUAL AND UNEQUAL COMPARISONS → *Las comparaciones iguales y desiguales*

 ## A) THE PROGRESSIVE TENSE

The **progressive** is a verb tense that gives extra emphasis to an act that is actually <u>in progress</u> — an event that is occurring at the exact moment that a speaker is describing. It can describe an event in the present or an event from the past.

 EXAMPLES: *El teléfono **está sonando** ahora, pero yo **estoy cortando** el césped.*
The phone is ringing right now, but I am cutting the lawn.

*Mi novio **estaba durmiendo** cuando llegué a su casa.*
My boyfriend was sleeping when I arrived at his house.

HOW IS THE PROGRESSIVE TENSE FORMED?

This tense is normally constructed by combining a form of the verb *"estar"* (usually the present or the imperfect) with a present participle. The present participle is equivalent to the "–ing" form of a verb in English.

The present participle in Spanish is formed as follows:

> **-AR verbs: Remove the *"ar"* from the infinitive and add *"ando."***

 EXAMPLES: *bailar*   →   *bailando*   (dancing)
hablar   →   *hablando*   (speaking)
trabajar   →   *trabajando*   (working)

-ER verbs: Remove the *"er"* from the infinitive and add *"iendo."*

✳ **EXAMPLES:**

comer	→	comiendo	(eating)
romper	→	rompiendo	(breaking)
vender	→	vendiendo	(selling)

-IR verbs: Remove the *"ir"* from the infinitive and add *"iendo."*

✳ **EXAMPLES:**

abrir	→	abriendo	(opening)
escribir	→	escribiendo	(writing)
vivir	→	viviendo	(living)

IRREGULAR FORMS

-IR "boot" verbs have a special vowel change, the same vowel change that occurs in the 3rd person of the preterite:

dormir	→	du*rmiendo*
pedir	→	p*i*diendo
repetir	→	repi*tiendo*
sentir	→	s*i*ntiendo

Note: *"decir"* → d*i*ciendo

You will need to memorize these other common irregular forms:

caer	→	cayendo
ir	→	yendo
leer	→	leyendo
traer	→	trayendo

Here is the formula for the progressive tense:

PRESENT	estoy	estamos		
	estás	estáis		**hablando**
	está	están	**+**	**comiendo**
IMPERFECT	estaba	estábamos		**viviendo**
	estabas	estabais		
	estaba	estaban		

Here are some more examples of sentences using the progressive tense:

✳ **EXAMPLES:** *¡Qué mala suerte!* **Está lloviendo** *y no podemos ver la luna.*
       What bad luck! It's raining and we can't see the moon.

*Arturo Sandoval **estaba tocando** la trompeta anoche en Boston durante las celebraciones del 4 de julio cuando comenzaron los fuegos artificiales.*
> Arturo Sandoval was playing the trumpet last night in Boston during the Fourth of July celebrations when the fireworks began.

*Un momento . . . **estoy pensando** . . . no sé qué voy a hacer.*
> One moment . . . I am thinking . . . I don't know what I'm going to do.

*María **estaba charlando** con su mamá cuando el cartero llegó.*
> María was chatting with her mom when the mailman arrived.

***Estamos esperando** la llegada del próximo autobús.*
> We're waiting for the arrival of the next bus.

Helpful Tip: The progressive is a combination of verb forms. The present participle does not have a feminine or plural form . . . i.e., it will always be *"hablando,"* for example, and never *hablanda or *hablandos!

If you ever have an object pronoun associated with the progressive tense, you have the option of putting this pronoun before the form of *"estar,"* or attaching it to the end of the present participle. If you attach the pronoun, be certain to add an accent mark.

 EXAMPLES: *¿La música de Shakira? **La** estoy escuchando (Estoy **escuchándola**).*
> The music of Shakira? I'm listening to it.

*¿Los tulipanes? **Los** estamos cortando (Estamos **cortándolos**).*
> The tulips? We're cutting them.

PRACTICE EXERCISES

1. Change these verbs into the corresponding form of the progressive:

Examples: comes → **estás comiendo**   vivían → **estaban viviendo**

a. bebe → _____

b. estudian → _____

c. vivo → _____

d. leíamos → _____

e. duermes → _____

f. caminan → _____

g. vendía → _____

h. sirvo → _____

i. escribían → _____

j. aprendes → _____

2. **Complete the following sentences by writing the correct form of the progressive tense. Be careful when deciding whether to use the present progressive** (estoy hablando) **or the imperfect progressive** (estaba hablando)**:**

   a. Mi amiga _____ ahora y no puede ir al Museo del Prado conmigo. (estudiar)

   b. Anoche la policía _____ cuando el ladrón entró en el jardín. (esperar)

   c. Mucha gente _____ durante la película, y por eso no podía oír nada. (hablar)

   d. Sé que tú _____ una carta ahorita, pero ¿no puedes hablar conmigo por un minuto? (escribir)

   e. ¡Caramba! _____ mucho y no podemos ver los árboles. (nevar)

   f. ¿El desayuno? Loretta Sánchez lo _____ cuando su hermana Silvia la llamó por teléfono. (comer)

   g. Nosotras _____ las noticias cuando el hombre misterioso llamó a la puerta. (leer)

   h. Ella no desea ir contigo a la piscina porque _____ en este momento. (dormir)

   i. Muchas personas _____ anoche en Puerto Rico los resultados de la pelea con Daniel Santos. (celebrar)

   j. En este momento creo que nuestros amigos _____ del avión. (salir)

   k. ¿En qué dirección _____ (nosotros) ahora — este, oeste, norte o sur? –Pues, no lo sé. (viajar)

B) REFLEXIVE AND RECIPROCAL CONSTRUCTIONS

1) REFLEXIVE CONSTRUCTIONS

In *Lección Siete*, we had the chance to look at sentences that use a reflexive construction.

 EXAMPLES: *Cada noche **me lavo** las manos antes de comer.*
Each night I wash my hands before eating.

*Mi hermano siempre **se mira** en el espejo cuando está en el cuarto de baño.*
My brother always looks at himself in the mirror when he is in the bathroom.

In these sentences, the verb and the object pronoun refer to the same person. Reflexive sentences make use of one of these pronouns:

me	nos
te	os
se	se

 EXAMPLES: *Me **hablo a mí misma** cuando estoy nerviosa.*
I talk to myself when I am nervous.

*Siempre **te dices a ti mismo** que lo sabes todo.*
You always tell yourself that you know everything.

*¿No recuerdan Uds. que **nos compramos** boletos para el concierto de Christina Aguilera?*
Don't you all remember that we bought ourselves tickets for the Christina Aguilera concert?

Helpful Tip: Do you remember that for extra emphasis or clarity, you can add the following words after the verb: *a mí (mismo/a), a ti (mismo/a), a sí (mismo/a), a nosotros (mismos), a nosotras (mismas), a vosotros (mismos), a vosotras (mismas), a sí (mismos/as)?*

---

2) RECIPROCAL CONSTRUCTIONS

What happens, however, when you want to say that you do something for each other rather than for yourselves? How would I say "They write each other" rather than "They write themselves"?

Spanish speakers make use of the following three pronouns for reciprocal action:

nos
os
se

You will notice that these object pronouns are the same ones used with plural verbs (we, you all, they). In order to have a reciprocal action, you need more than one person!

WHAT EXACTLY IS A RECIPROCAL ACTION?

Reciprocal action conveys a sense of "back and forth": I do something to you that you do to me, he does something to her that she does to him, one group of people does something to another group that the other group does to the first group, etc.

EXAMPLES: *Raúl Castro y yo **nos hablamos** por teléfono anoche.*
Raúl Castro and I spoke to each other last night by phone.

*Marco y Ana siempre **se besan** antes de despedirse.*
Marco and Ana always kiss each other before saying goodbye.

*Vosotros **os insultáis** frecuentemente. ¡No me gusta!*
You all insult each other frequently. I don't like that!

Although the translations above indicate that the sentences are reciprocal in nature, they theoretically could be interpreted as being reflexive (Raúl and I talk to ourselves . . . Marco and Ana kiss themselves . . . You all insult yourselves). Although the context of the sentence would probably give the listener the clue, how do we make a reciprocal sentence unambiguous?

For emphasis, or to distinguish a reciprocal sentence from a reflexive one, a Spanish speaker will simply add one of the following: *(el) uno a (al) otro, (la) una a (la) otra, (los) unos a (los) otros, (las) unas a (las) otras.*

EXAMPLES: *Mis amigos siempre **se hablan (el) uno a (al) otro** cuando tienen problemas.*
My friends always talk to each other when they have problems.

*Serena Williams y Dinara Safina **se felicitaron (la) una a (la) otra** después de su partido emocionante.*
Serena Williams and Dinara Safina congratulated each other after their exciting match.

*Nosotros **nos prometimos (los) unos a (los) otros** que nunca íbamos a pelear otra vez.*
All of us promised each other that we weren't going to fight again.

*Vosotras **os escribisteis (la) una a (la) otra** dos veces el verano pasado.*
You all wrote each other twice last summer.

¡CUIDADO! It is not possible to "mix" genders: *"una a otro" is incorrect. In a group of men and women, you must use the *"o"* ending: *"uno a otro"* or *"unos a otros."*

1. **Insert one of the following words to complete the following REFLEXIVE sentences** (*me, te, se, nos, os, se, mí, ti, sí, nosotros/as, vosotros/as, mismo, misma, mismos, mismas*)**:**

   a. _____ llamo Sergio García, no Andy García.

   b. Antes de comer, _____ lavamos las manos y la cara.

   c. Soy artista y siempre me digo a _____ que debo pintar estrellas, el cielo y puestas del sol bonitas.

   d. Cuando entras en la clase, normalmente _____ sientas en la primera fila, ¿verdad?

   e. David Bisbal y Elena Tablada se miraron a _____ en el televisor de al lado del podio.

   f. Uds. nunca _____ afeitan por la mañana. ¿Por qué?

2. **Now insert one of the following to complete the following RECIPROCAL sentences** (*nos, os, se, uno a otro, una a otra, unos a otros, unas a otras*)**:**

   a. Ramón Castro y Raúl Castro se saludaron _____ esta mañana en una calle de la Habana.

   b. Mi novia y yo _____ besamos por última vez cuando me fui de viaje la semana pasada.

   c. Pedro Almodóvar y Penélope Cruz se hablaban mucho _____ cuando hacían la película *Volver*.

   d. Las chicas en ese equipo nunca _____ ayudan unas a otras; por eso, pierden frecuentemente.

   e. Mis tías se dicen _____ que no hay mal que por bien no venga. ("Every cloud has a silver lining.")

3. Translate the following three sentences into Spanish. Use emphasis in "b" and "c":

a. We call ourselves cooks, but we don't know how to do anything in the kitchen.

_____

b. They promised to see each other in the summer.

_____

c. I sat myself down in the chair, and you and I told each other the secrets.

_____

C) EQUAL AND UNEQUAL COMPARISONS

Often a person wants to compare one thing to another. There are two basic types of comparative sentences: those that express equality, and those that express inequality.

1) EQUAL COMPARISONS

It is common to compare nouns, adjectives, adverbs, and verbs. When you want to say that you have as many as, or that someone is as tall as, or that someone runs as quickly as, or dances as much as someone else, you will need a construction of equality. In Spanish, these sentences of equal comparison are constructed as follows:

a) Nouns

When comparing nouns, use the adjectives _"tanto,"_ _"tanta,"_ _"tantos,"_ or _"tantas"_ (meaning "as much" or "as many") <u>before</u> a noun and use the word _"como"_ (meaning "as") <u>after</u> the noun.

> _tanto/tanta/tantos/tantas_ **+** Noun **+** _como_
> (as many, as much)   (as)

EXAMPLES: _Compré **tantas flores como** tú._
I bought as many flowers as you.

María tiene **tanta paciencia como** su madre.
María has as much patience as her mother.

Julio Iglesias, Jr. no **tiene tanto talento como** su papá.
Julio Iglesias, Jr. doesn't have as much talent as his dad.

b) Adjectives/adverbs

When comparing adjectives or adverbs, use the adverb *"tan"* (meaning "as") <u>before</u> the adjective or adverb, and the word *"como"* (meaning "as") <u>after</u> the adjective or adverb.

> ***tan*** **+ Adjective/Adverb +** ***como***
> (as)   (as)

EXAMPLES: *Serena juega **tan bien como** su hermana Venus.*
Serena plays as well as her sister Venus.

*Jamie lee **tan rápidamente como** sus amigos.*
Jamie reads as quickly as his friends.

La película Ratatouille *no es **tan buena como*** Wall-E.
The movie *Ratatouille* is not as good as *Wall-E.*

c) Verbs

When comparing verbs, the expression *"tanto como"* (meaning "as much as") follows the verb. Notice that in both languages, the second verb in the comparison is understood but not usually expressed.

> **Verb +** *tanto como*
> (as much as)

EXAMPLES: *Paula no baila **tanto como** Jennifer (baila).*
Paula doesn't dance as much as Jennifer.

*Leemos **tanto como** nuestros padres.*
We read as much as our parents.

*No estudié **tanto como** mi amiga.*
I didn't study as much as my friend.

2) UNEQUAL COMPARISONS

The following chart offers the construction for all sentences that express an unequal comparison:

Subject	+	Verb	+	*más/menos* (more/less)	+	Adjective <u>Adverb</u> Noun	+	*que* (than)	+	Noun Pronoun

a) Nouns

When comparing nouns, the words *"más"* and *"menos"* (meaning "more" and "less") precede a noun, and the word *"que"* (meaning "than") follows it.

> ✸ **EXAMPLES:** *Yo tengo **más amigas que** mi hermana.*
> I have more friends than my sister.
>
> *Los gatos comen **menos** carne **que** los perros.*
> Cats eat less meat than dogs.
>
> *Condujimos el coche **más** millas **que** tú.*
> We drove the car more miles than you.

b) Adjectives/adverbs

When comparing adjectives or adverbs, the words *"más"* and *"menos"* (meaning "more" and "less") precede an adjective or adverb, and the word *"que"* (meaning "than") follows it.

> ✸ **EXAMPLES:** *Yo corro **más despacio que** mi hermano*
> I run more slowly than my brother.
>
> *Lola es **más alta que** Mario.*
> Lola is taller than Mario.
>
> *A veces me siento **menos inteligente que** mis amigos.*
> At times I feel less intelligent than my friends.
>
> *Los soldados lucharon **más intensamente que** sus enemigos.*
> The soldiers fought more intensely than their enemies.

c) Verbs

When comparing verbs, the expression *"más que"* (meaning "more than") or the expression *"menos que"* (meaning "less than") is used.

> ✸ **EXAMPLES:** *Yo me equivoco **más que** Ud.*
> I make more errors than you.
>
> *Yo grito **menos que** ellos.*
> I shout less than they do.

¡CUIDADO! Some comparatives have special forms:

- The comparative form of *bueno* is *mejor,* not *más bueno.
- The comparative form of *malo* is *peor,* not *más malo.

1. **Choose the word or words that you feel best complete the following sentences that offer comparisons. You should choose one of the following** (*tanto, tanta, tantos, tantas, tanto como, tan, como, más, menos, más que, menos que, que*)**:**

   a. Tengo _____ discos compactos como tú.

   b. Estudié _____ Ana, pero saqué una nota más baja

   _____ ella.

   c. Hay _____ días en diciembre _____ en enero.

   d. Hay _____ días en febrero _____ en marzo.

   e. Cristina Seralegui es _____ famosa como Oprah Winfrey.

   f. No podemos trabajar _____ Uds.

   g. Lindsey Vonn es más atlética _____ yo.

   h. Bode Miller esquía _____ rápidamente como los otros miembros del equipo nacional de esquí.

   i. Yo tengo diez libros; mi amigo tiene ocho. Yo tengo _____

   libros _____ mi amigo.

   j. Todos dicen que Brad Pitt es _____ guapo que Antonio

   Banderas, pero yo creo que Antonio es más guapo _____ Brad.

2. Now translate these sentences into Spanish:

a. We work as much as our parents.

_____

b. There are more chairs than tables here.

_____

c. Do you have as much talent as Ricky Martin?

_____

3. The following paragraph contains five errors. Underline each error and write the correction above it:

Mi amigo Will se casó ayer con Diana. Todos lloraron durante

la misa; Will lloró tan como Diana. Will tiene treinta y ocho años y Diana

tiene treinta y uno. Will es profesor. Diana es médica. Los dos trabajan

mucho. Will trabaja tanta como Diana. Will y Diana tienen muchísimos

amigos . . . Will tiene tan amigos como Diana. Después de la luna de

miel, van a vivir cerca de Boston. Boston no es tanto vieja como muchas

otras ciudades en Europa, pero es mucho más buena.

These two sets of questions use grammatical structures and vocabulary from this lesson. Working with a partner, alternate asking and answering each question. When you get to the bottom of each list, start over at the top, switching roles. As a variation, write out the answers in complete sentences.

A) ¿Estás hablando en inglés o en español?

¿Estás llorando ahora?

¿Quién estaba charlando cuando entraste en la clase hoy?

¿Adónde vas para tu luna de miel?

¿Te gustan las personas humildes?

¿Cómo se llama una actriz pelirroja famosa?

¿Te equivocas frecuentemente?

B) ¿Te cantas a ti mismo/a cuando te bañas?

¿Se hablan tus padres uno a otro mucho?

¿Se felicitan los republicanos y los demócratas frecuentemente?

¿Compras tantos regalos como tus amigos?

¿Lees tan rápidamente como tus amigos?

¿Ves más películas que tus padres?

¿Hablas español más despacio que tus amigos?

1. Answer in complete sentences:

a. ¿Estás escribiendo con lápiz o con pluma ahora?

_____

b. ¿Estabas viendo la televisión anoche a las nueve?

_____

c. ¿Se escriben tus amigos unos a otros en el verano?

_____

d. ¿Te hablas a ti mismo/misma cuando te bañas?

_____

e. ¿Viste más películas que tus padres este año?

_____

2. Change these verbs into the corresponding form of the progressive:

a. vuelves ⟶ _____   **d.** tenía ⟶ _____

b. dormís ⟶ _____   **e.** comemos⟶ _____

c. preparan⟶ _____   **f.** piden ⟶ _____

3. Complete the following sentences by writing the correct form of the progressive tense:

a. Mi madre _____ con una amiga cuando llegué a casa. (charlar)

b. Ahora yo _____ porque mi luna de miel fue un desastre. (llorar)

c. Ramón no está en casa ahorita porque _____ un examen en la escuela. (hacer)

d. Nosotros _____ las instrucciones ahora porque nadie nos escuchó la primera vez. (repetir)

e. Tú no _____ tu parte en el incidente; voy a llamar a la policía. (admitir)

f. Acabo de volver de la tienda . . . hoy ellos _____ televisores por un precio increíble: ¡200 dólares! (vender)

4. Insert one of the words or expressions that you learned this lesson to give emphasis to the following reflexive and reciprocal sentences:

a. Mi amiga y yo nos hablamos _____ por teléfono todas las noches.

b. José se miró _____ en el espejo grande del baño.

c. Mis vecinos nunca se invitan _____ a ningún evento.

d. Nosotros tenemos que admitirnos a _____ que nuestro equipo va a perder todos los partidos este año.

e. Cuando Raúl está en Santo Domingo y Olivia está en Tokio, se escriben

_____ frecuentemente.

f. Por no haber muchos asistentes de vuelo en el avión, mis padres tuvieron

que sentarse _____.

5. **Choose the word or words that you feel best complete the following sentences that express comparison** *(tanto, tanta, tantos, tantas, tanto como, tan, como, más, menos, que, más que, menos que)*:

a. Yo tengo tres discos; tú tienes dos. Yo tengo _____ discos

_____ tú.

b. Nosotros nunca podemos correr _____ tú.

c. Hay _____ días en diciembre _____ en enero.

d. Mi madre es _____ alta que yo.

e. Ellos juegan _____ intensamente como nosotros.

f. Martina Navratilova no tenía _____ paciencia como Chris Evert Lloyd.

g. Hay _____ personas en California que en Rhode Island.

h. No te creo. Tú no comiste tantas pizzas _____ yo.

i. Alex Rodríguez gana _____ dinero que otros jugadores de béisbol.

6. **Translate the following sentences into Spanish:**

a. I am showering now; I can't talk with you.

_____

b. The girls are taller than the boys.

_____

c. The actors congratulated themselves after the movie.

_____

d. I already bought the television set . . . it cost more than the VCR.

_____

7. The following police report contains six errors. Underline each error and write the correction above it:

Anoche yo estaba conducido el coche cuando vi a un hombre pelirrojo con un televisor en las manos. El televisor era más grande como un elefante. El hombre era tan bajo que un tostador. La situación era un poco cómico. Le dije: "Señor, ¿adónde va Ud. caminanda con ese televisor?" El hombre no quería charlar. Comenzó a llorar. Después me dijo: "Lo siento". Yo dije: "¿Quiere Ud. acompañarme?" Luego el hombre me insultió y ahora está en la cárcel.

PARAGUAY & URUGUAY

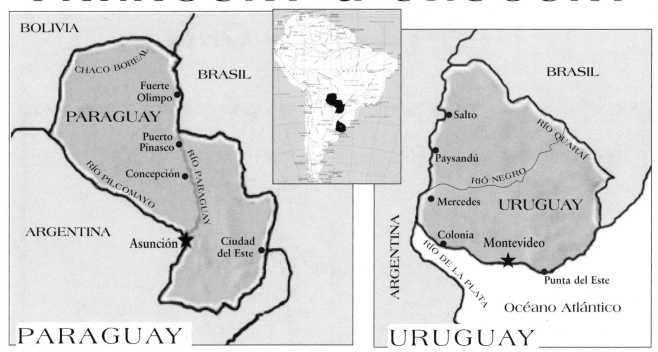

PARAGUAY

CAPITAL:	Asunción
POBLACIÓN:	6.800.000
GOBIERNO:	república constitucional
PRESIDENTE:	Fernando Lugo Méndez
DINERO ($):	guaraní
PRODUCTOS:	agricultura, algodón, ganadería, madera, maíz
MÚSICA, BAILE:	danza de la botella, polka
SITIOS DE INTERÉS:	Chaco, Ciudad del Este, El río Paraguay, Las Ruinas Jesuitas
COMIDA TÍPICA:	bori-bori, chipas, palmitos, so'o ku'i, sopa paraguaya, tereré

PARAGUAYOS FAMOSOS:

Agustín Barrios
(MÚSICO)

Augusto Roa Bastos
(ESCRITOR)

José Luis Chilavert
(FUTBOLISTA)

Luis Alberto
del Paraná
(CANTANTE)

URUGUAY

CAPITAL:	Montevideo
POBLACIÓN:	3.500.000
GOBIERNO:	república constitucional
PRESIDENTE:	Tabaré Vázquez Rosa
DINERO ($):	peso uruguayo
PRODUCTOS:	carne, cemento, cuero, vino
MÚSICA, BAILE:	música gauchesca, tango, vals
SITIOS DE INTERÉS:	Colonia del Sacramento, Punta del Este
COMIDA TÍPICA:	asado, cazuela, chivitos, mate, parrillada, puchero

URUGUAYOS FAMOSOS:

Juan Manuel Blanes
(PINTOR)

José Gervasio Artigas
(HÉROE NACIONAL)

Pedro Figari (PINTOR)

Juan Carlos Onetti
(ESCRITOR)

Horacio Quiroga
(ESCRITOR)

Enrique Rodó
(ESCRITOR)

VOCABULARIO LECCIÓN ONCE

THEME WORDS: "MUSIC"

el	acordeón	accordion
la	banda	band
el	clarinete	clarinet
el	concierto	concert
la	flauta	flute
la	guitarra	guitar
la	orquesta	orchestra
el	piano	piano
el	saxofón	saxophone
los	tambores	drums
el	trombón	trombone
la	trompeta	trumpet
el	violín	violin

OTHER NOUNS

el	actor	actor
la	actriz	actress
el	billete	ticket
la	boda	wedding
el	episodio	episode
el	luchador	wrestler

el	mensaje	message
la	mentira	lie
la	respuesta	reply

ADJECTIVES

contaminado/a	contaminated
tonto/a	foolish, silly, stupid
último/a	last (of a group)

VERBS

fumar	to smoke
invitar	to invite
mojar	to moisten, to wet
pasar (tiempo)	to spend (time)
perder (tiempo)	to waste (time)
preocuparse	to worry
regresar	to return

ADVERBS

cerca	near(by)
lejos	far (away)

LECCIÓN ONCE

KEY GRAMMAR CONCEPTS

A) FORMAL COMMAND FORMS USING UD. AND UDS. → *Mandatos con Ud. y Uds.*

B) DEMONSTRATIVE ADJECTIVES → *Los adjetivos demostrativos*

C) SOME USEFUL IDIOMATIC EXPRESSIONS AND PROVERBS → *Algunas expresiones idiomáticas y refranes útiles*

A) FORMAL COMMAND FORMS USING UD. AND UDS.

Commands express a desire that someone else either do or not do something. In Spanish, the endings of the verb forms themselves show that a command is intended. When reading, you will often find exclamation points acting as brackets, framing the beginning and the end of the command! Most interesting to English speakers is the fact that the first exclamation point is upside down.

Here are some sentences that use commands:

EXAMPLES: *¡Cierre Ud. la puerta!*
Close the door!

¡Abra Ud. el libro!
Open the book!

¡Escriban Uds. la composición ahora mismo!
Write the composition right now!

¡No cierre Ud. la puerta!
Don't close the door!

¡No abra Ud. el libro!
Don't open the book!

¡No escriban Uds. la composición ahora mismo!
Don't write the composition right now!

In this section, we will study the formula for creating these formal commands. Right off the bat, do you notice that the verb endings are exactly the same whether a *Ud./Uds.* command is affirmative or negative *(¡Abra! → ¡No abra!, ¡Cierre! → ¡No cierre!, ¡Escriban! → ¡No escriban!)*?

1) Regular verbs

Here are the forms for formal commands of regular verbs:

	Ud. (+)	Ud. (–)	Uds. (+)	Uds. (–)
HABLAR	¡Hable Ud.!	¡No hable Ud.!	¡Hablen Uds.!	¡No hablen Uds.!
COMER	¡Coma Ud.!	¡No coma Ud.!	¡Coman Uds.!	¡No coman Uds.!
VIVIR	¡Viva Ud.!	¡No viva Ud.!	¡Vivan Uds.!	¡No vivan Uds.!

Note: Affirmative and negative *Ud./Uds.* commands are exactly the same.

As you noticed in this chart, **-AR** verbs end with *"e"* or *"en,"* while **-ER** and **-IR** verbs end with *"a"* or *"an."* These endings are often described as the "opposite" of what you use in the regular present tense. Hearing these endings alerts a listener that the speaker has just barked out an order!

2) Stem-changing "boot" verbs

What happens with stem-changing "boot" verbs? To form the *Ud.* and *Uds.* command forms, follow the same idea as above, but remember the stem change!

	Ud. (+)	Ud. (–)	Uds. (+)	Uds. (–)
CERRAR	¡Cierre Ud.!	¡No cierre Ud.!	¡Cierren Uds.!	¡No cierren Uds.!
VOLVER	¡Vuelva Ud.!	¡No vuelva Ud.!	¡Vuelvan Uds.!	¡No vuelvan Uds.!
PEDIR	¡Pida Ud.!	¡No pida Ud.!	¡Pidan Uds.!	¡No pidan Uds.!

3) Irregular verbs

How do we form commands using verbs that are irregular in the *"yo"* form — words like *hacer, tener,* or *salir*? The process is simple — begin with the irregular *"yo"* form of the present tense. Then add the new endings that you have seen throughout this section.

		"yo" form of present	*"Ud."* command form	*"Uds."* command form
EXAMPLE:	**TENER**	tengo	tenga	tengan

	Ud. (+)	Ud. (–)	Uds. (+)	Uds. (–)
CONDUCIR	¡Conduzca Ud.!	¡No conduzca Ud.!	¡Conduzcan Uds.!	¡No conduzcan Uds.!
DECIR	¡Diga Ud.!	¡No diga Ud.!	¡Digan Uds.!	¡No digan Uds.!
HACER	¡Haga Ud.!	¡No haga Ud.!	¡Hagan Uds.!	¡No hagan Uds.!
PONER	¡Ponga Ud.!	¡No ponga Ud.!	¡Pongan Uds.!	¡No pongan Uds.!
SALIR	¡Salga Ud.!	¡No salga Ud.!	¡Salgan Uds.!	¡No salgan Uds.!

4) SUPER-IRREGULAR VERBS

Finally, there are some verbs whose command forms you simply need to memorize. They do not follow the rules that have been presented thus far. Practice them carefully; because they are such common words, you will use them all the time.

	Ud. (+)	Ud. (–)	Uds. (+)	Uds. (–)
IR	¡Vaya Ud.!	¡No vaya Ud.!	¡Vayan Uds.!	¡No vayan Uds.!
SABER	¡Sepa Ud.!	¡No sepa Ud.!	¡Sepan Uds.!	¡No sepan Uds.!
SER	¡Sea Ud.!	¡No sea Ud.!	¡Sean Uds.!	¡No sean Uds.!

FINALLY, WHAT HAPPENS TO OBJECT PRONOUNS AND COMMANDS?

The rules are simple:

◆ Attach all object pronouns to the end of AFFIRMATIVE (+) commands.

◆ Place all object pronouns before NEGATIVE (–) commands.

EXAMPLES: *¿Los perritos calientes? ¡Cómalos Ud.! . . . ¡No los coma Ud.!*
The hot dogs? Eat them! . . . Don't eat them!

¿Los vecinos? ¡Invítenlos Uds! . . . ¡No los inviten Uds!
The neighbors? Invite them! . . . Don't invite them!

¡CUIDADO! When you attach an object pronoun to a command of two syllables or more, you must add an accent mark: *¡Invítenlos! ¡Hágame! ¡Cómalos!*

PRACTICE EXERCISES

1. **Review the instructions for forming** *"Ud./Uds."* **commands carefully. Now fill in this table, following the example provided. The "+" and "−" indicate affirmative and negative respectively:**

	Ud. (+)	Uds. (−)
Example: bailar	¡Baile!	¡No bailen!
a. trabajar		
b. aprender		
c. vivir		
d. entender		
e. mostrar		
f. repetir		
g. salir		
h. sentarse		
i. tener		
j. ir		
k. ser		

2. Complete the following sentences by conjugating the verb in parentheses into the appropriate "Ud." or "Uds." command form. In the last three sentences, you will need to insert an object pronoun:

a. ¡_____ Uds. las respuestas en la pizarra! (Escribir)

b. ¡_____ Ud. el televisor ahora mismo! ¡Está comenzando el último episodio de *American Idol*! (Encender)

c. ¡No me _____ Ud. otra mentira . . . necesito la verdad! (decir)

d. ¡_____ Uds. todos los vegetales! (Comer)

e. ¡_____ Ud. la tarea primero, y después _____ con los amigos! (Hacer/salir)

f. ¡No me _____ Uds. más preguntas tontas! (repetir)

g. ¿Las chicas? ¡_____ Uds. a la fiesta! (Invitarlas)

¡CUIDADO! *(Remember, __attach__ the object pronoun to the end of an affirmative command!)*

h. ¿La canción de Coldplay, *Viva la vida*? ¡No _____ Ud. aquí! (cantarla)

¡CUIDADO! *(Remember, put the object pronoun before the negative command!)*

i. ¿El nuevo disco de Luis Fonsi? ¡_____ Uds. en la tienda! (Comprarlo)

B) DEMONSTRATIVE ADJECTIVES

Demonstrative adjectives help to identify and distinguish one noun from other nouns of the same type. These adjectives generally precede the noun that they modify. The corresponding words in English are "this," "these," "that," and "those."

Here are the demonstrative adjectives:

Demonstrative Adjectives		
este	*esta*	this
estos	*estas*	these
ese	*esa*	that
esos	*esas*	those
aquel	*aquella*	that (way over there)
aquellos	*aquellas*	those (way over there)

Aquel, aquella, aquellos, and *aquellas* help to identify something that is a great distance away, the farthest distance away of a number of objects, or something quite removed in time from the speaker's framework.

 **EXAMPLES:**

este libro	this book
esta mesa	this table
estos libros	these books
estas mesas	these tables
ese actor	that actor
esa actriz	that actress
esos actores	those actors
esas actrices	those actresses
aquel árbol	that tree (over yonder)
aquella montaña	that mountain (over yonder)
aquellos árboles	those trees (over yonder)
aquellas montañas	those mountains (over yonder)

Helpful Tip: Some students have trouble remembering if *"este"* means "this" or "that," or if *"estos"* means "these" or "those." The following rhyme may help to keep these forms straight in your mind:

"This" and "these" have "t's." (es*t*e/es*t*a and es*t*os/es*t*as)

PRACTICE EXERCISES

1. Translate the demonstrative adjective in parentheses into Spanish, being certain that it agrees with the noun it describes:

a. _____ flautas (these)

f. _____ padre (this)

b. _____ reloj (that, over yonder)

g. _____ restaurantes (those, over yonder)

c. _____ hamburguesa (that)

h. _____ trompeta (that)

d. _____ guitarras (those)

i. _____ hospitales (those)

e. _____ día (this)

j. _____ computadoras (these)

2. The following narrative contains seven errors. Underline each error and write the correction above it:

Esta chicas no saben nada. Cuando yo era niña nunca hablaba con eso tipo de chicas. Sé que aquelos días eran diferentes, pero a veces pienso que los jóvenes de hoy están locos. Por ejemplo, mi nieta, quien va a ese escuela cerca de la casa, siempre habla con el chico del trombón . . . ¿lo conoces? Es eso chico con el bigote que siempre fuma aquellas cigarrillos. Un día ella va a casarse con él. No importa. Voy a ese boda y no voy a decirle nada a nadie.

C) SOME USEFUL IDIOMATIC EXPRESSIONS AND PROVERBS

This section will present a number of **useful idiomatic expressions and proverbs.** Some of these expressions cannot be translated literally into English. Feeling at ease when using expressions such as the ones in the following chart is a sign of a good Spanish speaker.

Idiomatic Expressions and Proverbs	
a fines de →	around the end of
dar las gracias →	to thank
dar por entendido →	to consider it understood
dejar un recado →	to leave a message
de repente →	suddenly
de hoy en adelante →	from now on
echar al correo →	to mail
enamorarse (de) →	to fall in love (with)
estar de acuerdo (con) →	to agree (with)
extrañar el nido →	to be homesick
ida y vuelta →	roundtrip
La práctica hace al maestro. →	Practice makes perfect.
llamar a la puerta →	to knock on the door
llover a cántaros →	to rain a lot
Más vale tarde que nunca. →	Better late than never.
No hay mal que por bien no venga. →	Every cloud has a silver lining.
ponerse enfermo/a →	to become ill
sano y salvo →	safe and sound
tener cuidado →	to be careful
tener en cuenta →	to keep in mind
volverse loco/a →	to go crazy

Let's take a look at each of these expressions used in a sentence:

 EXAMPLES: *Voy a ver la película de Javier Bardem,* Killing Pablo, *a fines de este mes.*
I'm going to see the Javier Bardem movie, *Killing Pablo,* at the end of this month.

*Mi amigo no **me dio las gracias** después de la fiesta.*
My friend didn't thank me after the party.

***Doy por entendido** que todos van a llegar a las seis.*
I consider it understood that everyone will arrive at six.

*Penélope Cruz no me **dejó un recado** en el hotel.*
Penélope Cruz didn't leave me a message in the hotel.

De repente *sonó la alarma y tuvimos que salir.*
   Suddenly the alarm sounded, and we had to leave.

De hoy en adelante *sólo voy a decir la verdad.*
   From now on, I'm only going to tell the truth.

Mañana voy a ***echar al correo*** *una carta para mi novia.*
   Tomorrow I'm going to mail a letter to my girlfriend.

La infanta Cristina de Borbón ***se enamoró de*** *Iñaki Urdangarín hace muchos años.*
   The princess Cristina de Borbón fell in love with Iñaki Urdangarín many years ago.

Estoy de acuerdo *contigo; Derek Parra es uno de los mejores patinadores americanos.*
   I agree with you; Derek Parra is one of the best American skaters.

Como ***extrañaba*** *tanto* ***el nido,*** *volví a mi pueblo, Cuéllar.*
   Because I was so homesick, I returned to my hometown of Cuéllar.

Es mucho más barato comprar un billete de ***ida y vuelta.***
   It's much cheaper to buy a roundtrip ticket.

Mi profesora de piano siempre me decía: ***"La práctica hace al maestro".*** *Por eso, decidí no estudiar con ella.*
   My piano teacher always used to tell me: *"Practice makes perfect."* For that reason, I decided not to study with her.

Estaba llamando a la puerta *cuando alguien gritó: "¿Qué pasa?"*
   I was knocking on the door when someone shouted: "What's going on?"

Llovía a cántaros *cuando salí de casa, y por eso me mojé.*
   It was raining cats and dogs when I left home, and, therefore, I got wet.

Mi amigo se casó a la edad de cincuenta y cinco años. — ***Más vale tarde que nunca.***
   My friend got married at the age of fifty-five. — Better late than never.

Me rompí el brazo anoche, pero en el hospital conocí a un médico muy guapo . . . ***No hay mal que por bien no venga.***
   I broke my arm last night, but in the hospital I met a very handsome doctor . . . Every cloud has a silver lining.

El día de su boda con Jennifer López, Marc Anthony ***se puso enfermo*** *y no pudo cantar.*
   The day of his wedding to Jennifer López, Marc Anthony got sick and couldn't sing.

Al final de la película 101 Dálmatas, *todos los perritos volvieron a casa* ***sanos y salvos.***
   At the end of the movie *101 Dalmatians,* all of the puppies returned home safe and sound.

"¡Tengan cuidado!" gritó mi madre cuando mi hermano y yo salimos en
la Harley.

"Be careful!" shouted my mother when my brother and I left on the
Harley.

Si tocamos la canción "Quisiera" *de Alejandro Fernández, tenemos que*
tener en cuenta *que mi hermana va a llorar.*

If we play the song *"Quisiera"* by Alejandro Fernández, we have to keep
in mind that my sister is going to cry.

Cuando Ricky Martin canta "Livin' la vida loca", *todas las chicas todavía*
se vuelven locas.

When Ricky Martin sings *"Livin' la vida loca,"* all the girls still go crazy.

 PRACTICE EXERCISES

1. Choose one of the expressions in this section to complete the following sentences:

a. Creo que la comida que sirvieron estaba contaminada; por eso yo

_____ y tuve que ir al hospital.

b. Como estamos tan ocupados no podemos ir de vacaciones ahora . . . pero

_____ agosto vamos a tener mucho más
tiempo libre.

c. El cartero tenía un paquete urgente; por eso él _____
por cinco minutos. Por fin, dejó el paquete con el vecino.

d. Me robaron el dinero y el equipaje, pero aprendí muchas lecciones
importantes en el viaje . . . como siempre dice mi mamá:

_____ .

e. Lucille Ball y Desi Arnaz _____ cuando
eran jóvenes y decidieron casarse en seguida.

f. Cuando mis hijos nadan en la piscina del vecino, yo siempre les digo:

¡_____!

g. Necesito hacer algunos cambios importantes en mi vida:

_____ no voy a fumar más y voy a tocar el clarinete.

h. El novio llegó media hora tarde a la iglesia; todos estaban furiosos . . . pero

como decía mi abuela: _____.

i. Sí, tienes razón . . . yo _____ contigo;
Tito Puente fue uno de los mejores músicos del mundo — ¡su banda era
fantástica!

j. No me gustan las grandes ciudades; deseo regresar a mi pueblo lo más

pronto posible. Es verdad que yo _____.

**2. Now write some original sentences of your own using the following five
expressions:** *dejar un recado, de repente, ida y vuelta, la práctica hace al
maestro, volverse loco/a.* **Translate them afterwards:**

a. _____

_____

_____

_____

_____

b. _____

_____

_____

_____

_____

c. _____

_____

_____

_____

_____

d. _____

_____

_____

_____

_____

e. _____

_____

_____

_____

_____

These two sections use the grammatical structures and vocabulary from this lesson.

 (Alternate giving these commands with your partner . . . even though you are likely speaking with a friend, you will be practicing formal *"Ud."* commands . . . the person who receives the command must do it!)

A) ¡Hable Ud. un poco de inglés ahora!

¡Muéstreme su libro de español!

¡Pídame un autógrafo!

¡Levántese!

¡Cante una canción tonta!

¡Péinese!

¡Dígame un secreto!

B) ¿Te gustan estas preguntas?

¿Recuerdas aquellos días cuando eras bebé?

¿Viste esa película horrible de Jennifer López, *Gigli*?

¿De hoy en adelante vas a fumar más?

A fines de este año escolar, ¿me vas a invitar a una fiesta?

¿Te vuelves loco/a cuando canta Marc Anthony?

¿Siempre estás de acuerdo con tus padres?

DIALOGUE

The following dialogue contains grammar and vocabulary that you've seen in this lesson and in the introductory section. After listening to the CD, read this dialogue aloud, alone or with friends. Afterwards, try to answer the questions that follow either aloud or in written form.

 ## LAS AVENTURAS DE RAFAEL, ELISA Y "EL TIGRE"
ESCENA SEIS

Son las seis menos diez de la mañana. Elisa, "El Tigre", Rafael, Marisela y Javier esperan en el andén (platform) *al lado de un tren muy largo de Amtrak. En unos minutos van a abordar el tren para su viaje a Chicago.*

El Tigre: ¡Caramba! Es tan temprano.

Elisa: Tienes razón, Tigre. ¿No había otro tren, Rafael?

Rafael: No. Ese tren es ideal . . . va a llegar en veinticinco horas a Chicago. Llegamos a las seis de la mañana.

Javier: ¿A las seis? ¡Qué barbaridad! ¿En qué estábamos pensando?

Marisela: ¡No se preocupen! Podemos dormir en el tren esta tarde y toda la noche. Sé que hay tantas cosas que hacer en Chicago que no vamos a tener sueño.

Rafael: Es verdad. *La Torre Sears* es el edificio más alto de este país y *El Museo de Ciencia e Industria* es uno de los mejores del mundo.

Elisa: Además, me dicen que el lago Michigan es muy bonito y Chicago tiene playas preciosas.

El Tigre: Tengo hambre. ¿Sirven desayuno en el tren?

Javier: Caramba, Tigre. Es verdad lo que dicen tus amigos. Sólo piensas en la comida.

Todos se ríen. Entonces se escucha un anuncio.

Voz: Saliendo en la plataforma dos el tren para Chicago. Por favor, aborden inmediatamente.

En este momento el hombre del bigote y la mujer vestida de blanco llegan al andén.

Elisa: Tigre, Rafael. ¿Ven Uds. a esas dos personas? Creo que los vi recientemente en otro lugar.

Marisela: Esto (This) ocurre frecuentemente en Nueva York, Elisa. Después de unos días, uno cree que conoce a todo el mundo. ¡Abordemos! (Let's board!)

| **El Tigre:** | Pero creo que Elisa tiene razón. El hombre ese con el bigote . . . creo que es el mismo que me robó la mochila. |
| **Marisela:** | ¿El hombre aquel con la mujer? Pues los vi anoche en la cafetería, también. |

El hombre del bigote y la mujer vestida de blanco comienzan a acercarse a los jóvenes.

Javier:	Ellos vienen. ¿Qué hacemos? ¿Llamamos a la policía?
Elisa:	Tengo mi teléfono celular.
Rafael:	No, no. No hay tiempo. Subamos al tren.

Los cinco jóvenes suben al tren un segundo antes de que se cierren las puertas. Se oye un silbido (whistle) *y el tren se pone en marcha.*

Elisa:	¿Saben Uds. si el hombre y la mujer abordaron también?
El Tigre:	Creo que no.
Elisa:	Tengo miedo.
Marisela:	¡No te preocupes! No pasa nada. Somos cinco y ellos sólo son dos.
Javier:	Además, vamos a Chicago y ellos se quedan en Nueva York.

En otra parte del tren el hombre del bigote y la mujer vestida de blanco se sientan.

El hombre:	¡Qué suerte! Por poco nos deja el tren.
La mujer:	Pero saltamos (we jumped) muy bien . . . y ahora no van a poder escaparse de nosotros.
El hombre:	Sí, querida. En unas horas, vamos a hacerles una visita. Por ahora, vamos a descansar un poquito.

1) ¿Qué hora es cuando comienza esta escena?

_____

2) ¿Adónde van los jóvenes?

_____

3) ¿De cuántas horas es el viaje a Chicago?

_____

4) ¿Cómo se llama el edificio más alto de los Estados Unidos?

_____

5) ¿Qué museo de Chicago es muy famoso?

_____

6) ¿A quiénes ven ahora en el andén?

_____

7) ¿Van a llamar a la policía? ¿Por qué sí o por qué no?

_____

8) ¿De qué tiene miedo Elisa?

_____

9) ¿Quiénes hablan juntos al final de la escena y dónde están?

_____

10) ¿Qué van a hacer en unas horas?

_____

PRUEBA DE REPASO

1. Answer in complete sentences:

a. ¿Es bueno fumar en la biblioteca?

_____

_____

b. ¿Te gusta esta escuela o prefieres otra escuela?

_____

_____

c. ¡No escriba Ud. nada aquí!

_____

_____

d. ¿Dejaste un mensaje ayer en la mesa de tu profesor favorito?

_____

_____

e. ¿Normalmente se pone enferma una persona después de beber agua contaminada?

_____

_____

2. Write formal *"Ud."* commands as indicated:

	Ud. (+)	Ud. (−)
a. hablar	_____	_____
b. vivir	_____	_____
c. volverse	_____	_____
d. decir	_____	_____
e. conocer	_____	_____

	Uds. (+)	Uds. (−)
f. hacer	_____	_____
g. ser	_____	_____
h. ir	_____	_____
i. pedir	_____	_____
j. sentarse	_____	_____

3. Change these five negative commands to affirmative commands, remembering to add an accent mark when needed:

a. ¡No me diga el secreto!

_____

b. ¡No se sienten en esas sillas!

_____

c. ¡No nos muestre los vegetales!

_____

d. ¡No me inviten a la fiesta!

_____

e. ¡No se laven las manos en el río!

_____

4. Translate the demonstrative adjectives in parentheses into Spanish:

a. _____ piano (that)

b. _____ actrices (these)

c. _____ billete (that, over yonder)

d. _____ boda (this)

e. _____ saxofones (those)

f. _____ vegetales (these)

g. _____ orquesta (that)

h. _____ montañas (those, over yonder)

5. Choose one of the following expressions or proverbs for each space in the following sentences (*ida y vuelta, la práctica hace al maestro, llamar a la puerta, llover a cántaros, más vale tarde que nunca, no hay mal que por bien no venga, ponerse enfermo/a, sano y salvo, tener cuidado, tener en cuenta*)**:**

a. El accidente fue horrible, pero yo estoy bien . . . ¿no ves? Aquí estoy

_____ .

b. Cuando comencé a estudiar el violín, no sabía nada. Esta noche voy a tocar

en Carnegie Hall. Como decía mi abuelo : _____ .

c. Me mojé cuando salí de casa porque _____ .

d. "¡_____ con el enemigo!" les dijo el general
a los soldados.

e. Prefiero comprar billetes de _____ porque
normalmente son más baratos.

f. Mi amigo llegó dos horas tarde al concierto . . . ¡_____

_____ !

g. Cuando bebí agua contaminada, _____ .

6. Translate the following sentences into Spanish:

a. Don't smoke at the wedding!

_____

b. The actress fell in love with the actor.

_____

c. Do you prefer this flute or that accordion?

_____

7. The following narrative contains five errors. Underline each error and write the correction above it:

Mi hermano prefiere este árbol de Navidad, pero yo prefiero

aquella árbol. El hombre de la tienda nos dijo: "¡No se preocupan Uds.!

Pueden comprar eses dos árboles". Se los mostré a mi madre. Mi madre

estaba de acuerda con mi hermano. De hoy en adelanta, nunca voy con

él a la tienda.

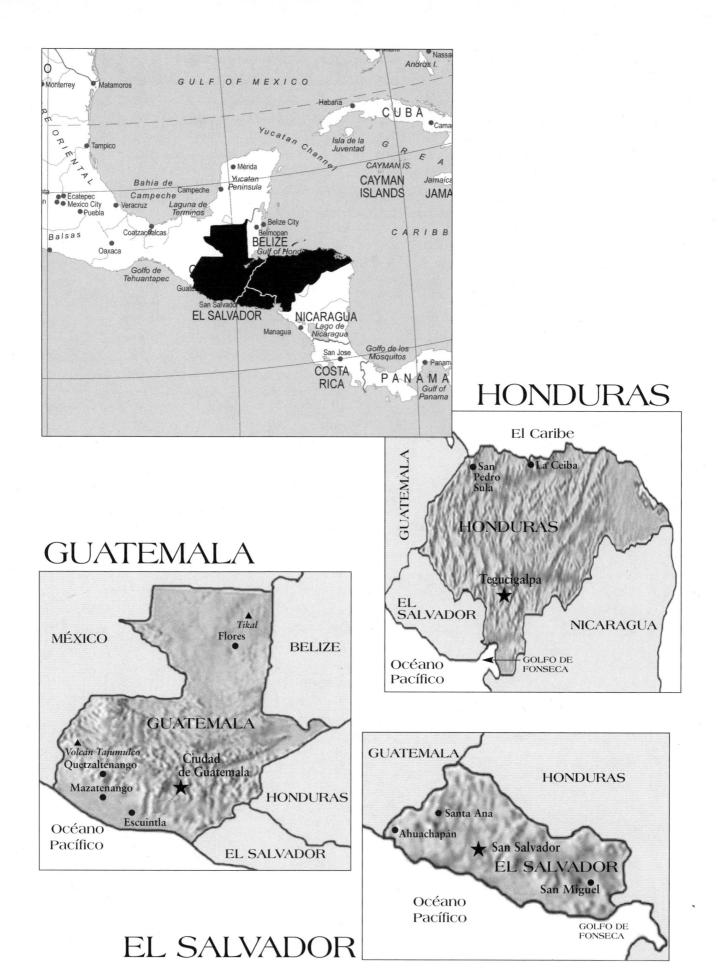

GULF OF MEXICO

CUBA

CAYMAN ISLANDS

JAMA

CARIBB

Monterrey • Matamoros

Habana

Andros I.

Nassau

Cama

Isla de la Juventud

CAYMAN IS.

Jamaica

Tampico

Mérida

Yucatan Channel

Ecatepec
Mexico City
Puebla

Bahia de Campeche

Campeche

Yucatan Peninsula

Veracruz

Laguna de Terminos

Coatzacoalcos

Balsas

Oaxaca

Golfo de Tehuantepec

Belize City

Belmopan

BELIZE

Gulf of Hond

Guate

San Salvador

EL SALVADOR

NICARAGUA

Managua

Lago de Nicaragua

San Jose

Golfo de los Mosquitos

COSTA RICA

PANAMA

Panam

Gulf of Panama

HONDURAS

El Caribe

GUATEMALA

San Pedro Sula

La Ceiba

HONDURAS

Tegucigalpa ★

EL SALVADOR

NICARAGUA

Océano Pacífico

GOLFO DE FONSECA

GUATEMALA

MÉXICO

Tikal ▲
Flores ●

BELIZE

GUATEMALA

Volcán Tajumulco ▲

Quetzaltenango ●

Mazatenango ●

Escuintla ●

Ciudad de Guatemala ★

HONDURAS

Océano Pacífico

EL SALVADOR

GUATEMALA

HONDURAS

Santa Ana ●

Ahuachapán ●

San Salvador ★

EL SALVADOR

San Miguel ●

Océano Pacífico

GOLFO DE FONSECA

EL SALVADOR

GUATEMALA, HONDURAS & EL SALVADOR

GUATEMALA

CAPITAL:	La Ciudad de Guatemala
POBLACIÓN:	13.000.000
GOBIERNO:	república democrática constitucional
PRESIDENTE:	Álvaro Colom
DINERO ($):	quetzal
PRODUCTOS:	azúcar, bananas, café, carne
MÚSICA, BAILE:	marimba, son
SITIOS DE INTERÉS:	Chichicastenango, Islas de la Bahía, Lago Atitlán, El Petén, Tikal, Volcán Pacaya
COMIDA TÍPICA:	chiles rellenos, guacamole, pepián, pescaditos, tamales, tapado, tortillas

HONDURAS

CAPITAL:	Tegucigalpa
POBLACIÓN:	7.600.000
GOBIERNO:	república constitucional democrática
PRESIDENTE:	Manuel Zelaya
DINERO ($):	lempira
PRODUCTOS:	azúcar, bananas, cacao, carne, fruta, minerales, tabaco
MÚSICA, BAILE:	punta, sique
SITIOS DE INTERÉS:	Copán (ruinas de los mayas), Santa Bárbara
COMIDA TÍPICA:	aguacate, carne asada, casabe, plátanos, sopa de camarones, tortillas

EL SALVADOR

CAPITAL:	San Salvador
POBLACIÓN:	7.000.000
GOBIERNO:	república
PRESIDENTE:	Mauricio Funes
DINERO ($):	colón, dólar estadounidense
PRODUCTOS:	agricultura, artesanía, azúcar, café
MÚSICA, BAILE:	danza de los historiantes, marimba
SITIOS DE INTERÉS:	Joya de Cerén, Izalco, La Palma, San Andrés, Santa Ana
COMIDA TÍPICA:	pan con pavo, pupusas, tamales

GUATEMALTECOS FAMOSOS:

Ricardo Arjona
(CANTANTE)

Miguel Asturias
(ESCRITOR)

Rigoberta Menchú
(ACTIVISTA)

Carlos Mérida
(ARTISTA)

Augusto Monteroso
(ESCRITOR)

HONDUREÑOS FAMOSOS:

Guillermo Anderson
(MÚSICO)

Julio Escoto
(ESCRITOR)

Lempira
(HÉROE NACIONAL)

Francisco Morazán
(POLÍTICO)

Gabriela Núñez
(POLÍTICA)

José Antonio Velázquez
(PINTOR)

SALVADOREÑOS FAMOSOS:

Raúl Díaz Arce
(FUTBOLISTA)

Jorge González
(FUTBOLISTA)

Claudia Lars
(ESCRITORA)

Alberto Masferrer
(ESCRITOR)

Óscar Romero
(ACTIVISTA, ARZOBISPO)

VOCABULARIO LECCIÓN DOCE

THEME WORDS: "HIGH TECH"

la	aspiradora	vacuum cleaner
la	computadora	computer
el	congelador	freezer
el	contestador automático	answering machine
el	correo electrónico	e-mail
el	horno de microondas	microwave oven
la	lavadora	washer
el	lavaplatos	dishwasher
la	nevera	refrigerator
el	ordenador	computer (Spain)
el/la	radio	radio
el	refrigerador	refrigerator
la	secadora	dryer
el	teléfono celular	cell phone
la	televisión	television
el	televisor	television set

OTHER NOUNS

el/la	abogado/a	lawyer
la	carie	cavity
la	carretera	highway
la	docena	dozen
el	fin de semana	weekend
la	galleta	cookie
el	garaje	garage
el	inglés	English
el	perrito caliente	hot dog
el	principio	beginning
la	raqueta	racquet

ADJECTIVES

precioso/a	beautiful, adorable

VERBS

gastar	to spend, to waste
terminar	to finish

MISCELLANEOUS

ir de viaje	to travel
otra vez	again

LECCIÓN DOCE

KEY GRAMMAR CONCEPTS

A) THE IMMEDIATE FUTURE → *El futuro inmediato*

B) USES OF "POR" AND "PARA" → *Los usos de "por" y "para"*

C) MORE NUMBERS → *Más números*

 A) THE IMMEDIATE FUTURE

In future years of Spanish study, you will learn the verbal endings of the "true" future tense. In the meantime, however, you may want to know how to talk about events that occur subsequent to the present. The **immediate future** is used to refer to events that, in the speaker's mind, will occur relatively soon. You simply use the present tense of *"ir"* with the preposition *"a"* and an infinitive.

Here's the construction of the immediate future:

voy	vamos			
vas	vais	**+**	**"a"** +	**Infinitive**
va	van			

EXAMPLES: *Esta noche **voy a ver** a David Suazo, la estrella hondureña de fútbol.*
Tonight I'm going to see David Suazo, the Honduran soccer star.

***Vamos a regresar** de las vacaciones este fin de semana.*
We'll be back from vacation this weekend.

*A su hijo **le va a encantar** la nueva película de Harry Potter.*
Your son is going to love the new Harry Potter film.

*Wisín y Yandel **van a dar** un concierto en Tegucigalpa este año.*
Wisín and Yandel are going to give a concert in Tegucigalpa this year.

*Mi novio **me va a invitar** al próximo partido los Pistons.*
My boyfriend is going to invite me to the next Pistons game.

*Mis padres **van a darme** un regalo muy especial para mi cumpleaños: un viaje a Disney's California Adventure.*

My parents are going to give me a very special present for my birthday: a trip to *Disney's California Adventure.*

*Mi dentista **va a estar** muy contento porque tengo muchas caries.*

My dentist is going to be very happy because I have many cavities.

*Mañana **vas a desayunar** a las seis en punto.*

Tomorrow you are going to have breakfast at six sharp.

Helpful Tip: Did you notice that when you use object pronouns with the immediate future, you have the option of placing them before the form of *"ir"* (*le va a encantar, me va a invitar*) or attaching them to the infinitive *(van a dar**me**)*?

 PRACTICE EXERCISES ▶

1. Write out the six forms of the immediate future with the following two infinitives:

cantar (to sing)   **levantarse** (to get up)

_____ _____   _____ _____

_____ _____   _____ _____

_____ _____   _____ _____

2. Complete the following sentences with the appropriate form of the immediate future:

a. Tenemos mucha suerte porque mañana _____ sol y podemos ir a la playa. (hacer)

b. Creo que Juanes _____ otro Grammy este año. (ganar)

c. Mi hermana y yo _____ el nuevo episodio de *Prison Break*. (ver)

d. Esta noche ellos _____ en ese nuevo restaurante hondureño. (comer)

e. Mañana nosotros _____ muy temprano porque vamos a visitar algunas ruinas mayas. (levantarse)

f. Tú _____ enfermo si comes tantos perros calientes. (ponerse)

g. Nadie _____ ahora porque comienza *CSI: Miami* con David Caruso y Adam Rodríguez. (salir)

h. Yo _____ que es buena idea trabajar primero y jugar después. (tener en cuenta)

i. Mi amigo _____ su iPod para escuchar las canciones más recientes. (usar)

B) USES OF "POR" AND "PARA"

In *Lección Cuatro,* you were introduced briefly to the prepositions *"por"* and *"para."* These words are used frequently in Spanish! In English, they can mean "for," "by," "in order to," "along," and "through." Non-native speakers often take a little while to learn which of these prepositions to choose. This section will present four common uses of each of these words.

1) USES OF "POR"

a) *"Por"* **can mean "in exchange for."** It is used when one person gives something to another person in exchange for something else.

EXAMPLES: *Te doy diez dólares **por** tu raqueta de tenis vieja.*
I'll give you ten dollars for your old tennis racquet.

*Muchas gracias **por** la invitación.*
Many thanks for the invitation.

(Here the speaker gives thanks in exchange for the invitation!
"Gracias por" = *"Thank you for"* — remember the rhyme!)

b) *"Por"* **can measure a duration of time.** When you say for how long you did something, you could use *"por."*

 EXAMPLES: *Esta mañana sólo estudié (por) diez minutos.*
    I only studied for ten minutes this morning.

Esta noche vamos a dormir (por) ocho horas.
    We are going to sleep for eight hours tonight.

Note: *"Por"* can be omitted in these sentences. In fact, in Spain, *"por"* would not be used here.

c) *"Por"* **expresses rate.**

 EXAMPLES: *Normalmente mi amigo conduce a sesenta millas por hora en la autopista.*
    Normally my friend drives sixty miles an hour on the highway.

El noventa por ciento de mis amigos hablan español.
    Ninety percent of my friends speak Spanish.

d) *"Por"* **describes movement through space.**

 EXAMPLES: *Siempre caminamos por la playa después de las siete.*
    We always walk along the beach after seven.

¡Salgan Uds. por esa puerta verde!
    Leave through that green door!

2) USES OF "PARA"

a) *"Para"* **is used to indicate a destination.**

 EXAMPLES: *Caminamos para la plaza central.*
    We are walking to (towards) the central plaza.

Este tren sale para las afueras.
    This train is heading to the suburbs.

b) *"Para"* **can mean "intended for."** It identifies the recipient of a gift or favor. It also can mean the place where you plan to put something.

 EXAMPLES: *"Este anillo es para ti", le dijo el cantante y actor Pablo Montero a su mujer, Sandra Vidal.*
    "This ring is for you," said the singer and actor Pablo Montero to his wife, Sandra Vidal.

La nueva alfombra azul y roja es para el comedor.
    The new blue and red rug is for the dining room.

c) *"Para"* indicates a deadline, a time by which something will be completed.

    ❋ **EXAMPLES:** *La tarea **para** mañana es leer los correos electrónicos.*
        The homework for tomorrow is to read your e-mail.

        ***Para** las cinco esta noche voy a terminar este proyecto.*
        I'm going to finish this project by five tonight.

d) *"Para"* can be used before an infinitive to mean "in order to."

    ❋ **EXAMPLES:** ***Para** comprender la película, es necesario leer el libro primero.*
        In order to understand the movie, it is necessary to read the
        book first.

        *"Dios me trajo a este mundo **para** ser músico", dijo una vez
        Tito Puente.*
        "God brought me to this world in order to be a musician,"
        Tito Puente once said.

Helpful Tip: If we want to say "in order to" in English (though we may choose not to), we <u>must</u> use *"para"* in Spanish.

 # PRACTICE EXERCISES ▶

1. Complete the following sentences by using the word *"por"* or *"para"*:

a. _____ ganar el partido, tenemos que practicar de sol a sol.

b. Vamos a pasar _____ la casa de la abuela.

c. Estuvimos en Santa Ana _____ tres semanas el verano pasado.

d. Estos regalos son _____ ti, amor mío.

e. Este maíz cuesta cinco dólares _____ docena.

f. ¿Me das tu radio _____ mi lavadora?

g. Tengo que terminar toda la tarea _____ esta noche.

h. ¿Puedes venir a mi casa _____ preparar el guacamole conmigo?

i. Estas flores preciosas son _____ mi abuela.

j. "Voy a cantar _____ tres horas", anunció Shakira al principio del concierto.

k. Este avión sale _____ Tegucigalpa en media hora.

2. The following paragraph contains five errors of *"por"* and *"para."* Underline each error and write the correction above it:

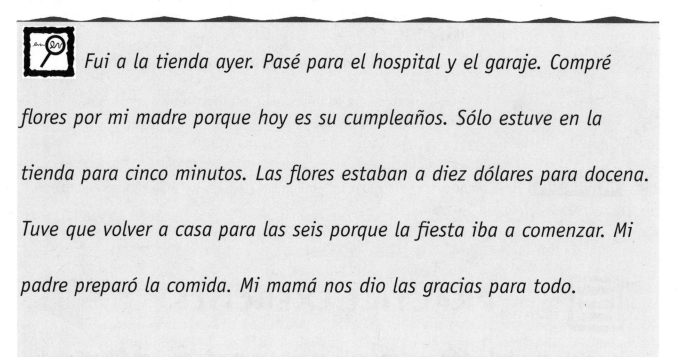

Fui a la tienda ayer. Pasé para el hospital y el garaje. Compré flores por mi madre porque hoy es su cumpleaños. Sólo estuve en la tienda para cinco minutos. Las flores estaban a diez dólares para docena. Tuve que volver a casa para las seis porque la fiesta iba a comenzar. Mi padre preparó la comida. Mi mamá nos dio las gracias para todo.

This final section will help you to expand your knowledge of numbers.

1) CARDINAL NUMBERS

In the preliminary pages, you learned to count to thirty-one. Do you remember all of the numbers? All of these numbers are called cardinal numbers.

1	*uno*	11	*once*
2	*dos*	12	*doce*
3	*tres*	13	*trece*
4	*cuatro*	14	*catorce*
5	*cinco*	15	*quince*
6	*seis*	16	*dieciséis (diez y seis)*
7	*siete*	17	*diecisiete (diez y siete)*
8	*ocho*	18	*dieciocho (diez y ocho)*
9	*nueve*	19	*diecinueve (diez y nueve)*
10	*diez*	20	*veinte*

The cardinal numbers 21–29 can be written as either one word or as three. Note the accents on *veintidós, veintitrés* and *veintiséis.*

21	*veintiuno (veinte y uno)*	26	*veintiséis (veinte y seis)*
22	*veintidós (veinte y dos)*	27	*veintisiete (veinte y siete)*
23	*veintitrés (veinte y tres)*	28	*veintiocho (veinte y ocho)*
24	*veinticuatro (veinte y cuatro)*	29	*veintinueve (veinte y nueve)*
25	*veinticinco (veinte y cinco)*		

The compound numbers from 31–99 must be written as three words.

30	*treinta*	34	*treinta y cuatro, etc.*	70	*setenta*
31	*treinta y uno*	40	*cuarenta*	80	*ochenta*
32	*treinta y dos*	50	*cincuenta*	90	*noventa*
33	*treinta y tres*	60	*sesenta*	100	*cien(to)*

Helpful Tips: **1)** The word *"ciento"* is shortened to *"cien"* before any noun *(cien televisores, cien mesas)* or before a larger number *(cien mil).*

2) The word *"y"* is only used in Spanish between groups of tens and ones *(cuarenta y seis).*

101	*ciento uno*		600	*seiscientos*
200	*doscientos*		700	*setecientos*
300	*trescientos*		800	*ochocientos*
400	*cuatrocientos*		900	*novecientos*
500	*quinientos*		1000	*mil*

Helpful Tips: **1)** When describing a feminine noun, the numerals 200–900 change to agree with that noun *(doscientos libros, doscientas sillas)*.

2) Also, note that the word *"uno"* changes, too. (641 women = ***seiscientas*** *cuarenta y* ***una*** *mujeres*; 641 men = ***seiscientos*** *cuarenta y* ***un*** *hombres*).

2) ORDINAL NUMBERS

Ordinal numbers describe numbers in order (sequence). The most common ordinal numbers in Spanish are the first ten. After that, a Spanish speaker will most often choose to use a cardinal number even though more ordinal numbers exist.

1ST	*primero*		5TH	*quinto*		8TH	*octavo*
2ND	*segundo*		6TH	*sexto*		9TH	*noveno*
3RD	*tercero*		7TH	*séptimo*		10TH	*décimo*
4TH	*cuarto*						

Helpful Tips: **1)** The words *primero* and *tercero* lose their *"o"* **before** a masculine, singular noun *(el primer libro, el tercer episodio)*. All other ordinal numbers retain the *"o"* before a masculine, singular noun *(el quinto hombre, el décimo año)*.

2) All ordinal numbers change the final *"o"* to an *"a"* when describing a singular, feminine noun *(la primera chica, la novena lección, etc.)*.

3) In Spanish, "1ST" is written *"1º"* or *"1ª"*; "2ND" is *"2º"* or *"2ª"*, etc.

PRACTICE EXERCISES

1. **Translate the following words into Spanish:**

   a. twenty-eight computers _____

   b. fifth _____

   c. two hundred thirty-one chairs _____

   d. the sixth book; the sixth week _____

   e. thirteen telephones _____

   f. first _____

   g. eight hundred sixty-nine _____

   h. second _____

   i. nine hundred twenty-five _____

   j. ninth _____

2. **Insert the correct ordinal or cardinal number in the spaces below:**

   a. El _____ presidente de los Estados Unidos fue Thomas Jefferson. (3RD)

   b. Hay _____ días en julio. (31)

   c. ¡Comí _____ galletas ayer! (31)

   d. La _____ lección de este libro es excelente. (5TH)

   e. Encontré _____ dólares en la calle Main. (200)

   f. Vi el _____ perrito que nació en casa de la vecina. (1ST)

   g. ¡Esa palabra tiene _____ letras! (16)

   h. El _____ mes del año es mi favorito. (2ND)

   i. Hay _____ alumnos en mi colegio. (341)

   j. Hay _____ aspiradoras en la casa. (10)

ORAL PRACTICE
PREGUNTAS EN GRUPOS DE DOS

These two sets of questions use grammatical structures and vocabulary from this lesson. Working with a partner, alternate asking and answering each question. When you get to the bottom of each list, start over at the top, switching roles. As a variation, write out the answers in complete sentences.

 A) ¿Vas a gastar mucho dinero este fin de semana?

¿Vas a llevar la secadora y la nevera a tu casa nueva?

¿Van a viajar tus padres esta primavera?

¿Vas a poner tu coche en el garaje esta noche?

¿Vas a hablar mucho conmigo hoy?

¿Cuánto dinero me das por mi microondas?

¿Qué tienes que hacer para jugar bien al baloncesto?

B) ¿Te gustan más las hamburguesas o los perritos calientes?

¿ Aproximadamente cuántas caries tienes?

¿Por cuánto tiempo hablas español en un día típico?

¿Cuál es el tercer mes del año?

¿Cuál es la quinta letra en la palabra "refrigerador"?

¿Cuál es tu número favorito?

¿Vamos a terminar estas preguntas pronto?

1. Answer in complete sentences:

a. ¿Vas a acostarte antes de las diez esta noche?

_____

b. ¿Cuándo va a llover otra vez?

_____

c. ¿Por cuántos años vas a estudiar español?

_____

d. ¿Cuál es el primer día de la semana?

_____

e. ¿Es posible comer trescientas galletas en un día?

_____

2. Write the full conjugations of the following two infinitives in the immediate future:

        vender (to sell)   **vestirse** (to dress)

_____ _____   _____ _____

_____ _____   _____ _____

_____ _____   _____ _____

3. Complete the following five sentences with the appropriate form of the immediate future:

a. Este fin de semana yo _____ con mi novio. (salir)

b. Esta tarde nosotras _____ mucho dinero en la tienda nueva. (gastar)

c. ¿A qué hora _____ tú esta noche? (acostarse)

d. Mi amigo no _____ su tarea pronto. (terminar)

e. Uds. _____ la verdad ahora mismo. (confesar)

4. Write either *"por"* or *"para"* in the following sentences:

a. Voy a darte quince dólares _____ tu libro de español.

b. _____ llegar a la Ciudad de Guatemala, tienes que seguir todo derecho _____ 20 kilómetros.

c. Normalmente paseamos _____ el parque cuando estamos en Nueva York.

d. Ese tren va _____ los suburbios; yo necesito ir al centro.

e. La estrella sólo habló con los fotógrafos _____ cinco minutos.

f. "Este perrito caliente es _____ Ud.", me dijo el hombre en Yankee Stadium.

g. Cuando viajo a ochenta millas _____ hora en mi moto, siempre me pongo un poco nervioso.

h. "Necesito la ropa _____ este viernes a las cinco", anunció la mujer en la lavandería.

i. Muchas gracias _____ dejarme tu coche este fin de semana.

j. "Estoy aquí _____ mostrarte fotos nuevas de mis preciosos nietos", anunció la abuela muy orgullosa.

5. Translate the following into Spanish:

a. thirty-five lawyers _____

b. the first star _____

c. two hundred and one racquets _____

d. the fifth cavity _____

e. 2010 _____

6. Now translate these words to fit into the following sentences:

a. El _____ momento bueno fue cuando Cristina entrevistó a Óscar de la Hoya. (1ST)

b. Bebimos _____ botellas de agua mineral este fin de semana. (21)

c. En mi opinión la _____ lección es la mejor. (5TH)

d. Dicen que Imelda Marcos tenía _____ pares de zapatos. (2341)

e. El _____ fin de semana de agosto pienso ir de viaje con mis cuñados. (2ND)

f. Para tu cumpleaños, te compré _____ rosas. (14)

g. Hay _____ mujeres en esa universidad. (431)

h. Para la boda, van a hacer muchísimo guacamole. Necesitan

_____ aguacates, _____

cebollas, jugo de _____ limones y

_____ tomates. (120, 21, 42, 35)

7. The following note from your teacher contains seven errors. Underline each error and write the correction above it:

No vas a escribes más ejercicios en este libro. ¡Increíble! Es el fin del libro. Vas a estas muy alegre ahora. Estudiaste para un año y aprendiste mucho español. ¿Fue tu primero año de español o tu segund año? Por hablar bien, tienes que practicar mucho. ¡La práctica hace al maestro! ¿Vas a hablar español este verano con amigos o sólo vas hablar inglés? Ahora, no importa. Tienes que celebrar. ¡Felicidades!

¡Felicidades!
YOU'VE BROKEN THE 1ST BARRIER!

CONJUGACIONES DE HABLAR, COMER, VIVIR

REGULAR VERBS

infinitivo	participio	presente	pretérito	imperfecto	Mandatos (commands) Ud./Uds., (+/–)
hablar (to talk, speak)	hablando	hablo hablas habla hablamos habláis hablan	hablé hablaste habló hablamos hablasteis hablaron	hablaba hablabas hablaba hablábamos hablabais hablaban	hable hablen
comer (to eat)	comiendo	como comes come comemos coméis comen	comí comiste comió comimos comisteis comieron	comía comías comía comíamos comíais comían	coma coman
vivir (to live)	viviendo	vivo vives vive vivimos vivís viven	viví viviste vivió vivimos vivisteis vivieron	vivía vivías vivía vivíamos vivíais vivían	viva vivan

IRREGULAR VERBS

infinitivo	participio	presente	pretérito	imperfecto	Mandatos (commands) Ud./Uds., (+/–)
andar (to walk)	andando	ando andas anda andamos andáis andan	anduve anduviste anduvo anduvimos anduvisteis anduvieron	andaba andabas andaba andábamos andabais andaban	ande anden
caber (to fit)	cabiendo	quepo cabes cabe cabemos cabéis caben	cupe cupiste cupo cupimos cupisteis cupieron	cabía cabías cabía cabíamos cabíais cabían	quepa quepan
caer (to fall)	cayendo	caigo caes cae caemos caéis caen	caí caíste cayó caímos caísteis cayeron	caía caías caía caíamos caíais caían	caiga caigan
comenzar (to begin)	comenzando	comienzo comienzas comienza comenzamos comenzáis comienzan	comencé comenzaste comenzó comenzamos comenzasteis comenzaron	comenzaba comenzabas comenzaba comenzábamos comenzabais comenzaban	comience comiencen
conducir (to drive)	conduciendo	conduzco conduces conduce conducimos conducís conducen	conduje condujiste condujo condujimos condujisteis condujeron	conducía conducías conducía conducíamos conducíais conducían	conduzca conduzcan

infinitivo	participio	presente	pretérito	imperfecto	Mandatos (commands) Ud./Uds., (+/−)
conocer (to know)	conociendo	conozco conoces conoce conocemos conocéis conocen	conocí conociste conoció conocimos conocisteis conocieron	conocía conocías conocía conocíamos conocíais conocían	conozca conozcan
construir (to build)	construyendo	construyo construyes construye construimos construís construyen	construí construiste construyó construimos construisteis construyeron	construía construías construía construíamos construíais construían	construya construyan
dar (to give)	dando	doy das da damos dais dan	di diste dio dimos disteis dieron	daba dabas daba dábamos dabais daban	dé den
decir (to say)	diciendo	digo dices dice decimos decís dicen	dije dijiste dijo dijimos dijisteis dijeron	decía decías decía decíamos decíais decían	diga digan
dormir (to sleep)	durmiendo	duermo duermes duerme dormimos dormís duermen	dormí dormiste durmió dormimos dormisteis durmieron	dormía dormías dormía dormíamos dormíais dormían	duerma duerman
estar (to be)	estando	estoy estás está estamos estáis están	estuve estuviste estuvo estuvimos estuvisteis estuvieron	estaba estabas estaba estábamos estabais estaban	esté estén
hacer (to do, make)	haciendo	hago haces hace hacemos hacéis hacen	hice hiciste hizo hicimos hicisteis hicieron	hacía hacías hacía hacíamos hacíais hacían	haga hagan
ir (to go)	yendo	voy vas va vamos vais van	fui fuiste fue fuimos fuisteis fueron	iba ibas iba íbamos ibais iban	vaya vayan
jugar (to play)	jugando	juego juegas juega jugamos jugáis juegan	jugué jugaste jugó jugamos jugasteis jugaron	jugaba jugabas jugaba jugábamos jugabais jugaban	juegue jueguen

infinitivo	participio	presente	pretérito	imperfecto	Mandatos (commands) Ud./Uds., (+/−)
negar (to deny)	negando	niego niegas niega negamos negáis niegan	negué negaste negó negamos negasteis negaron	negaba negabas negaba negábamos negabais negaban	niegue nieguen
oír (to hear)	oyendo	oigo oyes oye oímos oís oyen	oí oíste oyó oímos oísteis oyeron	oía oías oía oíamos oíais oían	oiga oigan
oler (to smell)	oliendo	huelo hueles huele olemos oléis huelen	olí oliste olió olimos olisteis olieron	olía olías olía olíamos olíais olían	huela huelan
pedir (to ask for)	pidiendo	pido pides pide pedimos pedís piden	pedí pediste pidió pedimos pedisteis pidieron	pedía pedías pedía pedíamos pedíais pedían	pida pidan
poder (to be able)	pudiendo	puedo puedes puede podemos podéis pueden	pude pudiste pudo pudimos pudisteis pudieron	podía podías podía podíamos podíais podían	pueda puedan
poner (to put)	poniendo	pongo pones pone ponemos ponéis ponen	puse pusiste puso pusimos pusisteis pusieron	ponía ponías ponía poníamos poníais ponían	ponga pongan
querer (to want, to like)	queriendo	quiero quieres quiere queremos queréis quieren	quise quisiste quiso quisimos quisisteis quisieron	quería querías quería queríamos queríais querían	quiera quieran
reír (to laugh)	riendo	río ríes ríe reímos reís ríen	reí reíste rió reímos reísteis rieron	reía reías reía reíamos reíais reían	ría rían

infinitivo	participio	presente	pretérito	imperfecto	Mandatos (commands) Ud./Uds., (+/−)
saber (to know)	sabiendo	sé sabes sabe sabemos sabéis saben	supe supiste supo supimos supisteis supieron	sabía sabías sabía sabíamos sabíais sabían	sepa sepan
seguir (to follow)	siguiendo	sigo sigues sigue seguimos seguís siguen	seguí seguiste siguió seguimos seguisteis siguieron	seguía seguías seguía seguíamos seguíais seguían	siga sigan
ser (to be)	siendo	soy eres es somos sois son	fui fuiste fue fuimos fuisteis fueron	era eras era éramos erais eran	sea sean
tener (to have)	teniendo	tengo tienes tiene tenemos tenéis tienen	tuve tuviste tuvo tuvimos tuvisteis tuvieron	tenía tenías tenía teníamos teníais tenían	tenga tengan
traer (to bring)	trayendo	traigo traes trae traemos traéis traen	traje trajiste trajo trajimos trajisteis trajeron	traía traías traía traíamos traíais traían	traiga traigan
venir (to come)	viniendo	vengo vienes viene venimos venís vienen	vine viniste vino vinimos vinisteis vinieron	venía venías venía veníamos veníais venían	venga vengan
ver (to see)	viendo	veo ves ve vemos veis ven	vi viste vio vimos visteis vieron	veía veías veía veíamos veíais veían	vea vean

SPANISH-ENGLISH DICTIONARY

SPANISH-ENGLISH DICTIONARY

(Bold indicates vocabulary from the beginning of each lesson.)

A

a . . . . **at, to**
a la derecha . . . . **to the right**
a la izquierda . . . . **to the left**
a menudo . . . . often
a veces . . . . **at times, sometimes**
abierto/a . . . . **open**
abogado/a (el/la) . . . . **lawyer**
abordar . . . . to board
abrigo (el) . . . . **coat**
abril . . . . April
abrir . . . . **to open**
abuela (la) . . . . grandmother
abuelo (el) . . . . grandfather
aburrido/a . . . . bored, boring
acabar de . . . . to finish
accidente (el) . . . . **accident**
acompañar . . . . **to accompany**
acondicionador de
  aire (el) . . . . **air conditioner**
acordeón (el) . . . . **accordion**
acostarse (ue) . . . . **to go to bed**
actor (el) . . . . **actor**
actriz (la) . . . . **actress**
adelante . . . . forward, ahead
admitir . . . . **to admit**
aeropuerto (el) . . . . **airport**
afeitar(se) . . . . **to shave (oneself)**
afueras (las) . . . . suburbs
agosto . . . . August
agua (el) (f.) . . . . **water**
ahora . . . . **now**
alcalde (le) . . . . mayor
alcoba (la) . . . . bedroom
alegre . . . . **happy**
alfombra (la) . . . . **carpet, rug**
algo . . . . **something**
alguien . . . . someone
allí . . . . **there**
almorzar (ue) . . . . to have lunch
alto/a . . . . **tall**
amar . . . . **to love**
amarillo/a . . . . yellow
anaranjado/a . . . . orange
amigo/a (el/la) . . . . **friend**
amor (el) . . . . **love**
ancho/a . . . . **wide**
anoche . . . . **last night**
andar . . . . to walk
anillo (el) . . . . ring
antes (de) . . . . **before**
año (el) . . . . **year**
apagar . . . . to turn off
aprender . . . . **to learn**
aquí . . . . **here**
árbol (el) . . . . **tree**

arbusto (el) . . . . **bush**
arete (el) . . . . **earring**
armario (el) . . . . **closet**
arroz (el) . . . . **rice**
asado/a . . . . roasted
asiento (el) . . . . **seat**
asistente de vuelo
  (el/la) . . . . **flight attendant**
aspiradora (la) . . . . . **vacuum cleaner**
atestado/a . . . . **crowded**
atlético/a . . . . **athletic**
atrás . . . . behind
aunque . . . . **although**
autobús (el) . . . . **bus**
autopista (la) . . . . highway
avión (el) . . . . **airplane**
ayer . . . . **yesterday**
azúcar (el) . . . . **sugar**
azul . . . . blue

B

bailar . . . . **to dance**
bajar . . . . **to go down**
bajo/a . . . . **short**
ballena (la) . . . . whale
baloncesto (el) . . . . **basketball**
banda (la) . . . . **band**
bandera (la) . . . . **flag**
bañarse . . . . **to take a bath**
bañera (la) . . . . **tub**
baño (el) . . . . bathroom
barato/a . . . . **cheap**
barco (el) . . . . **boat**
bebé (el) . . . . **baby**
beber . . . . **to drink**
bebida (la) . . . . **drink**
béisbol (el) . . . . **baseball**
besar . . . . **to kiss**
beso (el) . . . . **kiss**
biblioteca (la) . . . . **library**
bicicleta (la) . . . . **bicycle**
bien . . . . fine, well
bigote (el) . . . . **mustache**
billete (el) . . . . **ticket**
billetera (la) . . . . **wallet**
blanco/a . . . . white
blusa (la) . . . . **blouse**
boca (la) . . . . **mouth**
boda (la) . . . . **wedding**
boleto (el) . . . . **ticket**
bonito/a . . . . **pretty**
bota (la) . . . . **boot**
botella (la) . . . . **bottle**
brazo (el) . . . . **arm**
buenas noche . . . . good evening
buenas tardes . . . . good afternoon

bueno/a . . . . **good**
buenos días . . . . good morning
bufanda (la) . . . . **scarf**
buscar . . . . to look for
buzón (el) . . . . **mailbox**

C

caballo (el) . . . . horse
caber . . . . **to fit**
cada . . . . each, every
caer . . . . **to fall**
café (el) . . . . **coffee**
calcetines (los) . . . . **socks**
calendario (el) . . . . **calendar**
caliente . . . . **warm, hot**
calle (la) . . . . **street**
cama (la) . . . . bed
camarero/a (el/la) (mesero/a) . . **waiter**
cambiar . . . . **to change**
cambio (el) . . . . change
caminar . . . . **to walk**
camión (el) . . . . **truck**
camisa (la) . . . . **shirt**
campana (la) . . . . **bell**
campeonato (el) . . . . . **championship**
canción (la) . . . . **song**
cansado/a . . . . **tired**
cantante (el/la) . . . . singer
cantar . . . . to sing
cara (la) . . . . face
cárcel (la) . . . . **jail**
carie (la) . . . . **cavity**
cariñoso/a . . . . **affectionate**
carne (la) . . . . **meat**
caro/a . . . . **expensive**
carrera (la) . . . . race, career
carretera (la) . . . . **highway**
carta (la) . . . . **letter**
cartel (el) . . . . **poster**
cartero/a (el/la) . . . . mail carrier
casa (la) . . . . house
casarse . . . . **to get married**
casarse con . . . . . . **to get married to**
cebra (la) . . . . zebra
celoso/a . . . . jealous
centro (el) . . . . center, downtown
cepillarse . **to brush one's (hair, teeth)**
cerca . . . . **near(by)**
cerca (de) . . . . **near**
cerrado/a . . . . **closed**
cerrar (ie) . . . . **to close**
césped (el) . . . . **lawn**
chaqueta (la) . . . . **jacket**
charlar . . . . **to chat**
chica (la) . . . . **girl**
chicle (el) . . . . **gum**

chico (el) . . . . **boy**
chiste (el) . . . . **joke**
cielo (el) . . . . **sky**
cine (el) . . . . **movie theater**
cinturón (el) . . . . **belt**
ciudad (la) . . . . **city**
clarinete (el) . . . . **clarinet**
clase (la) . . . . **class**
clima (el) . . . . **climate**
coche (el) . . . . **car**
cocina (la) . . . . kitchen
cocinar . . . . to cook
coco (el) . . . . .coconut
código postal (el) . . . . **zip code**
coger . . . . to take, to catch
colegio (el) . . . . high school
colgar (ue) . . . . to hang (up)
comedor (el) . . . . dining room
comenzar (ie) . . . . **to begin**
comer . . . . **to eat**
comida (la) . . . . food
comisaría (la) . . . . police station
como . . . . **as, since, like**
¿cómo? . . . . how?
cómodo/a . . . . .comfortable
compartir . . . . **to share**
competir (i) . . . . to compete
comprar . . . . **to buy**
comprender . . . . to understand
computadora (la) . . . . **computer**
con . . . . **with**
concierto (el) . . . . **concert**
conducir . . . . **to drive**
congelador (el) . . . . **freezer**
conocer . . **to know (a person or place)**
conseguir (i) . . . . **to get, to obtain**
construir . . . . to build, to construct
contaminado/a . . . . **contaminated**
contar (ue) . . . . to count, to tell
contestador automático (el)
. . . . **answering machine**
contestar . . . . to answer
continente (el) . . . . **continent**
corbata (la) . . . . **tie**
cordial . . . . cordial, polite
corregir (i) . . . . to correct
correo electrónico (el) . . . . **e-mail**
correr . . . . **to run**
cortar . . . . **to cut**
cortés . . . . courteous, polite
cortinas (las) . . . . **curtains**
corto/a . . . . **short**
cosa (la) . . . . **thing**
costar (ue) . . . . to cost
crear . . . . **to create, to make**
creer . . . . **to believe**
¿cuál(es)? . . . . which one(s)?
¿cuándo? . . . . when?
cuánto/as . . . . how much/many
cuarto (el) . . . . . room, quarter, fourth
(cuarto de) baño (el) . . . . . . **bathroom**

cuchara (la) . . . . **spoon**
cuchillo (el) . . . . **knife**
cuenta (la) . . . . **bill**
cuento (el) . . . . story, tale
cuero (el) . . . . **leather**
culpable . . . . guilty
cumpleaños (el) . . . . **birthday**
cuñada (la) . . . . sister-in-law
cuñado (el) . . . . brother-in-law

D

dar . . . . **to give**
de . . . . of, from
de la mañana . . **A.M. (in the morning)**
de la tarde/noche
. . . . **P.M. (in the afternoon/evening)**
de nuevo . . . . **again**
débil . . . . **weak**
década (la) . . . . **decade**
decidir . . . . **to decide**
decir . . . . **to say, to tell**
dedo (el) . . . . **finger**
demasiado/a
. . . . **too much (pl., too many)**
deporte (el) . . . . **sport**
desaparecer . . . . to disappear
desayunar . . . . to have breakfast
descubrir . . . . **to discover**
desear . . . . **to desire**
despacio . . . . **slowly**
despertarse (ie) . . . . . . **to wake up**
después (de) . . . . **after**
detener . . . . **to detain, to stop**
devolver (ue) . . . . . to return (an object)
día (el) . . . . **day**
diciembre . . . . December
diente (el) . . . . **tooth**
difícil . . . . **difficult**
dinero (el) . . . . **money**
disco compacto (el) . .compact disc (CD)
divino/a . . . . **divine**
docena (la) . . . . **dozen**
dominar . . . . to dominate
domingo . . . . Sunday
¿dónde? . . . . where?
dormir (ue) . . . . **to sleep**
dos veces . . . . **twice**
ducha (la) . . . . **shower**
ducharse . . . . **to shower**
durante . . . . **during**

E

edificio (el) . . . . building
él . . . . he, him
eléctrico/a . . . . **electric**
elegir (i) . . . . **to choose, to elect**
ella . . . . she, her
ellas/os . . . . they, them
embajador (el) . . . . ambassador
emocionado/a . . . . **excited**

empezar (ie) . . . . **to begin**
empleo (el) . . . . **job**
en . . . . **in, on**
en voz alta . . . . **aloud**
encontrar (ue) . . . . . . to find, to meet
enemigo (el) . . . . **enemy**
enero . . . . January
enfermo/a . . . . **sick**
enfrente de . . . . **in front of**
enojarse . . . . **to become angry**
ensalada (la) . . . . **salad**
enseñar . . . . **to teach**
entender (ie) . . . . to understand
entrada (la) . . . . **admission, ticket,**
entrance
entrar . . . . to enter
entregar . . . . . . to deliver, to hand over,
to turn in
entrevista (la) . . . . **interview**
entrevistar . . . . to interview
enviar . . . . to send
episodio (el) . . . . **episode**
equipaje (el) . . . . luggage
equipo (el) . . . . **team**
equivocarse . . . . . . **to make a mistake**
escaleras (las) . . . . **stairs**
escapar . . . . to escape
escena (la) . . . . scene
escoba (la) . . . . **broom**
escoger . . . . to choose
escribir . . . . **to write**
escritorio (el) . . . . **desk**
escuchar . . . . to listen to
escuela (la) . . . . **school**
esencial . . . . essential
espacio (el) . . . . space
especial . . . . **special**
espejo (el) . . . . mirror
esperar . . . . **to hope, to wait**
esposa (la) . . . . wife
esposo (el) . . . . husband
esquí (el) . . . . **skiing**
esta mañana . . . . **this morning**
esta noche . . . . **tonight**
esta tarde . . . . **this afternoon**
estación de tren (la) . . . . . **train station**
estar . . . . to be
este . . . . **east**
estrecho/a . . . . **narrow**
estrella (la) . . . . **star**
estreno (el) . . debut, premiére, first night
estudiante (el/la) . . . . student
estudiar . . . . to study
estúpido/a . . . . **stupid**
examen (el) . . . . **test**
éxito (el) . . . . .success
explicar . . . . to explain
exposición (la) . . . exhibition, fair, show
extraño/a (raro/rara) . . . . **strange**

F

fábrica (la) . . . . factory
fácil . . . . **easy**
falda (la) . . . . **skirt**
febrero . . . . February
fecha (la) . . . . **date**
felicidades (las) . . . . . . congratulations
felicitar . . . . **to congratulate**
feliz . . . . **happy**
feo/a . . . . **ugly**
fideo (el) . . . . noodle
fiesta (la) . . . . **party**
fila (la) . . . . **row**
fin de semana (el) . . . . **weekend**
final (el) . . . . final, end
flaco/a . . . . thin, skinny
flauta (la) . . . . flute
flor (la) . . . . **flower**
foto(grafía) (la) . . . . . . **photo(graph)**
frecuentemente . . . . **frequently**
fregadero (el) . . . . . . **sink (in kitchen)**
freír (i) . . . . **to fry**
fresco/a . . . . fresh, cool
frío/a . . . . **cold**
frustrado/a . . . . **frustrated**
fuerte . . . . **strong**
fumar . . . . **to smoke**
furioso/a . . . . **furious, very mad**
fútbol (el) . . . . **soccer**
fútbol americano (el) . . . . **football**

G

galleta (la) . . . . **cookie**
ganar . . . . **to win, to earn**
garaje (el) . . . . **garage**
gasolinera (la) . . . . **gas station**
gastar . . . . **to spend, to waste**
gato (el) . . . . cat
generoso/a . . . . **generous**
gente (la) . . . . people
gordo/a . . . . fat
gorra (la) . . . . **cap, hat**
grabar . . . . to record
gracias . . . . **thanks**
graduarse . . . . **to graduate**
grande . . . . **big**
graniza . . . . it is hailing
gris . . . . grey
gritar . . . . **to shout**
guantes (los) . . . . gloves
guapo/a . . . . **good-looking**
guitarra (la) . . . . **guitar**

H

hablar . . . . **to talk, to speak**
hacer . . . . **to do, to make**
hamburguesa (la) . . . . **hamburger**
hasta . . . . until

hasta luego . . . . see you later
hecho (el) . . . . fact
helado (el) . . . . **ice cream**
hermana (la) . . . . sister
hermano (el) . . . . brother
hielo (el) . . . . ice
hierba (la) . . . . **grass**
hija (la) . . . . daughter
hijo (el) . . . . son
hockey sobre hielo (el) . . . . **ice hockey**
hombre (el) . . . . **man**
hora (la) . . . . hour
horno de microondas (el)
. . . . **microwave oven**
hoy . . . . today
huevo (el) . . . . **egg**
humilde . . . . **humble**

I

iglesia (la) . . . . **church**
increíble . . . . incredible
inglés (el) . . . . **English**
instrucciones (las) . . . . instructions
insultar . . . . **to insult**
intenso/a . . . . intense
interesante . . . . **interesting**
íntimo/a . . . . **intimate, close**
invierno (el) . . . . winter
invitar . . . . **to invite**
ir . . . . **to go**
ir de compras . . . . **to go shopping**
ir de viaje . . . . **to travel**

J

jamón (el) . . . . ham
jardín (el) . . . . **garden**
jirafa (la) . . . . giraffe
jóvenes (los) . . . . . . **youth, youngsters**
jueves . . . . Thursday
jugador/a (el/la) . . . . player
jugar (ue) . . . . **to play**
julio . . . . July
junio . . . . June
juntos/as . . . . together

L

lago (el) . . . . **lake**
lápiz (el) . . . . pencil
largo/a . . . . **long**
lavabo (el) . . . . . . **sink (in bathroom)**
lavadora (la) . . . . **washer**
lavaplatos (el) . . . . **dishwasher**
lavar . . . . to wash
lavarse . . . . **to wash oneself**
leal . . . . loyal
lección (la) . . . . lesson
leche (la) . . . . milk
leer . . . . **to read**

lejos . . . . **far (away)**
lejos (de) . . . . **far**
león (el) . . . . lion
letra (la) . . . . lyrics, letter
levantarse . . . . **to get up**
libertad (la) . . . . liberty
libra (la) . . . . **pound**
libre . . . . **free**
libro (el) . . . . **book**
limón (el) . . . . lemon
limonada (la) . . . . **lemonade**
limpiar . . . . **to clean**
loco/a . . . . crazy
lotería (la) . . . . **lottery**
luchador (el) . . . . **wrestler**
luego . . . . **later**
luna (la) . . . . **moon**
luna de miel (la) . . . . . . **honeymoon**
lunes . . . . Monday

LL

llamar . . . . **to call**
llama (la) . . . . llama
llegada (la) . . . . **arrival**
llegar . . . . **to arrive**
llevar . . . . **to take, to carry**
llorar . . . . **to cry**
llover (ue) . . . . to rain

M

madera (la) . . . . **wood**
madre (la) . . . . mother
malo/a . . . . **bad**
mano (la) . . . . **hand**
mantequilla (la) . . . . **butter**
manzana (la) . . . . **apple**
mañana . . . . tomorrow
mapa (el) . . . . **map**
marrón . . . . brown
martes . . . . Tuesday
marzo . . . . March
más . . . . **more**
matemáticas (las) . . . . math
mayo . . . . May
mayor . . . . **older**
mejor . . . . **better, best**
menor . . . . **younger**
menos . . . . **less**
mensaje (el) . . . . **message**
mentira (la) . . . . **lie**
mes (el) . . . . **month**
mesa (la) . . . . table
meteorólogo (el) . . . . . . **meteorologist**
mientras . . . . while
miércoles . . . . Wednesday
milla (la) . . . . **mile**
mirar . . . . **to look at**
misa (la) . . . . . . **mass, church service**
misterioso/a . . . . **mysterious**

mochila (la)	backpack
moda (la)	style, fashion
mojar	to wet, to moisten
montaña (la)	mountain
montar en bicicleta	to ride a bicycle
morado/a	purple
moreno/a	dark, brunette
morir (ue)	to die
mostrar (ue)	to show
moto(cicleta) (la)	motorcycle
mover (ue)	to move
mucho	a lot
mudarse	to move (relocate)
mujer (la)	woman
mundo (el)	world
música (la)	music
músico/a (el/la)	musician
muy	very

N

nacer	to be born
nada	nothing
nadar	to swim
nadie	no one
naranja (la)	orange
nariz (la)	nose
natación (la)	swimming
necesitar	to need
negar (ie)	to deny
negro/a	black
nevar (ie)	to snow
nevera (la), refrigerador (el)	refrigerator
ni	neither, nor
niebla (la)	fog
nieta (la)	granddaughter
nieto (el)	grandson
nieve (la)	snow
ninguno/a	none
niña (la)	girl
niño (el)	boy
no	no
noche (la)	night
norte	north
nosotros/as	we
noticias (las)	news
novela (la)	novel
novia (la)	girlfriend
noviembre	November
novio (el)	boyfriend
nublado/a	cloudy
nuevo/a	new
nunca	never

O

octubre	October
ocurrir	to occur, to happen
odiar	to hate
oeste	west

oficina (la)	office
oír	to hear
ojo (el)	eye
ordenador (el)	computer (Spain)
oreja (la)	ear
orgulloso/a	proud
original	original
orquesta (la)	orchestra
oso (el) (de peluche)	(teddy) bear
otoño (el)	fall
otra vez	again
otro/a	another, other

P

padre (el)	father
pagar	to pay
país (el)	country
pájaro (el)	bird
pala (la)	shovel
palabra (la)	word
pampas (las)	plains
pan (el)	bread
pantalones (los)	pants
papel (el)	paper
paquete (el)	package
para	by, for, in order to
parque (el)	park
partido (el)	game
pasado/a	past, last
pasar (tiempo)	to spend (time)
pasear	to take a stroll
pastel (el), torta (la)	cake
pedir (i)	to ask for, to order (food)
peinarse	to comb one's hair
pelea (la)	fight
pelear	to fight
película (la)	film (used in a camera), movie
pelirrojo/a	red-headed
pelo (el)	hair
pena (la)	pain
pendiente (el), arete (el)	earring
pensar (ie)	to think
peor	worse, worst
pequeño/a	small
perder (ie)	to lose
perder (tiempo)	to waste (time)
permitir	to permit, to allow
perro (el)	dog
perrito caliente (el)	hot dog
pescado (el)	fish
pez (el)	fish
piano (el)	piano
pie (el)	foot
pierna (la)	leg
piscina (la)	swimming pool
pizarra (la)	blackboard
plástico (el)	plastic
plato (el)	plate, dish
playa (la)	beach

pluma (la)	pen
pobre	poor
poco	a little
poder (ue)	to be able to
pollo (el)	chicken
poner	to put
ponerse	to put on
por	for, through
por eso	therefore
por fin	finally
por supuesto	of course
¿por qué?	why?
porque	because
precio (el)	price
precioso/a	beautiful, adorable
preocupado/a	upset
preferir (ie)	to prefer
premio (el)	prize
preocuparse	to worry
preparar	to prepare
prestar	to lend
primavera (la)	spring
primo/a (el/la)	cousin
principio (el)	beginning
probar (ue)	to taste, to try
profesor/a (el/la)	teacher
problema (el)	problem
prometer	to promise
pronto	soon
próximo/a	next
prueba (la)	proof, quiz, test
pueblo (el)	town, village
puerta (la)	door
puesta del sol (la)	sunset
pupitre (el)	student desk

Q

que	that, which
¿qué?	what?
quedar	to remain
querer (ie)	to want, to wish, to like
queso (el)	cheese
¿quién?	who?

R

radio (el/la)	radio
rana (la)	frog
rápidamente	quickly
raqueta (la)	racquet
ratón (el)	mouse
realidad (la)	reality
recibir	to receive
recibo (el)	receipt
reciente	recent
recordar (ue)	to remember
refrigerador (el), nevera (la)	refrigerator
regalo (el)	present
regresar	to return

reírse (i) . . . . to laugh
reloj (el) . . . . clock, watch
remo (el) . . . . rowing
repetir (i) . . . . to repeat
respuesta (la) . . . . reply
restaurante (el) . . . . restaurant
resultado (el) . . . . result
reunión (la) . . . . . . meeting, reunion
revista (la) . . . . magazine
rico/a . . . . rich
rígido/a . . . . rigid
río (el) . . . . river
rojo/a . . . . red
romper . . . . to break
ropa (la) . . . . clothes
rosa (la) . . . . rose
rosado/a . . . . pink

S

sábado (el) . . . . Saturday
saber . . . . to know (a fact)
saber de memoria . . to know by heart
sabroso/a . . . . tasty, delicious
sacar . . . . to take out
sala (de estar) (la) . . . . . . living room
salida del sol (la) . . . . sunrise
salir . . . . to leave
saxofón (el) . . . . saxophone
secadora (la) . . . . dryer
secreto (el) . . . . secret
seguir (i) . . . . to follow
según . . . . according to
semana (la) . . . . week
sentar (ie) . . . . to seat (someone)
sentarse (ie) . . . . to sit down
sentir (ie) . . . . to feel, to regret
septiembre . . . . September
ser . . . . to be
serpiente (la) . . . . serpent, snake
servir (i) . . . . to serve
si . . . . if
sí . . . . yes
siempre . . . . always
silla (la) . . . . seat, chair
simpático/a . . . . nice
sin . . . . without
sinagoga (la) . . . . synagogue
sitio (el) . . . . site, place
sobre . . . . over, about
sobrina (la) . . . . niece
sobrino (el) . . . . nephew
sofá (el) . . . . sofa
soldado (el) . . . . soldier
sólo . . . . only
solo/a . . . . alone
sombrero (el) . . . . hat
sonar (ue) . . . . to ring
soñar (ue) con . . . . to dream about
sopa (la) . . . . soup
sorprendido/a . . . . surprised

sorpresa (la) . . . . surprise
subir . . . . to go up
suéter (el) . . . . sweater
suegra (la) . . . . mother-in-law
suegro (el) . . . . father-in-law
suerte (la) . . . . luck
supermercado (el) . . . . . supermarket
sur . . . . south
susurrar . . . . to whisper

T

también . . . . also
tambores (los) . . . . drums
tan . . . . so
tanto (adv.) . . . . so much
tanto/a . . . . so many
tarde . . . . late
tarea (la) . . . . homework, task
taxi (el) . . . . taxi
té (el) . . . . tea
teatro (el) . . . . theater
teléfono (el) . . . . telephone
teléfono celular (el) . . . . cell phone
televisión (la) . . . . television
televisor (el) . . . . television set
tempestad (la), tormenta (la) . . . storm
temprano . . . . early
tenedor (el) . . . . fork
tener . . . . to have
tener razón . . . . to be right
tenis (el) . . . . tennis
terminar . . . . to finish
tía (la) . . . . aunt
tiempo (el) . . . . time
tienda (la) . . . . store
tierra (la) . . . . soil, earth
tigre (el) . . . . tiger
tío (el) . . . . uncle
típico/a . . . . typical
tiza (la) . . . . chalk
toalla (la) . . . . towel
tocar . . . . . . to play (an instrument),
. . . . to touch
todavía . . . . still
todavía no . . . . not yet
tomate (el) . . . . tomato
tonto/a . . . . . . foolish, silly, stupid
tormenta (la), tempestad (la) . . . storm
torta (la), pastel (el) . . . . cake
tostador (el) . . . . toaster
trabajar . . . . to work
traer . . . . to bring
traje de baño (el) . . . . swimsuit
tranquilamente . . . . calmly
tren (el) . . . . train
triste . . . . sad
trombón (el) . . . . trombone
trompeta (la) . . . . trumpet
tú . . . . you (familiar)
tulipán (el) . . . . tulip

U

último/a . . . . last (of a group)
una vez . . . . once
único/a . . . . only, unique
universidad (la) . . . . university
uno/a . . . . a, an
unos/as . . . . some
usted (Ud.) . . . . you (formal)
ustedes (Uds.) . . . . you all (formal)

V

vaca (la) . . . . cow
valer . . . . to be worth
vaso (el) . . . . glass
vecino/a (el/la) . . . . neighbor
vegetal (el) . . . . vegetable
vela (la) . . . . sailing
vender . . . . to sell
venir . . . . to come
ventana (la) . . . . window
ver . . . . to see
verano (el) . . . . summer
verdad (la) . . . . truth
¿verdad? . . . . isn't that so?
verde . . . . green
vestido (el) . . . . dress
viajar . . . . to travel
viaje (el) . . . . trip
vídeo (el) . . . . VCR, video
viejo/a . . . . old
viento (el) . . . . wind
viernes (el) . . . . Friday
vino (el) . . . . wine
violín (el) . . . . violin
vivir . . . . to live
volar (ue) . . . . to fly
volver (ue) . . . . to return
vosotros/as . . . . you all (familiar)
yo I

Y

y . . . . and
ya . . . . already
ya no . . . . no longer, anymore

Z

zanahoria (la) . . . . carrot
zapato (el) . . . . shoe

ENGLISH-SPANISH DICTIONARY

(Bold indicates vocabulary from the beginning of each lesson.)

A

a, an . . . . *uno/a*
able (to be) (to) . . . . *poder (ue)*
accident . . . . *(el) accidente*
accompany (to) . . . . *acompañar*
according to . . . . *según*
accordion . . . . *(el) acordeón*
actor . . . . *(el) actor*
actress . . . . *(la) actriz*
admission, ticket,
   entrance . . . . *(la) entrada*
admit (to) . . . . *admitir*
adorable, beautiful . . . . *precioso/a*
affectionate . . . . *cariñoso/a*
after . . . . *después (de)*
afternoon (this) . . . . *esta tarde*
again . . . . *de nuevo, otra vez*
ahead, forward . . . . *adelante*
air conditioner
   . . . . *(el) acondicionador de aire*
airplane . . . . *(el) avión*
airport . . . . *(el) aeropuerto*
allow (to), to permit . . . . *permitir*
alone . . . . *solo/a*
aloud . . . . *en voz alta*
already . . . . *ya*
also . . . . *también*
although . . . . *aunque*
always . . . . *siempre*
A.M. (in the morning) . . *de la mañana*
ambassador . . . . *(el) embajador*
an, a . . . . *uno/a*
and . . . . *y*
angry (to become) . . . . *enojarse*
another, other . . . . *otro/a*
answer (to) . . . . *contestar*
answering machine . . *(el) contestador*
                                          automático
anymore, no longer . . . . *ya no*
apple . . . . *(la) manzana*
April . . . . *abril*
arm . . . . *(el) brazo*
arrival . . . . *(la) llegada*
arrive (to) . . . . *llegar*
as, since, like . . . . *como*
ask (for) (to), to order (food) . *pedir (i)*
at, to . . . . *a*
at times, sometimes . . . . *a veces*
athletic . . . . *atlético/a*
August . . . . *agosto*
aunt . . . . *(la) tía*

B

baby . . . . *(el) bebé*
backpack . . . . *(la) mochila*

bad . . . . *malo/a*
band . . . . *(la) banda*
baseball . . . . *(el) béisbol*
basketball . . . . *(el) baloncesto*
bath (to take a) . . . . *bañarse*
bathroom . . . . . . *(el) (cuarto de) baño*
be (to) . . . . *estar, ser*
be able to (to) . . . . *poder (ue)*
be born (to) . . . . *nacer*
be worth (to) . . . . *valer*
beach . . . . *(la) playa*
bear . . . . *(el) oso*
beautiful, adorable . . . . *precioso/a*
because . . . . *porque*
bed . . . . *(la) cama*
bed (to go to) . . . . *acostarse (ue)*
bedroom . . . . *(la) alcoba*
before . . . . *antes (de)*
begin (to) . . *comenzar (ie), empezar (ie)*
beginning . . . . *(el) principio*
behind . . . . *atrás*
believe (to) . . . . *creer*
bell . . . . *(la) campana*
belt . . . . *(el) cinturón*
better, best . . . . *mejor*
bicycle . . . . *(la) bicicleta*
bicycle (to ride a) . . *montar en bicicleta*
big . . . . *grande*
bill . . . . *(la) cuenta*
bird . . . . *(el) pájaro*
birthday . . . . *(el) cumpleaños*
black . . . . *negro/a*
blackboard . . . . *(la) pizarra*
blouse . . . . *(la) blusa*
blue . . . . *azul*
board (to) . . . . *abordar*
boat . . . . *(el) barco*
book . . . . *(el) libro*
boot . . . . *(la) bota*
bored, boring . . . . *aburrido/a*
bottle . . . . *(la) botella*
boy . . . . *(el) chico, (el) niño*
boyfriend . . . . *(el) novio*
bread . . . . *(el) pan*
break (to) . . . . *romper*
bring (to) . . . . *traer*
broom . . . . *(la) escoba*
brother . . . . *(el) hermano*
brown . . . . *marrón*
brunette, dark . . . . *moreno/a*
brush one's (to) (hair, teeth)
   . . . . *cepillarse*
build (to), to construct . . . . . . *construir*
building . . . . *(el) edificio*
bus . . . . *(el) autobús*
bush . . . . *(el) arbusto*

butter . . . . *(la) mantequilla*
buy (to) . . . . *comprar*
by, for, in order to . . . . *para*

C

cake . . . . *(la) torta, (el) pastel*
calendar . . . . *(el) calendario*
call (to) . . . . *llamar*
calmly . . . . *tranquilamente*
cap . . . . *(la) gorra*
car . . . . *(el) coche*
career, race . . . . *(la) carrera*
carpet, rug . . . . *(la) alfombra*
carrot . . . . *(la) zanahoria*
carry (to), to take . . . . *llevar*
cat . . . . *(el) gato*
catch (to), to take . . . . *coger*
cavity . . . . *(la) carie*
cell phone . . . .*(el) teléfono celular*
center, downtown . . . . *(el) centro*
chair, seat . . . . *(la) silla*
chalk . . . . *(la) tiza*
championship . . . . . . *(el) campeonato*
change . . . . *(el) cambio*
change (to) . . . . *cambiar*
chat (to) . . . . *charlar*
cheap . . . . *barato/a*
cheese . . . . *(el) queso*
chicken . . . . *(el) pollo*
choose (to), to elect . *elegir (i), escoger*
church . . . . *(la) iglesia*
church service, mass . . . . . . *(la) misa*
city . . . . *(la) ciudad*
clarinet . . . . *(el) clarinete*
class . . . . *(la) clase*
clean (to) . . . . *limpiar*
climate . . . . *(el) clima*
clock, watch . . . . *(el) reloj*
closed . . . . *cerrado/a*
close, intimate . . . . *íntimo/a*
close (to) . . . . *cerrar (ie)*
closet . . . . *(el) armario*
clothes . . . . *(la) ropa*
cloudy . . . . *nublado/a*
coat . . . . *(el) abrigo*
coconut . . . .*(el) coco*
coffee . . . . *(el) café*
cold . . . . *frío/a*
comb one's hair (to) . . . . . . *peinarse*
come (to) . . . . *venir*
comfortable . . . .*cómodo/a*
compact disc (CD)
   . . . . *(el) disco compacto*
compete (to) . . . . *competir (i)*
computer . . . . *(la) computadora*
computer (Spain) . . . . *(el) ordenador*

concert	*(el) concierto*
congratulate (to)	*felicitar*
congratulations	*(las) felicidades*
construct (to), to build	*construir*
contaminated	*contaminado/a*
continent	*(el) continente*
cook (to)	*cocinar*
cookie	*(la) galleta*
cool, fresh	*fresco/a*
cordial, polite	*cordial*
correct (to)	*corregir (i)*
cost (to)	*costar (ue)*
count (to), to tell	*contar (ue)*
country	*(el) país*
courteous, polite	*cortés*
cousin	*(el/la) primo/a*
cow	*(la) vaca*
crazy	*loco/a*
create (to), to make	*crear*
crowded	*atestado/a*
cry (to)	*llorar*
curtains	*(las) cortinas*
cut (to)	*cortar*

D

dance (to)	*bailar*
dark, brunette	*moreno/a*
date	*(la) fecha*
daughter	*(la) hija*
day	*(el) día*
debut, premiére, first night	*(el) estreno*
decade	*(la) década*
December	*diciembre*
decide (to)	*decidir*
delicious, tasty	*sabroso/a*
deliver (to), to turn in, to hand over
	entregar
deny (to)	*negar (ie)*
desire (to)	*desear*
desk	*(el) escritorio*
detain (to), to stop	*detener*
die (to)	*morir (ue)*
difficult	*difícil*
dining room	*(el) comedor*
discover (to)	*descubrir*
disappear (to)	*desaparecer*
dish, plate	*(el) plato*
dishwasher	*(el) lavaplatos*
divine	*divino/a*
do (to), to make	*hacer*
dog	*(el) perro*
dominate (to)	*dominar*
door	*(la) puerta*
down (to go)	*bajar*
downtown, center	*(el) centro*
dozen	*(la) docena*
dream about (to)	*soñar (ue) con*
dress	*(el) vestido*
drink	*(la) bebida*
drink (to)	*beber*

drive (to)	*conducir*
drums	*(los) tambores*
dryer	*(la) secadora*
during	*durante*

E

each, every	*cada*
ear	*(la) oreja*
early	*temprano*
earn (to), to win	*ganar*
earring	*(el) arete, (el) pendiente*
earth, soil	*(la) tierra*
east	*este*
easy	*fácil*
eat (to)	*comer*
eat lunch (to)	*almorzar (ue)*
egg	*(el) huevo*
elect (to), to choose	*elegir (i)*
electric	*eléctrico/a*
e-mail	*(el) correo electrónico*
end, final	*(el) final*
enemy	*(el) enemigo*
English	*(el) inglés*
enter (to)	*entrar*
entrance, admission, ticket
	(la) entrada
episode	*(el) episodio*
escape (to)	*escapar*
essential	*esencial*
every, each	*cada*
excited	*emocionado/a*
exhibition, fair, show	*(la) exposición*
expensive	*caro/a*
explain (to)	*explicar*
eye	*(el) ojo*

F

face	*(la) cara*
fact	*(el) hecho*
factory	*(la) fábrica*
fall	*(el) otoño*
fall (to)	*caer*
far	*lejos (de)*
far (away)	*lejos*
fashion, style	*(la) moda*
fat	*gordo/a*
father	*(el) padre*
father-in-law	*(el) suegro*
February	*febrero*
feel (to), to regret	*sentir (ie)*
fight	*(la) pelea*
fight (to)	*pelear*
film (used in a camera), movie
	(la) película
final, end	*(el) final*
finally	*por fin*
find (to), to meet	*encontrar (ue)*
fine, well	*bien*
finger	*(el) dedo*

finish (to)	*acabar de, terminar*
first night, première, debut	*(el) estreno*
fish	*(el) pez, (el) pescado*
fit (to)	*caber*
flag	*(la) bandera*
flight attendant
	(el/la) asistente de vuelo
flute	*(la) flauta*
flower	*(la) flor*
fly (to)	*volar (ue)*
fog	*(la) niebla*
follow (to)	*seguir (i)*
food	*(la) comida*
foolish, silly, stupid	*tonto/a*
foot	*(el) pie*
football	*(el) fútbol americano*
for, by, in order to	*para*
for, through	*por*
fork	*(el) tenedor*
forward, ahead	*adelante*
fourth, quarter, room	*(el) cuarto*
free	*libre*
freezer	*(el) congelador*
frequently	*frecuentemente*
fresh, cool	*fresco/a*
Friday	*(el) viernes*
friend	*(el/la) amigo/a*
frog	*(la) rana*
from, of	*de*
frustrated	*frustrado/a*
fry (to)	*freír (i)*
furious, very mad	*furioso/a*

G

game	*(el) partido*
garage	*(el) garaje*
garden	*(el) jardín*
gas station	*(la) gasolinera*
generous	*generoso/a*
get (to), to obtain	*conseguir (i)*
get up (to)	*levantarse*
giraffe	*(la) jirafa*
girl	*(la) chica, (la) niña*
girlfriend	*(la) novia*
give (to)	*dar*
glass	*(el) vaso*
gloves	*(los) guantes*
go (to)	*ir*
good	*bueno/a*
good afternoon	*buenas tardes*
good evening	*buenas noche*
good morning	*buenos días*
good-looking	*guapo/a*
guitar	*(la) guitarra*
graduate (to)	*graduarse*
granddaughter	*(la) nieta*
grandmother	*(la) abuela*
grandfather	*(el) abuelo*
grandson	*(el) nieto*
grass	*(la) hierba*

grey . . . . *gris*
green . . . . *verde*
guilty . . . . *culpable*
gum . . . . *(el) chicle*

H

hair . . . . *(el) pelo*
ham . . . . *(el) jamón*
hamburger . . . . *(la) hamburguesa*
hand . . . . *(la) mano*
hand over (to), to deliver, to turn in
. . . . *entregar*
hang (up) (to) . . . . *colgar (ue)*
happen (to), to occur) . . . . *ocurrir*
happy . . . . *alegre, feliz*
hat, cap . . . . *(la) gorra*
hat . . . . *(el) sombrero*
hate (to) . . . . *odiar*
have (to) . . . . *tener*
have breakfast (to) . . . . *desayunar*
hear (to) . . . . *oír*
he, him . . . . *él*
her, she . . . . *ella*
here . . . . *aquí*
high school . . . . *(el) colegio*
highway . . *(la) autopista, (la) carretera*
him, he . . . . *él*
homework, task . . . . *(la) tarea*
honeymoon . . . . *(la) luna de miel*
hope (to), to wait . . . . *esperar*
horse . . . . *(el) caballo*
hot, warm . . . . *caliente*
hot dog . . . . *(el) perrito caliente*
hour . . . . *(la) hora*
house . . . . *(la) casa*
how? . . . . *¿cómo?*
how much/many . . . . *cuánto/as*
humble . . . . *humilde*
husband . . . . *(el) esposo*

I

I . . . . *yo*
ice . . . . *(el) hielo*
ice cream . . . . *(el) helado*
ice hockey . . . . *(el) hockey sobre hielo*
if . . . . *si*
in, on . . . . *en*
in front of . . . . *enfrente de*
in order to, by, for . . . . *para*
incredible . . . . *increíble*
instructions . . . . *(las) instrucciones*
insult (to) . . . . *insultar*
intense . . . . *intenso/a*
interesting . . . . *interesante*
interview . . . . *(la) entrevista*
interview (to) . . . . *entrevistar*
intimate, close . . . . *íntimo/a*
invite (to) . . . . *invitar*
isn't that so? . . . . *¿verdad?*

it is hailing . . . . *graniza*

J

jacket . . . . *(la) chaqueta*
jail . . . . *(la) cárcel*
January . . . . *enero*
jealous . . . . *celoso/a*
job . . . . *(el) empleo*
joke . . . . *(el) chiste*
July . . . . *julio*
June . . . . *junio*

K

kiss . . . . *(el) beso*
kiss (to) . . . . *besar*
kitchen . . . . *(la) cocina*
knife . . . . *(el) cuchillo*
know (to) (a fact) . . . . *saber*
know (to) (a person or place) . . *conocer*
know (to) (by heart)
. . . . *saber de memoria*

L

lake . . . . *(el) lago*
last (of a group) . . . . *último/a*
last night . . . . *anoche*
late . . . . *tarde*
later . . . . *luego*
laugh (to) . . . . *reírse (i)*
lawn . . . . *(el) césped*
lawyer . . . . *(el/la) abogado/a*
learn (to) . . . . *aprender*
leather . . . . *(el) cuero*
leave (to) . . . . *salir*
leg . . . . *(la) pierna*
lemon . . . . *(el) limón*
lemonade . . . . *(la) limonada*
lend (to) . . . . *prestar*
less . . . . *menos*
lesson . . . . *(la) lección*
letter . . . . *(la) carta*
letter, lyrics . . . . *(la) letra*
liberty . . . . *(la) libertad*
library . . . . *(la) biblioteca*
lie . . . . *(la) mentira*
like, as, since . . . . *como*
lion . . . . *(el) león*
listen to (to) . . . . *escuchar*
little (a) . . . . *poco*
live (to) . . . . *vivir*
living room . . . . . . *(la) sala (de estar)*
llama . . . . *(la) llama*
long . . . . *largo/a*
look (at) (to) . . . . *mirar*
look for (to) . . . . *buscar*
lose (to) . . . . *perder (ie)*
lot (a) . . . . *mucho*
lottery . . . . *(la) lotería*

love . . . . *(el) amor*
love (to) . . . . *amar*
loyal . . . . *leal*
luck . . . . *(la) suerte*
luggage . . . . *(el) equipaje*
lyrics, letter . . . . *(la) letra*

M

mad (very), furious . . . . *furioso/a*
magazine . . . . *(la) revista*
mail carrier . . . . *(el/la) cartero/a*
mailbox . . . . *(el) buzón*
make (to), to create . . . . *crear*
make (to), to do . . . . *hacer*
make a mistake (to) . . . . . *equivocarse*
man . . . . *(el) hombre*
map . . . . *(el) mapa*
March . . . . *marzo*
married (to get) . . . . *casarse*
married to (to get) . . . . . *casarse con*
math . . . . *(las) matemáticas*
May . . . . *mayo*
mayor . . . . *(el) alcalde*
mass, church service . . . . . . *(la) misa*
meat . . . . *(la) carne*
meet (to), to find . . . . . . *encontrar (ue)*
meeting, reunion . . . . . . *(la) reunión*
message . . . . *(el) mensaje*
meteorologist . . . . . . *(el) meteorólogo*
microwave oven
. . . . *(el) horno de microondas*
mile . . . . *(la) milla*
milk . . . . *(la) leche*
mirror . . . . *(el) espejo*
moisten (to), to wet . . . . *mojar*
Monday . . . . *lunes*
money . . . . *(el) dinero*
month . . . . *(el) mes*
moon . . . . *(la) luna*
more . . . . *más*
mother . . . . *(la) madre*
mother-in-law . . . . *(la) suegra*
motorcycle . . . . *(la) moto(cicleta)*
mountain . . . . *(la) montaña*
mouse . . . . *(el) ratón*
mouth . . . . *(la) boca*
move (to) . . . . *mover (ue)*
move (to) (relocate) . . . . *mudarse*
movie, film (used in a camera)
. . . . *(la) película*
movie theater . . . . *(el) cine*
music . . . . *(la) música*
musician . . . . *(el/la) músico/a*
mustache . . . . *(el) bigote*
mysterious . . . . *misterioso/a*

N

narrow . . . . *estrecho/a*
near . . . . *cerca (de)*

near(by)	*cerca*	pen	*(la) pluma*	remain (to)	*quedar*

near(by) . . . . *cerca*
need (to) . . . . *necesitar*
neighbor . . . . *(el/la) vecino/a*
neither, nor . . . . *ni*
nephew . . . . *(el) sobrino*
never . . . . *nunca*
new . . . . *nuevo/a*
news . . . . *(las) noticias*
next . . . . *próximo/a*
nice . . . . *simpático/a*
niece . . . . *(la) sobrina*
night . . . . *(la) noche*
no . . . . *no*
no longer, anymore . . . . *ya no*
no one . . . . *nadie*
none . . . . *ninguno/a*
noodle . . . . *(el) fideo*
nor, neither . . . . *ni*
north . . . . *norte*
nose . . . . *(la) nariz*
not yet . . . . *todavía no*
nothing . . . . *nada*
novel . . . . *(la) novela*
November . . . . *noviembre*
now . . . . *ahora*

O

obtain (to), to get . . . . . . *conseguir (i)*
occur (to), to happen . . . . *ocurrir*
October . . . . *octubre*
of, from . . . . *de*
of course . . . . *por supuesto*
office . . . . *(la) oficina*
often . . . . *a menudo*
old . . . . *viejo/a*
older . . . . *mayor*
on, in . . . . *en*
once . . . . *una vez*
only, unique . . . . *único/a*
only . . . . *sólo*
open . . . . *abierto/a*
open (to) . . . . *abrir*
orange . . . . *anaranjado/a*
orange . . . . *(la) naranja*
orchestra . . . . *(la) orquesta*
order (to) (food), to ask for . . *pedir (i)*
original . . . . *original*
other, another . . . . *otro/a*
over, about . . . . *sobre*

P

package . . . . *(el) paquete*
pain . . . . *(la) pena*
pants . . . . *(los) pantalones*
paper . . . . *(el) papel*
park . . . . *(el) parque*
party . . . . *(la) fiesta*
past, last . . . . *pasado/a*
pay (to) . . . . *pagar*

pen . . . . *(la) pluma*
pencil . . . . *(el) lápiz*
people . . . . *(la) gente*
permit (to), to allow . . . . *permitir*
photo(graph) . . . . *(la) foto(grafía)*
piano . . . . *(el) piano*
pink . . . . *rosado/a*
place, site . . . . *(el) sitio*
plains . . . . *(las) pampas*
plastic . . . . *(el) plástico*
plate, dish . . . . *(el) plato*
play (to) . . . . *jugar (ue)*
play (to) (an instrument),
    to touch . . . . *tocar*
player . . . . *(el/la) jugador/a*
P.M. (in the afternoon/evening)
    . . . . *de la tarde/noche*
police station . . . . *(la) comisaría*
polite, cordial . . . . *cordial*
polite, courteous . . . . *cortés*
poor . . . . *pobre*
poster . . . . *(el) cartel*
pound . . . . *(la) libra*
prefer (to) . . . . *preferir (ie)*
premiére, debut, first night . . *(el) estreno*
prepare (to) . . . . *preparar*
present . . . . *(el) regalo*
pretty . . . . *bonito/a*
price . . . . *(el) precio*
prize . . . . *(el) premio*
problem . . . . *(el) problema*
promise (to) . . . . *prometer*
proof, quiz, test . . . . *(la) prueba*
proud . . . . *orgulloso/a*
purple . . . . *morado/a*
put (to) . . . . *poner*
put on (to) . . . . *ponerse*

Q

quarter, fourth, room . . . . *(el) cuarto*
quickly . . . . *rápidamente*
quiz, proof, test . . . . *(la) prueba*

R

racquet . . . . *(la) raqueta*
race, career . . . . *(la) carrera*
radio . . . . *(el/la) radio*
rain (to) . . . . *llover (ue)*
read (to) . . . . *leer*
reality . . . . *(la) realidad*
receipt . . . . *(el) recibo*
receive (to) . . . . *recibir*
recent . . . . *reciente*
record (to) . . . . *grabar*
red . . . . *rojo/a*
red-headed . . . . *pelirrojo/a*
refrigerator . . . . *(el) refrigerador,*
    (la) nevera
regret (to) . . . . *sentir (ie)*

remain (to) . . . . *quedar*
remember (to) . . . . *recordar (ue)*
repeat (to) . . . . *repetir (i)*
reply . . . . *(la) respuesta*
restaurant . . . . *(el) restaurante*
result . . . . *(el) resultado*
return (to) . . . . . . *regresar, volver (ue)*
return (to) (an object) . . . . *devolver (ue)*
reunion, meeting . . . . *(la) reunión*
rice . . . . *(el) arroz*
rich . . . . *rico/a*
right (to be) . . . .*tener razón*
rigid . . . . *rígido/a*
ring . . . . *(el) anillo*
ring (to) . . . . *sonar (ue)*
river . . . . *(el) río*
roasted . . . .*asado/a*
room, quarter, fourth . . . . . . *(el) cuarto*
rose . . . . *(la) rosa*
row . . . . *(la) fila*
rowing . . . . *(el) remo*
rug, carpet . . . . *(la) alfombra*
run (to) . . . . *correr*

S

sad . . . . *triste*
sailing, candle . . . .*(la) vela*
salad . . . . *(la) ensalada*
Saturday . . . . *(el) sábado*
saxophone . . . . *(el) saxofón*
say (to), to tell . . . . *decir*
scarf . . . . *(la) bufanda*
scene . . . . *(la) escena*
school . . . . *(la) escuela*
seat . . . . *(el) asiento*
seat, chair . . . . *(la) silla*
seat (to) (someone) . . . . *sentar (ie)*
secret . . . . *(el) secreto*
see (to) . . . . *ver*
see you later . . . . *hasta luego*
sell (to) . . . . *vender*
send (to) . . . . *enviar*
September . . . . *septiembre*
serpent, snake . . . . *(la) serpiente*
serve (to) . . . . *servir (i)*
share (to) . . . . *compartir*
shave (to) (oneself) . . . . *afeitar(se)*
she, her . . . . *ella*
shirt . . . . *(la) camisa*
shoe . . . . *(el) zapato*
shopping (to go) . . . . . . *ir de compras*
short . . . . *bajo/a*
short . . . . *corto/a*
shout (to) . . . . *gritar*
shovel . . . . *(la) pala*
show, exhibition, fair . . . *(la) exposición*
show (to) . . . . *mostrar (ue)*
shower . . . . *(la) ducha*
shower (to) . . . . *ducharse*
sick . . . . *enfermo/a*

silly, foolish, stupid . . . . *tonto/a*
since, like, as . . . . *como*
sing (to) . . . . *cantar*
singer . . . . *(el/la) cantante*
sink (in bathroom) . . . . *(el) lavabo*
sink (in kitchen) . . . . *(el) fregadero*
sister . . . . *(la) hermana*
sister-in-law . . . . *(la) cuñada*
sit (down) (to) . . . . *sentarse (ie)*
site, place . . . . *(el) sitio*
skiing . . . . *(el) esquí*
skinny, thin . . . . *flaco/a*
skirt . . . . *(la) falda*
sky . . . . *(el) cielo*
sleep (to) . . . . *dormir (ue)*
slowly . . . . *despacio*
small . . . . *pequeño/a*
smoke (to) . . . . *fumar*
snake, serpent . . . . *(la) serpiente*
snow . . . . *(la) nieve*
snow (to) . . . . *nevar (ie)*
so . . . . *tan*
so many, so much . . . . *tanto/a*
so much (adv.) . . . . *tanto*
soccer . . . . *(el) fútbol*
socks . . . . *(los) calcetines*
sofa . . . . *(el) sofá*
soil, earth . . . . *(la) tierra*
soldier . . . . *(el) soldado*
some . . . . *unos/as*
someone . . . . *alguien*
something . . . . *algo*
sometimes, at times . . . . *a veces*
son . . . . *(el) hijo*
song . . . . *(la) canción*
soon . . . . *pronto*
soup . . . . *(la) sopa*
south . . . . *sur*
space . . . . *(el) espacio*
speak (to), to talk . . . . *hablar*
special . . . . *especial*
spend (to) (time) . . . . . *pasar (tiempo)*
spend (to), to waste . . . . *gastar*
spoon . . . . *(la) cuchara*
sport . . . . *(el) deporte*
spring . . . . *(la) primavera*
stairs . . . . *(las) escaleras*
star . . . . *estrella*
still . . . . *todavía*
stop (to), to detain . . . . *detener*
store . . . . *(la) tienda*
storm . . . *(la) tempestad, (la) tormenta*
story, tale . . . . *(el) cuento*
strange . . . . *extraño/a (raro/rara)*
street . . . . *(la) calle*
strong . . . . *fuerte*
student . . . . *(el/la) estudiante*
student desk . . . . *(el) pupitre*
study (to) . . . . *estudiar*
stupid . . . . *estúpido/a*

stupid, foolish, silly . . . . *tonto/a*
style, fashion . . . . *(la) moda*
suburbs . . . . *afueras (las)*
success . . . .*(el) éxito*
sugar . . . . *(el) azúcar*
summer . . . . *(el) verano*
Sunday . . . . *domingo*
sunrise . . . . *(la) salida del sol*
sunset . . . . *(la) puesta del sol*
supermarket . . . . . . *(el) supermercado*
surprise . . . . *(la) sorpresa*
surprised . . . . *sorprendido/a*
sweater . . . . *(el) suéter*
swim (to) . . . . *nadar*
swimsuit . . . . *(el) traje de baño*
swimming . . . . *(la) natación*
swimming pool . . . . *(la) piscina*
synagogue . . . . *(la) sinagoga*

T

table . . . . *(la) mesa*
take (to), to carry . . . . *llevar*
take (to), catch (to) . . . . *coger*
take a stroll (to) . . . . *pasear*
take out (to) . . . . *sacar*
tale, story . . . . *(el) cuento*
talk (to), to speak . . . . *hablar*
tall . . . . *alto/a*
task, homework . . . . *(la) tarea*
taste (to), to try . . . . *probar (ue)*
tasty, delicious . . . . *sabroso/a*
taxi . . . . *(el) taxi*
tea . . . . *(el) té*
teach (to) . . . . *enseñar*
teacher . . . . *(el/la) profesor/a*
team . . . . *(el) equipo*
telephone . . . . *(el) teléfono*
television . . . . *(la) televisión*
television set . . . . *(el) televisor*
tell (to), to count . . . . *contar (ue)*
tell (to), to say . . . . *decir*
tennis . . . . *(el) tenis*
test . . . . *(el) examen*
test, proof, quiz . . . . *(la) prueba*
thanks . . . . *gracias*
that, which . . . . *que*
theater . . . . *(el) teatro*
them, they . . . . *ellas/os*
there . . . . *allí*
therefore . . . . *por eso*
they, them . . . . *ellas/os*
thin, skinny . . . . *flaco/a*
thing . . . . *(la) cosa*
think (to) . . . . *pensar (ie)*
this morning . . . . *esta mañana*
through, for . . . . *por*
Thursday . . . . *jueves*
ticket, entrance, admission
. . . . *(la) entrada*

ticket . . . . *(el) billete, (el) boleto*
tie . . . . *(la) corbata*
tiger . . . . *(el) tigre*
time . . . . *(el) tiempo*
tired . . . . *cansado/a*
to, at . . . . *a*
to the left . . . . *a la izquierda*
to the right . . . . *a la derecha*
toaster . . . . *(el) tostador*
today . . . . *hoy*
together . . . . *juntos/as*
tomato . . . . *(el) tomate*
tomorrow . . . . *mañana*
tonight . . . . *esta noche*
too much, (pl. too many)
. . . . *demasiado/a (adj.)*
tooth . . . . *(el) diente*
touch (to), to play
(an instrument) . . . . *tocar*
towel . . . . *(la) toalla*
town, village . . . . *(el) pueblo*
train . . . . *(el) tren*
train station . . . . . *(la) estación de tren*
travel (to) . . . . . . *ir de viaje, viajar*
tree . . . . *(el) árbol*
trip . . . . *(el) viaje*
trombone . . . . *(el) trombón*
truck . . . . *(el) camión*
trumpet . . . . *(la) trompeta*
truth . . . . *(la) verdad*
tub . . . . *(la) bañera*
Tuesday . . . . *martes*
tulip . . . . *(el) tulipán*
turn in (to), to hand over,
to deliver . . . . *entregar*
turn off (to) . . . . *apagar*
twice . . . . *dos veces*
typical . . . . *típico/a*
try (to), to taste . . . . *probar (ue)*

U

ugly . . . . *feo/a*
uncle . . . . *(el) tío*
understand (to) . . . . *comprender,*
entender (ie)
unique, only . . . . *único/a*
university . . . . *(la) universidad*
until . . . . *hasta*
up (to go) . . . . *subir*
upset . . . . *preocupado/a*

V

vacuum cleaner . . . . . . *(la) aspiradora*
VCR, video . . . . *(el) vídeo*
vegetable . . . . *(el) vegetal*
very . . . . *muy*
video, VCR . . . . *(el) vídeo*
violin . . . . *(el) violín*

W

wait (to), to hope . . . . *esperar*
waiter . . *(el/la) camarero/a (mesero/a)*
wake (up) (to) . . . . . . *despertarse (ie)*
walk (to) . . . . *andar, caminar*
wallet . . . . *(la) billetera*
warm, hot . . . . *caliente*
want (to), to wish . . . . *querer (ie)*
wash (to) . . . . *lavar*
wash (to) (oneself) . . . . *lavarse*
washer . . . . *(la) lavadora*
waste (to), to spend . . . . *gastar*
waste (to) (time) . . . . . *perder (tiempo)*
watch, clock . . . . *(el) reloj*
water . . . . *(el) agua (f.)*
we . . . . *nosotros/as*
weak . . . . *débil*
wedding . . . . *(la) boda*
Wednesday . . . . *miércoles*
week . . . . *(la) semana*
weekend . . . . *(el) fin de semana*
well, fine . . . . *bien*
west . . . . *oeste*
wet (to), to moisten . . . . *mojar*
whale . . . . *(la) ballena*
what? . . . . *¿qué?*
when? . . . . *¿cuándo?*
where? . . . . *¿dónde?*
which one(s)? . . . . *¿cuál(es)?*
while . . . . *mientras*
whisper (to) . . . . *susurrar*
white . . . . *blanco/a*
who? . . . . *¿quién?*
why? . . . . *¿por qué?*
wide . . . . *ancho/a*
wife . . . . *(la) esposa*
win (to), to earn . . . . *ganar*
wind . . . . *(el) viento*
window . . . . *(la) ventana*
wine . . . . *(el) vino*
winter . . . . *(el) invierno*
wish (to), to want . . . . *querer (ie)*
with . . . . *con*
without . . . . *sin*
woman . . . . *(la) mujer*
wood . . . . *(la) madera*
word . . . . *(la) palabra*
work (to) . . . . *trabajar*
world . . . . *(el) mundo*
worry (to) . . . . *preocuparse*
worse, worst . . . . *peor*
wrestler . . . . *(el) luchador*
write (to) . . . . *escribir*

Y

year . . . . *(el) año*
yellow . . . . *amarillo/a*
yes . . . . *sí*

yesterday . . . . *ayer*
you (familiar) . . . . *tú*
you (formal) . . . . *usted (Ud.)*
you all (familiar) . . . . *vosotros/as*
you all (formal) . . . . *ustedes (Uds.)*
younger . . . . *menor*
youngsters, youth . . . . . . *(los) jóvenes*
youth, youngsters . . . . . . *(los) jóvenes*

Z

zebra . . . . *(la) cebra*
zip code . . . . *(el) código postal*

INDEX